Powers Brown Architecture Commodity and Virtue in Architecture

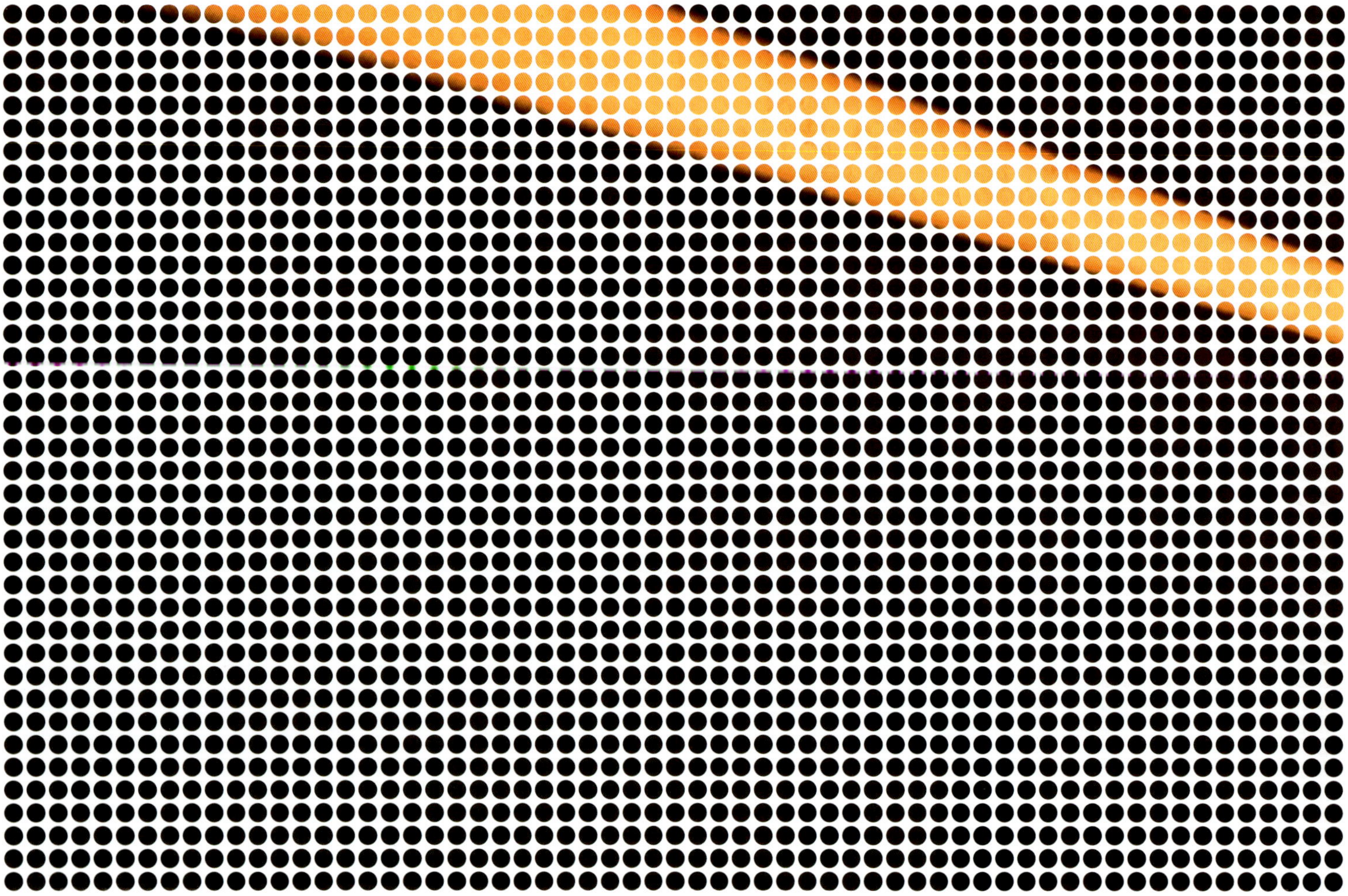

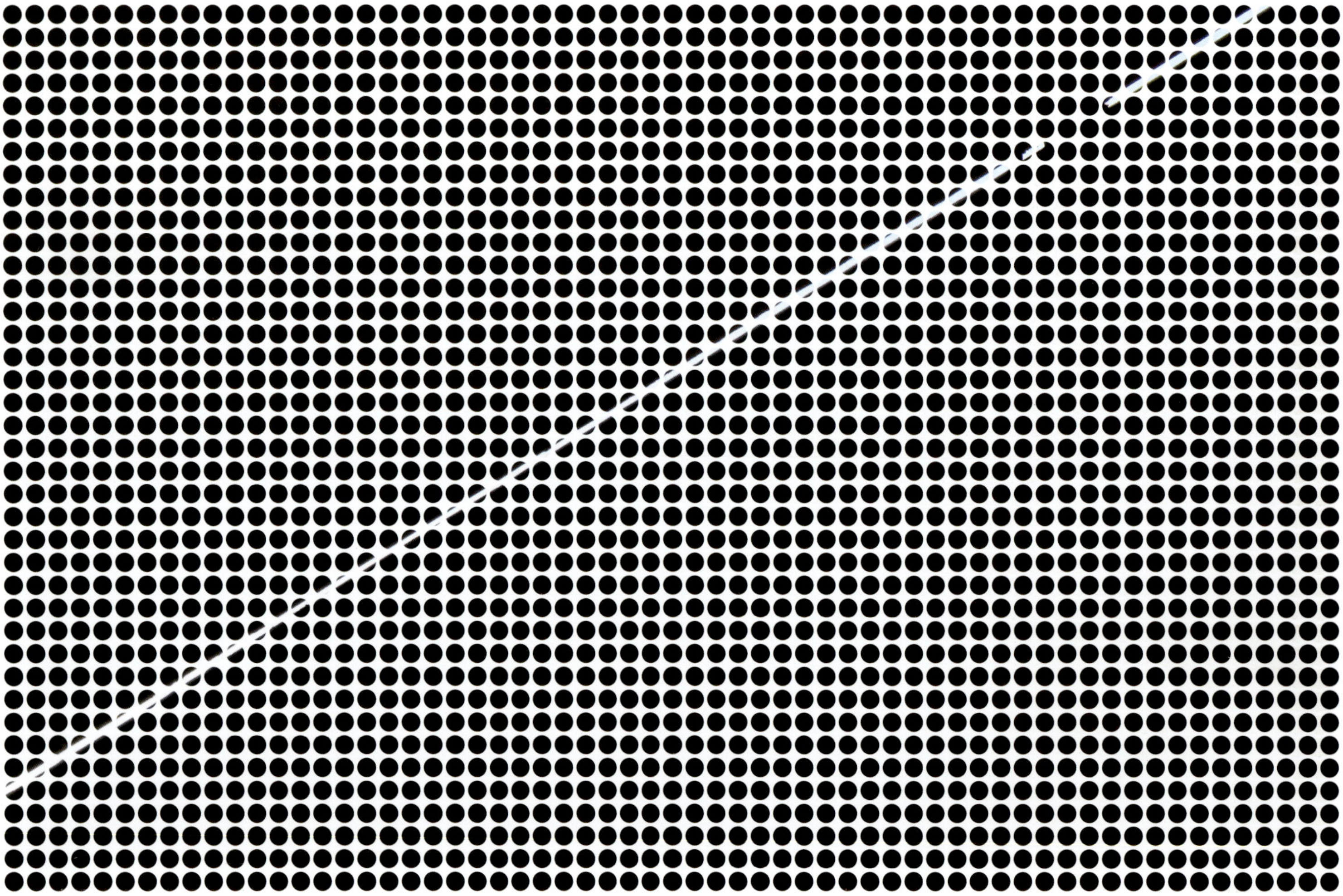

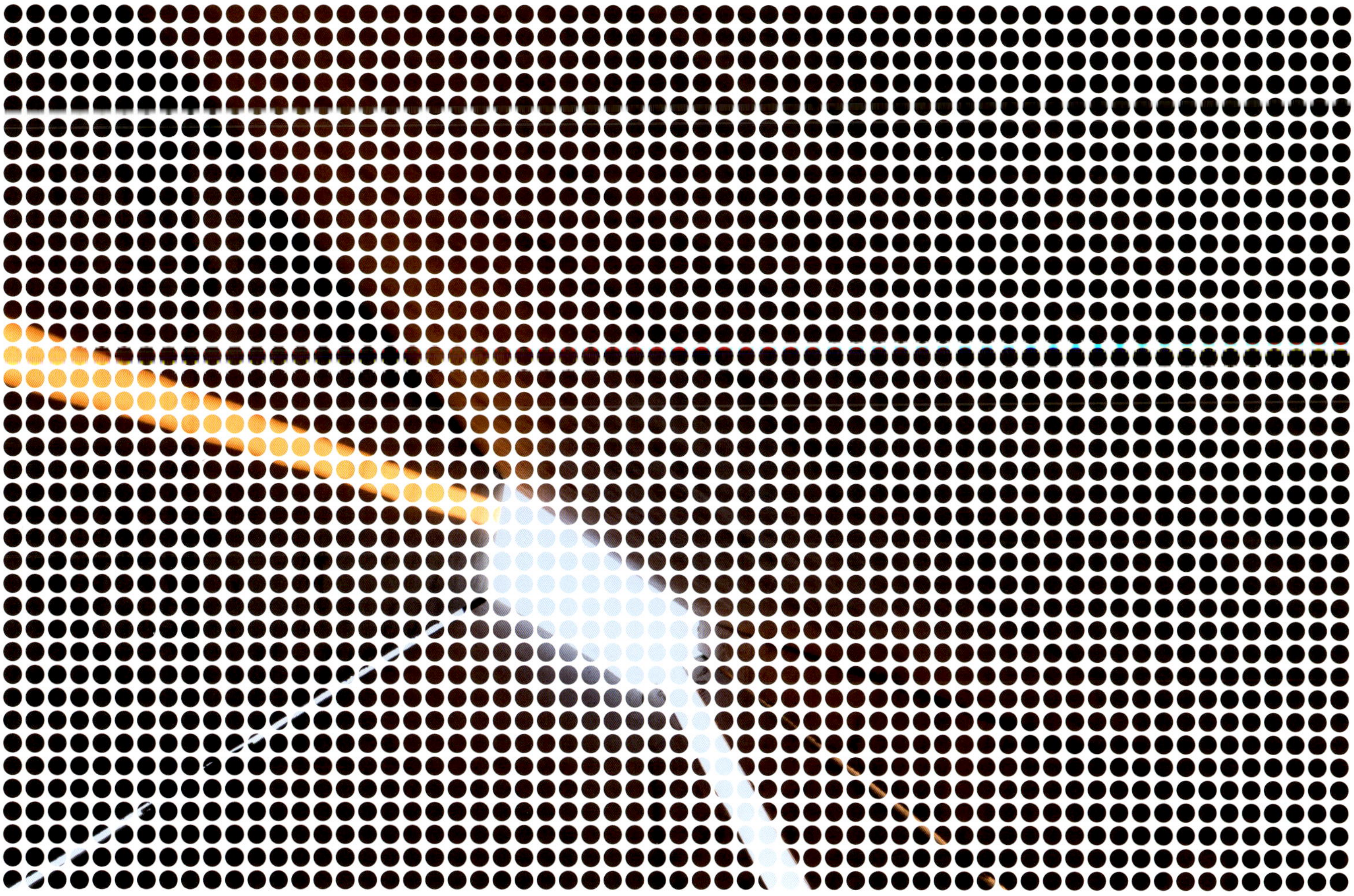

Powers Brown Architecture Commodity and Virtue in Architecture

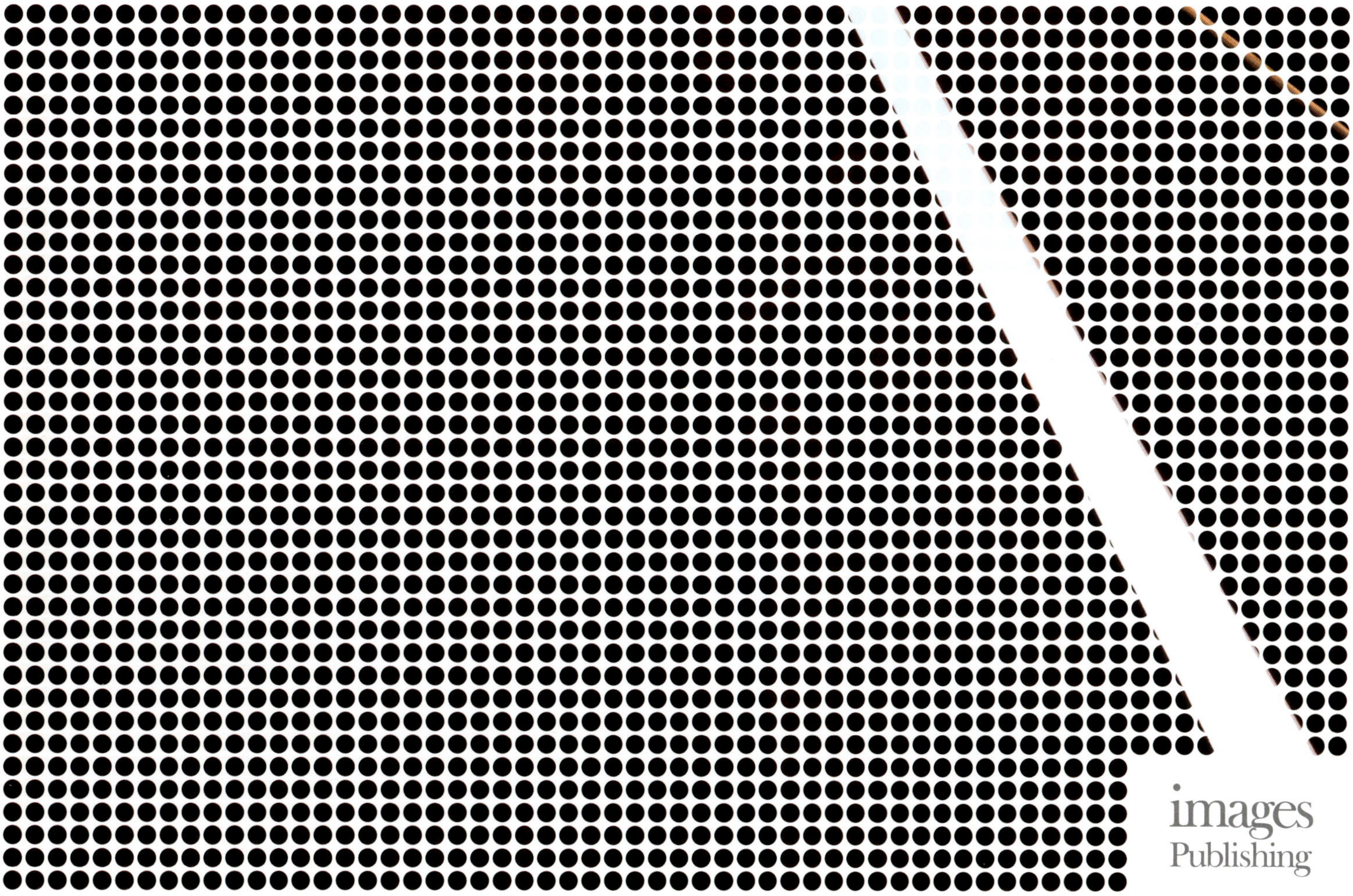

images Publishing

YHOUSE

Contents

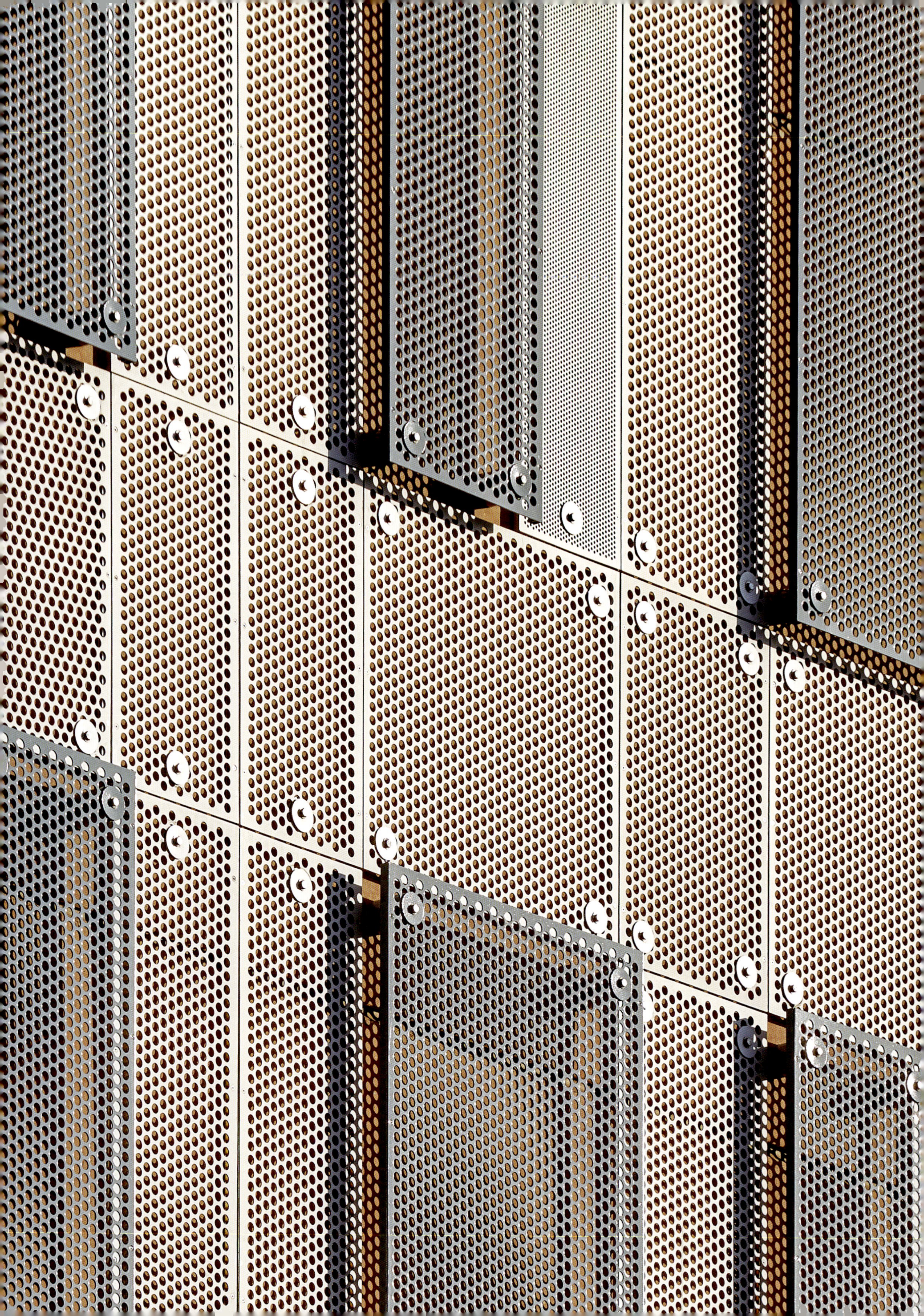

Innovating Toward Excellence

Stephen Sharpe

Twenty-five years ago, two young architects decided to join forces and open their own firm, Powers Brown Architecture. Ambitious and accomplished yet feeling increasingly sidelined in the large Houston office where they worked, Joe Powers and Jeffrey Brown agreed that the time was right to forge ahead together. I first became familiar with their work during that time as executive editor of *Texas Architect* Magazine and covered the firm's projects from 2000 to 2012. Over the following quarter century, their firm has flourished through successful partnerships with clients to create a broad range of building types and urban design strategies in several major North American markets. Along the way, Powers Brown Architecture has developed new technologies that have transformed the built environment of Houston while also leading the architecture profession toward greater capacity for research and innovation.

As the firm has continued to expand and evolve, Powers Brown maintains its founding partners' original dedication to working with clients to design buildings that are cost-effective and market-driven. The bulk of Powers Brown's work lies within an area of architectural practice that many firms avoid due to their belief that there's insufficient architectural potential. These building types are associated with commercial projects that are often dismissed as too mundane by the so-called "starchitects," the avant-garde of the profession who often seek design awards and media adulation over simply acknowledging their client's needs for well-designed and cost-efficient structures that respond to everyday programmatic requirements.

Bottom-Up Innovation

The stereotypical starchitect's "top-down" approach to design endeavors focuses on high-profile projects that are expected to garner accolades for their firm's brand, which means they only seek clients who will readily acquiesce to preset methods of experimentation. Instead, Powers Brown prefers a "bottom-up" method that eschews "experimentation" by re-calibrating often mundane systems of the everyday tools in the commercial environment and construction. As Jeffrey Brown explains in his essay "Mining for Virtue in Commodification", Powers Brown does not turn away clients or any type of project as long as there's a promise of a fair profit. "When we consider our practice, we seem to land first on our approach to clients, who our clients are, what they are. We observe that seems to be different to many of the firms we admire," he writes.

"Marketect" is the term Brown coined for the antithesis of the starchitect and he proudly proclaims Powers Brown to be the poster child of the market-driven strategy for striving for the best design solutions for any and all clients. Embracing the concept of the commodification of architecture—the notion that all clients deserve good design—affords Powers Brown the license to explore potential innovations regardless of building type. "Some architects do the right projects for their practice. Other architects do the required projects for their clients," notes Brown, unabashedly placing Powers Brown in the latter group.

Through its bottom-up approach, Powers Brown seeks cutting-edge solutions that often elevate a seemingly boring building type beyond client expectations. Perhaps the best examples in Powers Brown's portfolio are its tilt-wall projects, which belie preconceptions of simplistic concrete boxes with sophisticated compositions and state-of-the-art construction techniques. While tilt-wall (e.g., warehouses and big-box retail) is viewed within the profession as the epitome of unexciting and unvarying architecture, Powers Brown instead has literally transformed this system of construction. It's no surprise that Brown has written the definitive treatise on the subject. His *Tiltwallism* (Images Publishing, 2014) outlines the history of building with site-cast concrete panels and showcases some of the most impressive works by the nation's leading designers. More recently, Powers Brown has pushed the envelope of tilt-wall construction through research and development of affordable methodologies that meet high-level federally mandated anti-terrorism criteria for blast and progressive collapse resistance to accommodate clients such as the U.S. Department of Defense.

Neglected Territory

Brown wrote in Powers Brown's 2007 monograph that the firm finds fertile ground for enterprise and innovation within market segments viewed by some architects as unworthy of their creative focus. Using the term "neglected territory" to describe architectural projects that too often result in anonymous and facile buildings, Brown stated that the firm strives to respond to the market's need for thoughtfully designed structures such as corporate offices that respect their occupants' hopes for well-organized and enjoyable places to work. As he explained: "Neglected territory has guided our practice from its beginnings. Our vision for its meaning shaped our choice in relation to design process, business structure, and our close engagement with construction. Our team is structured to engage in the everyday projects overlooked by enlightened practice; the increments of the built environment not seen as having the artistic potential of project types we view as constituting the preferred architectural territory."

Another example illustrative of Powers Brown's expertise in ennobling otherwise ignored background elements of the built environment are its parking garages, projects that the firm sees as having potential to become essential urban components that transcend their utilitarian purpose as mere containers for idle vehicles. By manipulating form in response to environmental context and augmenting functional programming, the design team imbues this aspect of neglected territory with welcoming neighborliness and unexpected elegance.

Sustainability is an equally important facet of Powers Brown's approach to neglected territory, which derives from the firm's research into low-impact materials and energy-efficient systems that enrich rather than detract from the design of its myriad projects. With an emphasis on performance capacities over performative appearances, the firm strategically integrates eco-friendly features that often offer their clients opportunities to achieve carbon-neutral operations.

In addition to realizing sustainability goals and life-saving innovations such as blast-resistant tilt-wall construction, Powers Brown excels in applying research for the benefit of its clients. Sometimes its research opens new markets where none existed before, such as the world's first use of vertical stacking of tilt-wall panels to six levels and its exploration of formal expression for high-rise towers that challenge traditional architectural standards. Expounding on the firm's attitude toward market-driven experimentation, Brown states, "Research in our practice has exposed new and unforeseen possibilities in what we call the Virtues of Commercial Architecture. Through the vehicle of what we are presented by clients as design needs and under cover of the notion of research, we have looked inward at our practice and made discoveries."

Recognition

Beyond responding to its clients' desires with applied research and professional aplomb, Powers Brown's pursuit of excellence has brought the firm more than its share of awards from the field of design and the construction industry. Many of the firm's projects have been featured in national and regional periodicals and recognized by cultural institutions as exemplary by inclusion in exhibitions ranging from the digital publication *Archinect* to the Museum of Fine Arts Houston, among others.

Without question, Powers Brown has refined its own practice from its beginnings as a small firm that Powers and Brown opened in Houston in 1999, ultimately branching out across North America. Today the firm employs a total of 160 people who staff offices in Houston, Washington, D.C. (opened in 2006), Denver (2012), St. John's, Newfoundland and Labrador, Canada (2016), Toronto (2017), Atlanta (2021), and Chicago (2024).

Following Joe Powers' retirement in 2017, Jeffrey Brown reorganized the firm to accommodate its national stature while providing the same close relationships with its clientele as before and maintaining a progressive office culture, particularly in terms of diversity, equity and inclusion. Adhering to the principle of lateral interoffice communications, Brown leads monthly town-hall style meetings across all the firm's offices with an "ask me anything" coda at the end of each session. "I don't ever talk about us as a family," Brown says, "We are not a family, that term is exclusive to the private lives of employees. We are a team related to work and I think the generation working for us appreciates that we don't pander that way. Otherwise, we are a learning and teaching environment as we understand our newest employees have very little of the technical knowledge they will need in the practice of architecture." By nurturing new arrivals, Brown adds, Powers Brown is preparing to extend its track record of success with future innovations to serve a new generation of clients.

This monograph spans the entire twenty-five years of Powers Brown's practice and includes projects not extensively covered in earlier publications. The body of work collected herein evinces the singularly disciplined structure of the practice itself—the firm's defining characteristic—over a predominant style or argument about form. I look forward to what the next quarter century holds for this unique approach to the architecture all of us encounter every day of our lives.

Mining for Virtue in Commodification

Jeffrey Brown, FAIA

> "Innovation is a development that people find useful or meaningful. To be innovative, architects—and works of architecture themselves—must become more responsive to their users and environments. In other words, they must incorporate feedback from their physical and cultural contexts rather than relying solely on conventional analytical or internal processes of development ... from design to construction."[1]
>
> Ali Rahim

An architectural monograph inevitably explicates buildings as the gathering of some type of observed or preconceived forces, influences, and concerns aesthetically synthesized across a single building or body of work into a physical proposition. As a whole, an approach to creating content is communicated, often as a philosophy or a proposition the work makes or in how it is decoded—its "theory," or in its "innovation." All architecture is innovation. It forms in the resistance to massive headwinds. It also comes in a variety of types, two of which, top-down and bottom-up innovation, are currently sponsoring a cleaving force in the profession of architecture.

When we reconsider our practice, we seem to land first on our approach to clients, who our clients are, what they are. We observe that seems to be different from many of the firms we admire. Client typology seems to be a difference between what we were doing and those firms who hold the leading narratives in architecture. A choice we made intuitively, early on, to take all clients, closed as many doors of opportunity to us as it opened. Our client base travels in quotidian building types. The anonymous warehouses, office buildings, and apartment complexes that constitute many more actual built structures than all "culturally significant" buildings combined. However, some architects rigorously curate their clients, which in turn closes off many problem types, and appears to us to narrow aspects of what represents "culture" as a whole. Yet many of those very firms are granted the mantle of defining culture through architecture. They lead by a top-down innovation on a minority of important but relatively rare building types. This makes us reflect upon our role as architects and as a practice engaging architecture as a cultural endeavor. We see connections between the significant building types and the "other" types in that the money to build the museum involved goods either stored or manufactured in a warehouse at some point. So, in working on so many of the less culturally infected building types, we employ a working heuristic of bottom-up innovation. This monograph allows us to re-inhabit some of the lessons innovating on the "mundane" that we have accumulated. For us, it turns out that some kinds of information transcend the moment of its making.

Recently, something unique happened in the 2023 Pritzker Prize acceptance speech by Sir David Chipperfield. He integrated, in what is likely to be one of the most important talks he will give, the state of architectural *practice* itself. I perceive this to be unique in so far as the press covering the speech took the lead in observing the inclusion of *practice* as a significant, if not surprising, aspect of understanding his oeuvre. It should not be surprising given his time in 2019 as guest editor for *Domus* magazine, where he employed "practice" as its organizing editorial theme. What is important is not so much *what* he said about it; rather it's the notion he mentioned practice at all. It's not often that practice, rather than the artifact itself, is considered an important aspect to understanding the work of an architect, determined by the fact it is rarely mentioned as a subject by any leading practitioner. The design of practice, its structure, its presence in the public psyche itself, which is separate from the presence of *architecture* in the public psyche, is noteworthy.

Nonetheless, what he did describe was a conception of architectural practice writ large, engaged in a kind of friction with cultural possibilities, or responsibilities regarding care for resources, equitable urban planning, and general resiliency. He positioned architectural practice as a monolithic force engaging culture as a whole on a kind of conversational frontier, implying that somehow architectural practice has a duty to define, accommodate, and interpret a cultural correction. He implied it could work on a broad front in unity. He described how architecture has the elasticity to ameliorate the current spectrum of cultural challenges, or at least synthesize them. He seemed to elide a "one profession, one practice" construct that was both intriguing and troubling—troubling in that such unity does not show up in our experience in practice. Finally, what Chipperfield's proposed effort translates into is a form of innovation and what its subject matter in architecture actually could be. In consideration, we were stimulated to see a new way of looking at those core values through the lens of the concept of practice and its *multitude of manifestations*. We perceive a more fractured manner in which architecture is practiced. The place we stand in practice, very different from where his notion of practice is situated, has a potential to cover neglected aspects of the very territory he inspires us to engage.

Over the past few years, after I ended my twelve-year teaching career, I have re-engaged by looking at the state of practice. With fresh eyes, I was curious and questioning about its form and structure, its design. Our practice had an ethical basis as its binding matrix. We took every client and treated the project on its own terms as best we could divine them. We did what we could with what we had at the time. Partially we operated out of the expediency of making it in business. We were happy to have any client who could pay for services. I was finding that what was seen as leading architecture, as an abstract condition, seemed to slip, on a regular basis, through the filters of its implied purpose to serve the public. Instead, the through line in dominant architectural discourse focuses on limited works that fit the creative interests of certain individual architects, simultaneously excluding many problem types left out of consideration by their practices. Two conditions of architectural practice seemed to be acting like the two-slit experiment with light, in which it appears to act as both a particle and a wave. But light does it simultaneously. Architectural practice seems to accomplish it only as a set of independent bypassing systems sold as simultaneity. Some architects do the right projects for their practice. Other architects do the required projects for their clients.

Consider that for a lay consumer of architecture, the building where she went to work on Friday had an architect. The museum she went to on Saturday afternoon also had an architect. They were not the same architect. Nor were they the same *type* of architect. Almost ever. For some practitioners, architecture is an approach to form making reserved for special occasions, and for others it is a service to produce forms for everyday consumption. This is a radical departure from what the assumption of architecture seems to be in polite society. I see ample evidence for a condition quite different than the one-profession solidarity of Chipperfield.

Peter MacKeith, in writing the introduction to SOM's *Journal 8* on the subject of collaboration, offers the following observation:

> "In the present day, in which the public (at least) perceives architecture as a bi-polar profession, constituted in large part as an anonymous service industry, but given effervescent, near-manic distinction by an overarching constellation of 'star-architects,' each practicing in distinctive 'signature' styles, the conceptions of teamwork, collaboration, and collective design leadership can slip all too easily under pressures of ego, marketing tools and public relations—or so it may seem."[2]

Dan Willis, writing in *Harvard Design Magazine*, also previews two conditions of practice when he says:

> "The industrialized practice of architecture has not resolved the inherent tension between architecture as a business and architecture as a creative act. And it never will."[3]

Kenneth Frampton is a bit more aggressive in distinguishing a divide of sorts in practice:

> "architecture has become a brand in itself, particularly for the 'signature' architect, whose mediatic overvaluation finds a direct correspondence in the systematic undervaluation of other equally if not more-talented architects whose work has yet to be confirmed by the mediatic consensus as a discernable and desirable brand."

Frampton also offers:

> "that there is a world of difference between architecture as a critical act and building as a banal, almost metabolic activity."[4]

These tangential clues, that there is something two-sided and also unspoken in the practice of architecture, are less obvious but nonetheless involve a similar recognition. Supporting the observations with our own experience, the "one profession" edifice is not precisely what we have observed over the tenure of our practice. At least not when we pause and look outside of our own day-to-day experience over twenty-five years. We have developed a concrete sense of a bifurcated profession, two types of practice practicing two different professions, at the same time for different client classes. The place we have come to stand in the conversational frontier of what it is we are doing, and why, reveals a vision of architecture as a divided self.

One way to describe this condition is to think of practice from two frameworks: One that we work from, and one in which we receive signals that we ought to be working from. There is an apparent, never actually mentioned but obvious, hierarchy in practice that reliably produces two distinct architectural results. One produces meaning and cultural content; the other produces the background, the datum from which the above class of building distinguishes itself. It is in the DNA of architects to reject this kind of structure as a false binary. The originality and uniqueness clause in the genes of everyone who has aspired to be, or become, an architect resists categorization. It would be easy to list 200 architects in sixty seconds who would reject either category. But it is real. The question for us has been: what is the infrastructure of this condition?

The thesis for practice that I coalesced around in my academic wake was that there seemed to be two sets of books being kept by architecture. Or at least, two distinct camps organized by the way they practice, for whom they work and what they deliver as a product. Yet the participants in both halves of this dual bookkeeping operate under a single portmanteau title of Architecture. To an observer this is reliably obvious. As to exactly *why* there appear to be two camps, depends upon who the observer is. The general consumer, experiencer, or audience of architecture will sense the difference between an office building and a museum intuitively. For this *outside observer* (the cohort of general public) there are two results in architecture, from which two camps of architects wouldn't be a stretch. But to *inside observers* (the cohort of architecture) the difference in "kinds" of architects is what defines the two camps, not necessarily the buildings each engages.

Margaret Crawford describes the evolution of the practice of architecture in her essay "Can Architects Be Socially Responsible?"[5] She is concerned with the perceived exclusion of social values in favor of a curated aesthetic system evolving in current practice, and attacks it with an analysis of the profession itself via its 100-year-old structural development, history, the source of its agency, and its transformation. She describes a profession begun by *practicing* architecture, which is then transformed by the immigration during World War II of influential practitioners and teachers of modernism to the institutions of the United States into *theorizing* architecture. In so doing she proposes the evolution of architects fighting and succeeding in establishing a separate status from the building trades. They transform into stewards of cultural concerns outside of technological limitations. She captures a version of a division between practice and theory borne out of the principles of modernism or, better described, its failures:

> "The narrowing of architectural practice has been balanced by an expanding architectural avant-garde, who, opposing the corruption of architecture by business, take roles closer to that of artist. Avoiding the inevitable 'contamination,' of the professional world of building, these architects survive through teaching, publication, competitions, and the growing niche in the art market for architectural models and drawings."[6]

The phrase "avoiding the inevitable 'contamination' of the professional world of building" could just as easily include "and the architects that participate in that space." She also appears, in the prospect of one type of practice contaminating another, to describe a binary approaching the current level of polarization in the profession.

From this very small sample of commentary, we see the roots of what is now the two-books problem.

Thus, the "Two Books Theory" involves two types of architects who coalesce around two distinct types of practice. Two ways of being an architect in the world, two ways of performing the work an architect does, two distinct *practices*:

1. The first is the Starchitect. The theory sustaining the starchitect is the Avant-Garde. The Academics of architecture maintain the concept of and legitimization of the avant-garde.

2. The second is the Marketect. The theory around which this type operates is the Every-Day. Commodification of architecture and its services drives the characteristics of the marketect.

The difference between them is that the marketect does almost all the buildings an architect is involved in. The starchitect designs most of the comparatively small number of buildings that claim to distinguish architecture from mere construction. Encoded in this dichotomy is what is deemed important in architecture, how that is determined, and who actually has access to participating in meaningful cultural expression through architecture and design. How or if this can be discussed *productively* in some way, and whether it is sustainable long-term, is what fascinates us.

Starchitects

Forced to establish the first starchitect, and skipping Google's choice of Frank Lloyd Wright, one might propose Palladio. He at the very least would easily connect to Le Corbusier via "The mathematics of the ideal villa." It is also not overly facile to trace a line between Clement Greenberg's definition of avant-garde (which is described below, under The Avant-Garde Defined), the painters he was defining, and Le Corbusier as the first starchitect. This route links through painting as Le Corbusier was painting as a Purist artist in the tradition of the contemporary avant-garde painters like Picasso. Le Corbusier also received international attention for both his written theories and his buildings, which were some of the most influential works in the world at that time. Making a direct move from then until the recent instantiation of starchitects could be the connection to Richard Meier, whose practice was inspired by Le Corbusier and was, prior to his downfall, a starchitect of the first order in the 1980s, 1990s, and early 2000s. This is a minimalist timeline that establishes a bare but useful baseline for what a starchitect was, is, and has now become.

The critique by the academy of the avant-garde, around neoliberal industrialization and mass culture items that art theorist Clement Greenberg explored, have been absorbed via theory into architecture. As more money in the 1980s and 1990s came into play in architecture and art, critics like Dave Hickey described a *trahision des clercs* (treason of the intellectuals) argument around the failure of institutions and the academy to support work that broke boundaries in new ways, yet was suppressed by government regulation in the case of Robert Mapplethorpe, for example. In the same vein, architecture critics like Jeffrey Kipnis explored neoliberal and corporate forces sponsoring extreme versions of styles of architecture to become the brand of the corporation itself.

This trend has spawned many well-known architects. It was manifest in many instances as a kind of ersatz commodification in the form of signature styles—not for corporations but for the architects themselves, repeated again and again in limited building types. There is an urban legend about the University of Cincinnati campus needing an "Eisenman"[7] to add to its collection. (Columbus, Indiana, could be another easy example.)

More recently, transformation of starchitects into influencer architects is underway via social media. Style is being replaced by likes. Complicating matters are the subsets within starchitects: influencer architects and master architects. This really doesn't muddy the water much as they are all equally of a sort. How to tell the difference almost doesn't matter. But the game can be fun: Bjarke Ingels? Influencer architect, easy. Master architect, not so easy ...; Tadao Ando? Starchitect? Perhaps. Master architect? Indeed ...; Renzo Piano? Starchitect. Sure. Master builder. Positively. Influencer perhaps not.

Setting aside the spectrum of possible inclusion in the starchitect universe, the main organizing characteristics of established starchitects follow:

The careful curation of incoming clients appropriate for the kind of work said starchitect wants to pursue. It is not an easy exercise to identify the turning away of services by a licensed professional; in fact, architecture appears to be unique in this respect. This curation also appears to be blatant and systematized. An easy illustration of this is the Architectural League of New York's new interview series "I Would Prefer Not To." The project was conceived and produced by Critical Broadcasting Lab Director Ana Miljački and includes many luminaries in the starchitect world. In a blog piece on Archinect about the interview series, Josh Niland shares the concern:

> "'Decisions to refuse a commission, or withdraw from one, by definition, stay hidden from public scrutiny, and thus also hidden from architectural history,' the Architectural League notes. 'Withdrawals of this kind do not leave paper trails. If at all, they exist as specters of professional gossip, not easy to examine or learn from. And yet, the lessons contained in architects' deliberations about, and decisions not to engage, are politically relevant and urgent.'"[8]

The commodification of a style that identifies the work as a brand that differentiates itself in the market. The thrust of the above system, as a form of subsidized self-expression, requires attempts to stimulate the production of meaningful form. They are derived mostly from the influences happening in discourses outside of architecture—cultural issues, social, economic, ideological and technological or methodological—mediated by influences generated in the academy. They are put forth as original and unique interpretations and pertain to a preference for originality over creativity. And yet there appears to be an eerie similarity across the spectrum of work the starchitect group publishes. It has become very hard to tell a BIG building from an MVRDV building from a Ben van Berkel from an OMA, etc. Further, starchitects such as Daniel Libeskind develop motifs that repeat across project types, defeating the originality proposition. In his case, the motifs designed for the landmark Jewish Museum in Berlin reappear in a dormitory and a retail complex. This has not been lost on architectural observers like Nicolai Ouroussoff. Writing in *Harvard Design Magazine*, he creates a framework of architecture being in the middle of a long overdue ethical reckoning and the development of design software that manifests in "the tendency of some architects to dress up a corporate mindset in language that evokes radical designs of the past."[9] He observes:

> "Much of Ingels's [BIG] design output is made up of easily digestible one-liners, which tend to become blander and more meaningless as they are repeated ... Nor is Ingels alone in using vague and ultimately meaningless metaphors to obscure rather than clarify a building's meaning ... Such practices can be partly dismissed as a canny marketing strategy."[10]

But it is in the *practice* of starchitects, where the work and the supporting theory or apparatus of ideas behind them are sustained by selecting only the projects and clients that fit the theory.

There is a problem statement *a priori* for the work selected by the starchitect, rather than an acceptance of the work that comes in the door. It must be the right project, with an adequate budget (often to be blown past in the chase for immortality) and must be supported by the client in a patron-like way. They are no customer of mere services, but rather are willing to subsidize the self-expression of an impresario with the assumption that some symbolic cultural manifestation will always emanate from the work of this architect on their concern.

The starchitect has to be careful not to take on clients who are not interested in a form of subsidized self-expression lest the brand becomes impure. It is a strategy that appears to carry a heavy cultural mortgage, yet it is the manner of *practicing* employed by the celebrity architect. Chipperfield appears both aware of this when he talks of design *and* unaware there might be an alternative way of practice not exercising the same agency.

The Avant-Garde Defined

As the supporting meta theory of the starchitects, the term "avant-garde" itself, at least at is relates to this discussion, is a portmanteau word. It first appeared around 1825, casually mentioned in an essay on the artist's role in driving social reform. Its modern use was established by Clement Greenberg in the magazine *Partisan Review* defining the work of the abstract expressionist painters. In constructing his theory, he does two things: he points out something unprecedented is happening in painting and grants it a quality of superiority. Things not in that category are lower, less valuable; thus, they define "kitsch." The move he makes is hierarchical. Things that are not "unprecedented" are *inferior*, at least as genuine expressions of the zeitgeist aspect of culture at any moment. This notion of inferiority is important.[11]

In architectural use, "avant-garde" became the term summarizing the coalescence of modernist impulses in the transfer of Franco-German modernism to the United States in the form of international-style modernism. This entailed differentiating and underwriting the concept of architects who practiced a "correct" leading style that one either emulated or was seen to be out of step. The term continues to be used mostly in academia even if it continues its simplified meaning outside of it. Michael Hays captures a sense of how loaded, or unloaded for that matter, the term itself has become. A thorough reading of Hays's book *Architecture's Desire: Reading the Late Avant-Garde* gets one through the *historical* avant-garde all the way to the *late* avant-garde then onto the doorstep of its revival as *neo* avant-garde. In his book he observes:

> "The 'over and over' again indictment of the post-war avant-garde, numbing repetitions of forms left over from the presumed authentic historical avant-garde became something of a leftist critical trope ... the neo avant-garde institutionalizes the avant-garde as art and thus negates genuinely avant-garde intentions."[12]

One can go beyond Hays to find the zombie quality of the term. Tomes have been written exploring what avant-garde means; if it is dead as concept; if it led architecture astray as a discipline; if it ever applied to architecture rather than only to art; if indeed it ever existed, and many more topics that the term inspires. Avant-garde is in some ways a touchstone formulation or tenet of most architectural theory, or at least hierarchy. But it is a common understanding among architects that matters here. There is no confusion between something framed in a discussion between architects as avant-garde and something simply not; something banal. While it may, in that context, not necessarily be a compliment, the intention is clear even if the concept is incredibly complex. So why use the term? It is self-evident that it simply has not offloaded its common understanding of "cutting edge." That is not an assignment of quality to its use, simply an indictment of how the term is used and understood in common architectural discourse. Avant-garde, for purposes of this effort, is employed with a full understanding of the dilution of its once more precise meaning, a term that has had its currency debased in many ways, but also in recognition of its capacity to circumscribe the elements in a specific component of practice relevant to the discussion of starchitect practice.

If you want to know where architecture *is*, its status, what's current or "going on" you would look to starchitects. But be careful—it is not necessarily where to look if one wants to know what that work is supposed to mean. For content, one tracks what the next instantiation of the avant-garde is or is becoming in the support infrastructure of starchitects, the academy. It is academics where the content has traditionally been generated. It is also where the ethical DNA of architecture is formed, manipulated, and edited.

Academics

It is no secret that the star chamber for starchitects is the academy and academics. There are many debates around what should be taught in architecture programs, regulated by the N.A.A.B.[13] Design often fights for its life over technical and practical issues in what young architects need to learn before they practice. Some schools have remained design oriented; others have become more vocational. The design schools are where the proto-starchitect thrives best. While the roots perhaps go much deeper, the establishment in 1964 of the Institute for Architecture and Urban Studies in New York led by Peter Eisenman was the beginning of collapsing the European academic system into the American academic system from which the design schools evolved. Faculty like Rem Koolhaas, along with their work, had access to publication, which begat notoriety.

Academics also allow for the aspiring starchitect, or at least the faculty member who intuitively curates their clients, a steady paycheck, and an endless cheap labor pool. Often the teaching and the work of the academic architects are one and the same in the form of "research." Related to research, there exists in the architectural academy a subset of faculty teaching and establishing theory. Theory is the evolution of what was, pre-1970s, architectural history. The journals filled by the evolution from history to theory, established a foundation for the avant-garde theories' integration into architecture and thus the establishment of the starchitect. Early publications such as *Oppositions* integrated intellectual history, philosophy, and criticism into the teaching of architecture and into the theories by which architecture was deemed to be avant-garde. Later journals such as *Assemblage* seemed to shift emphasis to works of architecture and the interpretation of them. Most recently, in the most defined theoretical movement in terms of discourse and discussion, the shift away from the notion of criticality to the concept of projectivity, directly supports and advertises the work of starchitects. Simplified, this theory prefers the acceptance of work as response to hyper-contextual forces rather than criticality's stance against the typical. Projectivity relies on a feedback loop with the work of starchitects, just short of a form of rationalization. The academy and starchitects seem to be moving toward singularity and collapsing critical distance.

Under the mantra of publish or perish, many schools support academic journals, spots in which are highly coveted by faculty in order to establish bona fides sometimes related to the design of buildings. There are also academic industry publications that serve as the occasional launch pad for a young starchitect. Either way, the academy through a web of well-established connections to the professional architectural media, who are always looking for the competitive scoop, is ready to supply. The result of the closed system between starchitects and the academy is maintained by a highly regulated and programmed media narrative.

The most synthetic exposition on the origins of the mediated content in architecture is in several sections of Diane Ghirardo's 1991 book *Out of Site: A Social Criticism of Architecture*, particularly her introduction. She is writing in reaction to a conference held in 1989 entitled "Postmodernism and Beyond: Architecture as the Critical Art of Contemporary Culture," which explored architecture's response to contemporary problems through form. She observes numerous problems with this premise framed around the radicality of the notion that architecture could eschew social, economic, and political concerns by creating a rubric between architects and critics/academics for evaluating buildings exclusive of concerns other than form. In so doing, she argues media, through a class of practitioners and critics, controls the selection of what is relevant in architecture and what is not via curation of media and discourse. She states:

"This essentially self-serving scheme for determining what is legitimate and pertinent operates to mystify architecture."

She counters with objections that the 80 percent of all buildings done by non-architects, i.e., most of the built environment, simply cannot be empty of content on the basis of its relationship to mass or low culture. In her words:

"Excluding a certain class of questions and building also means not facing up to the whole range of problems they present."[14]

The balance of her argument describes and integrates the value of non-architect buildings, those done by builders and contractors, as having value, and highlights the danger in dismissing that value when trying to accurately assess cultural conditions by looking only at a curated set of concerns or values. Here, without granting her too much agency, can be seen the roots of the "class" distinction between starchitect and marketecture practices. For Ghirardo, it is a distinction between a narrowly defined set of cultural issues defined by architects against an equally important bottom-up set of cultural issues, in many ways more inclusive issues, embodied in the vast non-architect-built environment. While the dichotomies of commodity and art, market and culture are hinted at here, she doesn't establish that there are really two kinds of architects rather than one. That is, a great many of what she called non-architect buildings actually do have an architect involved in them, just not the right kind of architect, it turns out.

Marketecture

The marketecture group does not, in ecumenical terms, curate clients. If some agency causes the right projects to accumulate to starchitecture, the marketecture is an extreme contrast. The doors are open to all comers in the mainstream—it's the democratic underbelly of starchitecture. If you need architectural services, you have a right to get them, no matter the potential content or fit with ambition and interest, as it were. This inclusionary interface does not exclude firms built around building-type specialization. There are K–12 specialty firms and interior design firms and other types of specialization within this group. Yet the same rules apply: if you specialize in K–12 school work, *all* K–12 clients are welcome—not just the very high-end, high-budget private schools. All schools. In fact, the more the better for any type of specialist marketect.

Firm size seems to be as balanced in the marketecture practice format as it is in the starchitect format. There are some very small boutique firms and there are some quite large format practices with hundreds of employees in both practices. According to a recent Economic Census, there were 20,836 architecture firms in the United States. Less than 5 percent of them appear to be starchitect designed less than 5 percent of all projects. Approximately 20 percent of all firms employ 80 percent of all architects in the states. They form a cohort we see as the "Branded Band" firms. They are the likes of HOK, SOM, P&W, KPF; large-format firms packaged as alphabet-brand logos very much like LVMH, CNN, etc. The markecture firms on the large side still take all comers and perform about 60 percent of all projects done. The average number of architects in a firm not in the Branded Band hover around four employees. Average-sized firms make up an estimated 75 percent of all firms and undertake approximately 35 percent of all projects.

Beyond variable size and non-selectivity, marketecture firms share common reactions to two key trends and conditions:

The radical reaction to the market for architectural services. Post Great Recession of 2008, no business, profession, or trade took up where it left off before this historic economic event. They all get the new normal. Architects, however, gave every indication that they just needed to wait until the clients "come back." When it does return, we determined, it will not come back to us. Architects missed the meaning in the new normal: There are no more "clients" to hunt, only "markets" to participate in now. Breaking protocol, marketecture is a compounding of market and architecture.

Architects will have to "go to" the market with a product rather than waiting for the market to come back requesting services. The value proposition of architecture has changed. Innovation in mainstream everyday practice requires that we understand markets don't behave like clients. Most explicitly, rather than targeting a single client, you place a product in the market, which is open 24 hours a day, every day, and the clients come to you. So, in some ways the market is an abstraction, like a place that exists only virtually and thus is vulnerable to wide "interpretation" when it comes to its effect on, its interaction with, something like architecture. For marketects the market is where the sorting is done. We have often lectured around this topic to professional architectural audiences. Inevitably, we draw laughter when we state that you know you are a marketect if you have ever been selected on no other criteria than your fee for a project assignment. Almost everyone raises their hand when asked if this has ever been the case. We obviously are talking to marketects. This will cause tremors for starchitects.

The accommodation of the concept of commodification is architecture, or its building types. This framework of commodity is vastly different from the creation of a style of architecture as a brand. This application or interpretation of commodity has to do with the market pressures on the abandoned building types left over after the curation of the starchitects. Building types like speculative office buildings, warehouses, market-rate multifamily buildings, pad sites, all forms of retail from power centers to strip malls and many other of the miscellany that people anonymously drive by on the way home from work. These building types often come with up to 80 percent of all decisions regarding form, size, and format *before* the architect is brought on board. Decisions like how the *owner's brokers* think the *client's brokers* expects the core to be placed in an office building for optimum efficiency, the depth of retail typologies based on to whom they will be leased, and any other manner of form-influencing criteria that the financing of the project has more input on than does any aesthetic concern. Marketects work this neglected territory with as much ingenuity as any starchitect-designed museum, yet the aesthetic outcome is obviously limited. Deviate at peril from any force the market deems to preordain, and you will not be seen as clever or creative but rather as not a good investment. It's the stuff left out. It is the everyday aspect of architecture that constitutes the average *everyday* experience of the built environment.

The "Everyday" Defined

The notion of the everyday has fascinated artists, authors, and photographers, as a pursuit of authenticity. The term itself immediately establishes a tension with the notion of the avant-garde. In fact, one assumes it defines kitsch, the lesser of the results in operations of the avant-garde, the inferior. Any exploration of the notion of the everyday in architecture would brace itself against the work of Denise Scott Brown and Robert Venturi on Las Vegas. This work established the circumstantial, unplanned, and ad hoc as acceptable grounds for research and inspiration, to name a few of its achievements. Landmark exhibitions such as "The Family of Man" in 1955 at the Modern Museum of Art, which comprised photographs curated by Edward Steichen of everyday people in their everyday places and circumstances from all over the world, were transformative on numerous fronts from the political to the artistic conceptions of the everyday.

Everydayness as an architectural force has since spawned a robust lineage that includes a very good collection of essays under the title of *Architecture of the Everyday*, edited by Steven Harris and Deborah Berke in 1997. In his introductory essay Harris establishes the precept that the:

> "Consideration of everyday life as a political construct represents an attempt to suggest an architecture resistant to the ... commodification/consumption paradigm, a paradigm that has come to dominate contemporary architectural practice."[15]

This sounds as if everydayness's engagement with the concept of commodity is a legitimate force in marketecture, but in context Harris sees commodification, quite early in the game, as a problem with the avant-garde rather than with marketecture. The book is organized around the core notion of everydayness by philosopher Henri Lefebvre, and Mary McLeod's critique of it.

Lefebvre, in his seminal essay "The Everyday and Everydayness" defines his operational sense of the concept as follows:

> "The everyday can therefore be defined as a set of functions which connect and join together systems that might appear to be distinct. Thus defined, the everyday is a product, the most general of products in an era where production engenders consumption, and where consumption is manipulated by producers."[16]

He posited that intellectuals sought their references elsewhere than the everyday in subjects like language and politics and social structures. He saw the everyday as a referent framework to make the study of the banal exciting or at least important. Thus, it's a concept that opposes the basic keystones of avant-garde theory of hierarchy and inferiority in terms of refutation. Mary McLeod summarizes his mainline argument:

> "... stems from a relatively modest aesthetic and political program: a rejection of avant-garde escapism, pretension, and heroicism in favor of a more sensitive engagement with people's everyday environments and lives."[17]

If you want to know what the subject matter, the basis of study, and focus is of the marketect, the concept of the everyday describes the territory. The everyday exposes a world infrastructure of repetition and rational geometry as a deep structure in which one could operate subversively. It's a concept that simultaneously accepts and critiques homogenization. This is the operational theater of the marketect.

Commodification

The significant principal of commodification applied here is that of seeing architectural buildings as products within the financial and consumer audiences versus seeing them as expressions of culture with the style of the architects acting as the commodity. It is the notion of the former that architecture internally seems to consistently reject on multiple fronts. Buildings do exist as commodities for marketects. Karl Marx defined a commodity as "any good or service produced by human labor and offered as a product for sale in the general market."[18] Buildings are usable and otherwise undifferentiated articles of trade or commerce that are produced by human labor, subject to competitive pricing and driven to efficiency. All these commodity traits apply to certain building types, particularly the ones marketecture practices encounter without a functional theory to employ beyond *everydayness*.

In his introductory essay to the pamphlet "Commodification and Spectacle in Architecture" Frampton is unrelenting in his frustration that the contributing authors seem to miss the bigger issue of the growing challenges of consumerism and commodification. In his summary of Michael Benedikt's critique of the irrelevance of elitist aestheticism as he describes it, Frampton observes:

> "One can hardly be sanguine about his economic determinism rendered exclusively in terms of populist market forces. It is somehow unconscionable, given his realistic stance, that he has nothing to say about the not so benign neglect of public transport in the United States."[19]

Chipperfield's call to architectural practice to solve social injustices runs parallel to Kenneth Frampton's urgency in extending the evils of commodification well beyond architecture, indeed to the environment as well. Two opposing conditions of commodification have been presented—branding by aesthetic product (the style a starchitect establishes) and collaboration with commercial forces (direct accommodation of market criteria). They represent the supposed rejection of commodification in the presentation of starchitect work and the engagement of commodification by the practice of marketects. This brings two main themes together. The notion that one monolithic practice concept implied by Chipperfield can both navigate the market such as it is and simultaneously be the front of solutions to cultural ills does not hold up. We propose that it is precisely these conditions that cause two forms of practice. Architecture just doesn't seem to be able to equally engage on two fronts.

Conclusion

> "The basic criterion for any kind of human excellence is simply how heavy a demand it makes on the intelligence. How inclusive a consciousness does it focus? By this standard there is very little fiction in a century, very little music, and very little poetry or painting which deserves attention for its own sake. One function of the critic is to keep the best work free from the surrounding clutter. But, in order to free the mind from the debilitating confusion, it is not enough to claim priority for excellence without considering the bulk which is inferior. To win more and more attention for the best work it is necessary to demonstrate what constitutes the inevitably second rate, third rate, and so on. And in the course of doing this one finds the great work of a period has much in common with the poorest work ... The great artist necessarily has his roots very deep in his own time—roots which embrace the most vulgar and commonplace fantasies and aspirations."[20]
>
> Marshall McLuhan, "Money in Comics," *The Mechanical Bride*

By way of re-statement, the claim being made here by Marshall McLuhan is that practice is largely split between two types of architectural practices populated by two types of architects. McLuhan seems to suggest there may not be too much distance between the products both practice types produce, divided without a difference. But this does not overcome the separate spheres of operation as regards cultural relevance. There are also troubling developments in each camp to boot. In the starchitecture world, there has been a reversal of sorts regarding the flow from the academy to practice. More and more, it is practice that is leading the academy, particularly in what constitutes research. Theory has also become controversial around the facile accommodation of starchitecture. The post-critical theory described as performativity above in the academic section, has caused a fair amount of rancor in the journals. Critic Mark Wigley has come out describing it as theory being used to endorse and promote brand, "which is just a sort of powerfully naïve position." This is the polite disagreement he makes. He goes on to observe:

> "The problem was that this group [of performativity theorists] was not very accomplished, and so they had all these anxieties because very soon they became embarrassed at their own company ... I think it was, more or less, a cynical self-branding exercise that received currency only because there is a deeply anti-intellectual core in the American academy. So they tried to describe the need for architects to be praised in this uncritical way."[21]

The efficient machine of the starchitecture academic feedback mechanism appears to have confused the menu with the meal. In the marketecture world things are not much better. The problem in what has become such a service-based business is that it has become good business, and as such, business-like stuff is bound to snowball. Lately there has been massive consolidation in the marketecture sector, with bigger marketects buying the expertise of smaller marketects. There also has been a hot market for marketects to be purchased by engineering/architecture firms, that is, large engineering conglomerates buy smaller marketecture firms to enter the market as providers of all services. More insidiously, private equity has become interested in buying marketecture firms. This turns the business of architecture into ... *business*, as this owner group only looks at profit. So, the fraying of starchitects into celebrity architects, master architects, and influencer architects all combining to work on very few building types, alongside the marketecture firms combining with other types of businesses, may leave any notion of "unification" impossible.

How this came to be the current state of things may be less important than the silent distortive effect it is having on architecture's cultural role. Discussing it is less a case for revolting against this situation than it is elevating awareness that something transformative is happening in architectural practice and without announcement, new territory is being entered and simultaneously created and/or abandoned without a noise. Our practice has dwelled on this threshold, wondering whether this format can last forever. Can fewer and fewer buildings be the "subject" of architecture as "architecture" with the balance of building types left as mere architectural services? In context, Chipperfield challenges us to determine just what is an architecture's patch.

Practicing as marketects we have no other position to take than optimism in our efforts to operate within the constraints of the everyday building types and project types that are our lot. The most visionary projects here and the least visionary projects here are the result of the design of our architectural practice. We don't see it as a battle between bureaucracy and art; rather we see it as a challenge to innovate, from the bottom up, in smaller episodes than an entire building, to enter our own feedback loop with the market's financial pressures. For us it is a matter of optimizing architecture's potential within circumstances that chose us, not in circumstances we chose. And finally, we work toward mining for virtue in commodification.

Jeffrey Brown, FAIA
Gloucester, Massachusetts
November 2023

Endnotes

1 Ali Rahim, *Catalytic Formations: Architecture and Digital Design* (New York: Taylor & Francis, 2006), 3.

2 Peter MacKeith, "On Teamwork: Standards and Practices," *SOM Journal 8* (Chicago, IL: Skidmore, Owings & Merrill, 2011), 8.

3 Daniel Willis, "Are Charrettes Old School?" *Harvard Design Magazine* (Cambridge, MA: Harvard University Graduate School of Design, 2010), f/w vol. II, no. 33, 31.

4 Kenneth Frampton in the Introduction in *Out of Site: A Social Criticism of Architecture* (Seattle, WA: Bay Press, 1991), Kenneth Frampton & Diane Ghirardo (eds.), 17.

5 Margaret Crawford, "Can Architects Be Socially Responsible?" in *Out of Site: A Social Criticism of Architecture* (Seattle, WA: Bay Press, 1991), Kenneth Frampton & Diane Ghirardo (eds.), 27.

6 ibid., 42.

7 Author recalls the story as being circulated by Peter Eisenman himself.

8 Josh Niland, "I Would Prefer Not To," Archinect (August 30, 2023), accessed December 22, 2023, https://archinect.com/news/article/150363902/i-would-prefer-not-to-looks-at-refused-commissions-the-decisions-behind-them-and-their-impact-on-architecture

9 Nicolai Ouroussoff, *Harvard Design Magazine* (Cambridge, MA: Harvard University Graduate School of Design, 2022), s/s 22, no. 50, 71.

10 ibid., 74.

11 Clement Greenberg in "Avant-Garde and Kitsch," *Partisan Review* (New York: John Reed Club of New York, 1939). He defines it as an approach to art from a vanguard culture set against mainstream culture—what everyone else is doing in one sense, what culture expects in another. The vanguard work sets itself against mass culture and thus in a way capitalism, in Greenberg's use. He saw the mainstream cultural output as a result of mass industrialization, which produced what he called kitsch. In a way he was talking about, specifically in the abstract expressionist works he was describing, real creativity from market-driven innovation made to sell, rather than record in the work, new forms of interpretation and new territory.

12 K. Michael Hays, *Architecture's Desire: Reading the Late Avant-Garde* (Cambridge, MA: MIT Press, 2010), 4.

13 N.A.A.B. (National Architecture Accreditation Board). This organization approves and reviews architectural curriculums in schools and grants accreditation for the degree.

14 Diane Ghirardo in the "Introduction" in *Out of Site: A Social Criticism of Architectur*e (Seattle, WA: Bay Press, 1991), Kenneth Frampton and Diane Ghirardo (eds.), 14.

15 Steven Harris in *Architecture of the Everyday* (New York: Princeton Architectural Press, 1997), Deborah L. Berke and Steven Harris (eds.), 3.

16 Henri Lefebvre "The Everyday and Everydayness," *Yale French Studies*, Henri Lefebvre and Christine Levich (eds.), (New Haven, CT: Yale University Press, 1987), 7–11.

17 Mary McLeod in *Architecture of the Everyday* (New York: Princeton Architectural Press, 1997), Deborah L. Berke and Steven Harris (eds.), 11.

18 Karl Marx, *Capital: A Critique of Political Economy* (in German: *Das Kapital*), 1867.

19 Kenneth Frampton in the "Introduction" in *Commodification and Spectacle in Architecture: A Harvard Design Magazine Reader* (Cambridge, MA: Harvard University Graduate School of Design, 2005), William S. Saunders (ed.), 3.

20 Marshall McLuhan, "Money in Comics," *The Mechanical Bride: Folklore of Industrial Man* (Boston, MA: Beacon Press, 1967), 152.

21 Mark Wigley in *Oxymoron & Pleonasm: Conversations on American Critical and Projective Theory of Architecture*, (New York, Actar Publishers, 2015), Monika Mitášová (ed.), 88, 89–90.

"This monograph allows us to re-inhabit some of the lessons innovating on the 'mundane' we have accumulated. For us, it turns out that some kinds of information transcend the moment of its making."

NO SMOKING
NMF
PILOT
TUG

One of the foundational binaries in architectural design strategies related to space, private versus public, can also apply to building types. There are both public and private building types that resolve easily. A library is public, yet it may have "private" areas in its program, while a house is invariably private, but organized in a hierarchy of spaces the public enters (like the parlor) and others they cannot.

In the world of the mainstream architect, the determination of public or private can be reduced to funding. The source of the money of the desire of the client to privatize what could be considered inherently public—the private chapel, the private library—is not uncommon. Often a private building's macro program is to establish a company's brand via its statement, its architecture, thus messaging a population who will never be invited to enter the premises.

Consider **Frank's International** corporate headquarters on an industrial site in rural Louisiana, designed to "send a message" to the competitor just across the road; **Seismic Exchange** corporate headquarters and the desire to recall the genus loci of the home city of the owners in New Orleans made manifest in a single building in a satellite Houston business park; and **Pavilion**, which is an inherently public typology funded entirely by private resources to compete with numerous other outdoor venues in the greater Houston metro complex. The public nature of the rooftop garden in Seismic, the kinetic transformation of private to public room in the hangar door space in Frank's are reminders that the original public–private binary can be a "both/and" condition.

Private

Frank's

Frank's International is a five-level corporate headquarters for a global oil services company base in Lafayette, Louisiana. Our task was to create a core and shell condition with the anticipation of an interior design to be provided by the client at a later date. Thus, the challenge we had was creating specificity for the company, controlling only some of the variables. So, we proposed an outside-in process. By strategizing the façade with architectural hierarchies and interstitial spaces that blurred the boundaries between interior and exterior, we were able to inform the unknown future of the building's interior. We assigned a different architecture, varying in levels of transparency, to each unique department. A composition of punched openings applied to the south and west faces overlook the industrial facility. This area is intended for technicians administering various operations around the site. A curtain wall system with vertical fins diffusing west light faces outward, presenting a dominantly glass façade to the public side of the facility (intended for sales and marketing use). We used a beyond-the-wall approach as a device for separating visitors from operational uses. A two-level, triple-height zinc and curtain wall volume shelters a terrace over the glass box, offering panoramic views of the site. This element is intended to sponsor a conference center and spans both sides of the wall. We infused each skin strategy with exterior spaces nested within the building's massing at each level to provide access to air and light while encouraging collaboration between employees.

We infused each skin strategy with exterior spaces nested within the building's massing at each level providing access to air and light while encouraging collaboration between employees.

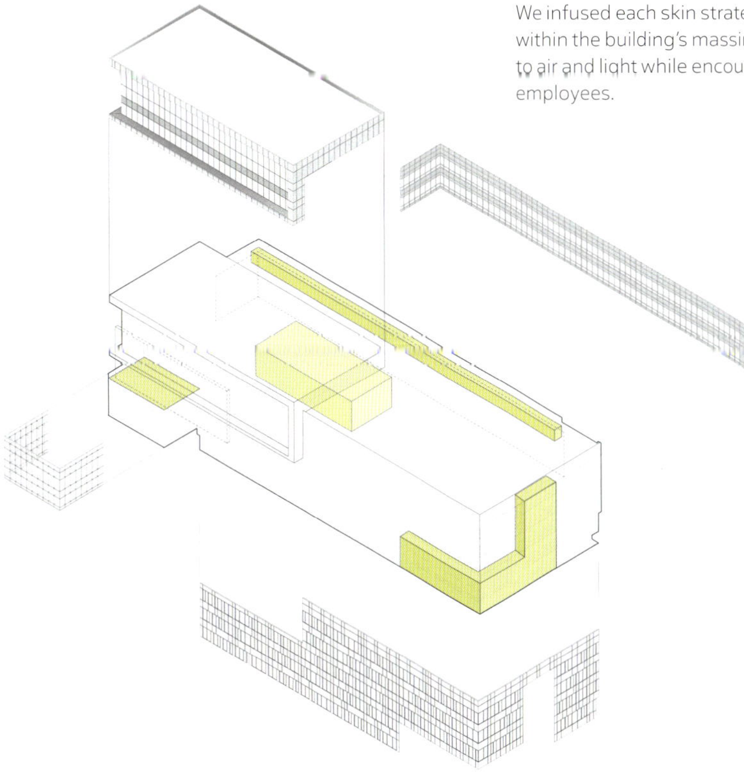

Axonometric—massing and skin strategy

700

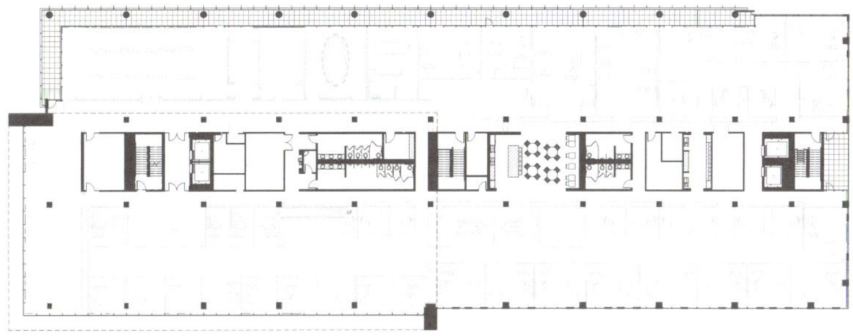

Fifth-floor plan

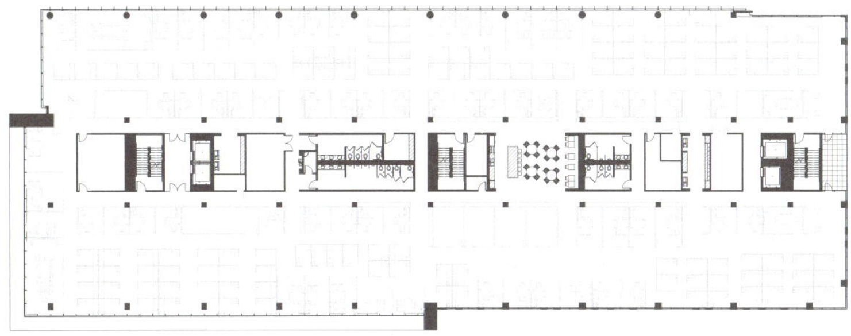

Fourth-floor plan

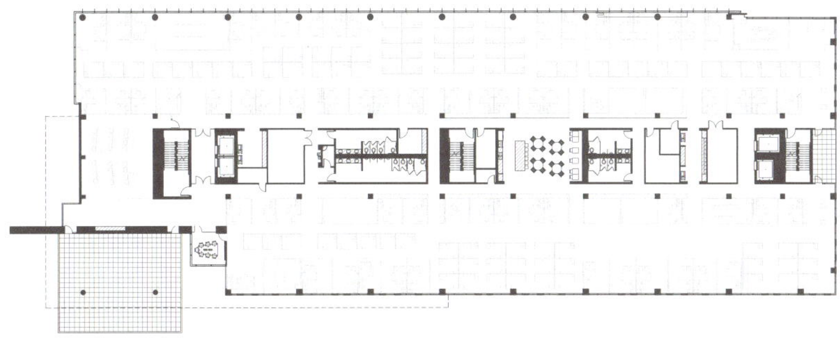

Third-floor plan

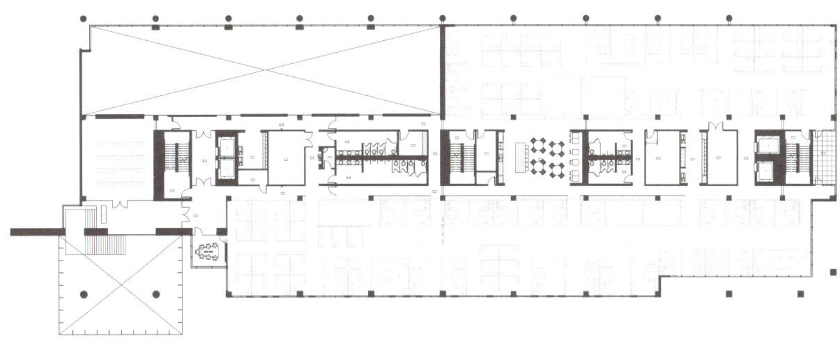

Second-floor plan

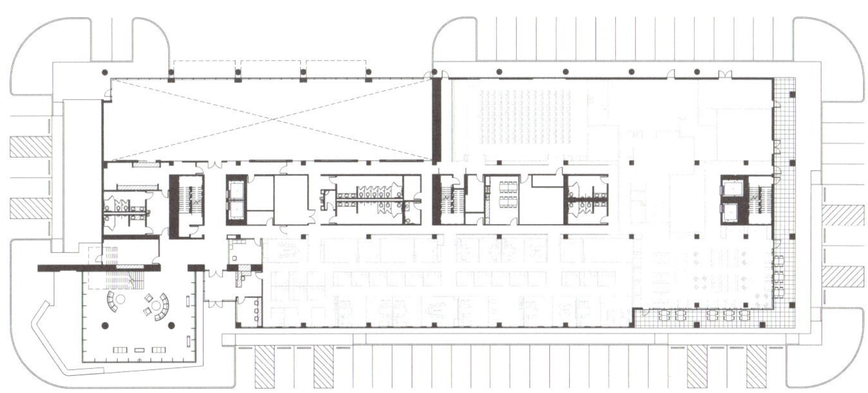

First-floor plan

Frank's Top 3 Safety
Years on Record!

Pavilion

The Westchase District is a 4.2-square-mile territory located in West Houston. The District has a population of nearly 25,000 residents, similar to that of Manhattan, and is served by two school districts, one public building (a library) and no dedicated public green space. Decimated and humiliated by office towers from the 1970s and 1980s, strip centers, surface parking, and aging apartment complexes, the District faced the problem of all future development requiring detention due to downstream flooding.

The District has implemented numerous projects with federal funds for situational sites over the last several years, like linear parks under utility easements and improvements of existing canals. It also has attracted several private developers by utilizing market-based theoretical urban interventions designed by us as incentives. It also has looked to compete with the many similar districts in the metropolitan agglomeration. Several competing districts provide cultural venues and Westchase is geographically situated in a non-overlapping pool of possible patrons, enough to support a new outdoor events venue.

The pavilion is designed to activate a parcel in the District with a combination park space and outdoor performance venue as an anchor to much-needed housing and service retail. The pavilion is proposed to seat 5,000 people undercover. The roof is a tensile fabric canopy held up by laminated structural wood set with tree-like columns that extend the park metaphor, linking the building architecture and its surrounds.

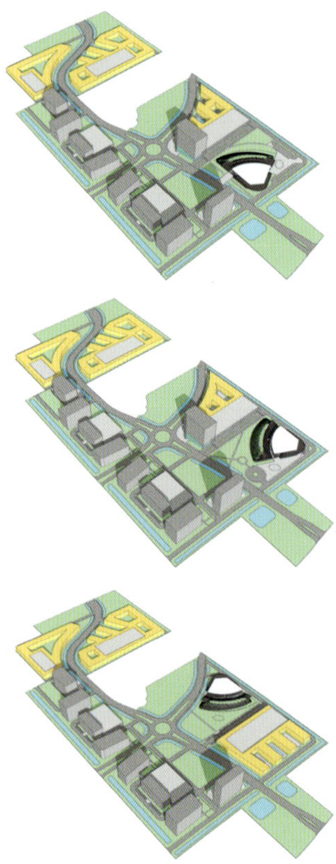

Site plan options

Overall site plan

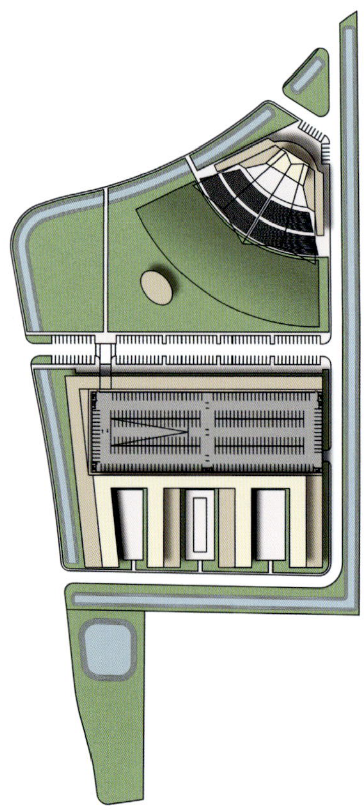

Enlarged site plan

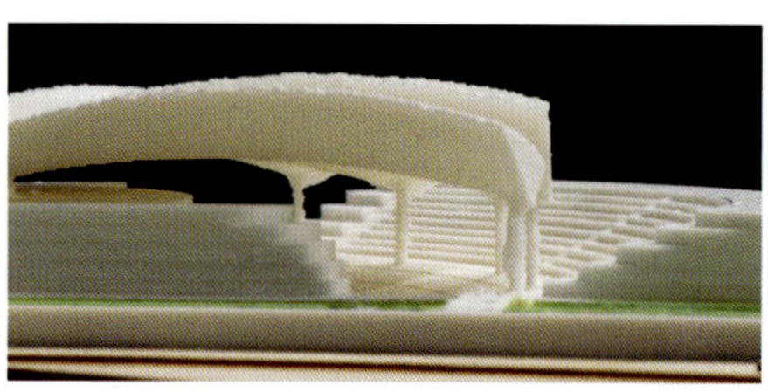

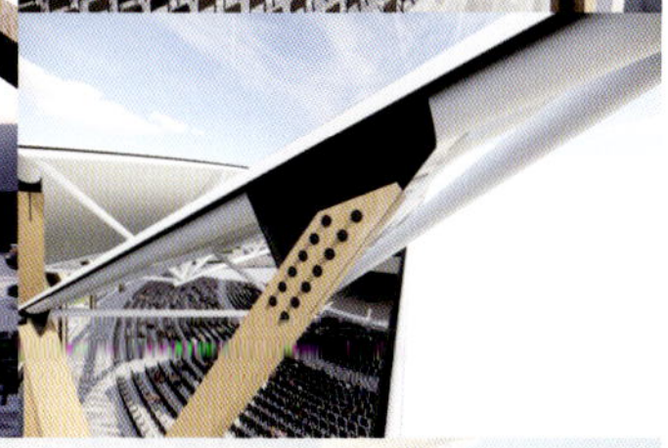

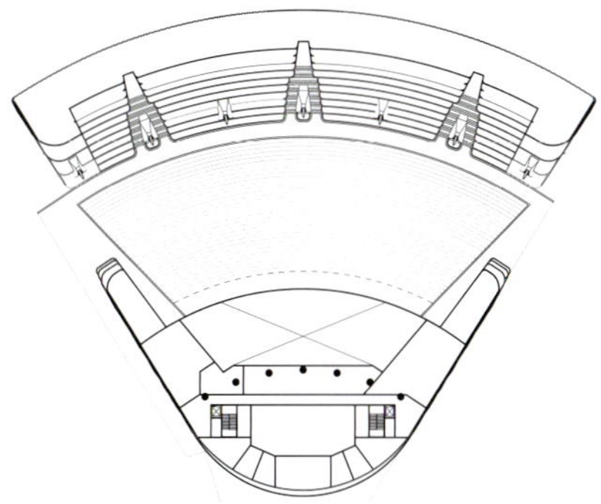

Second-level floor plan

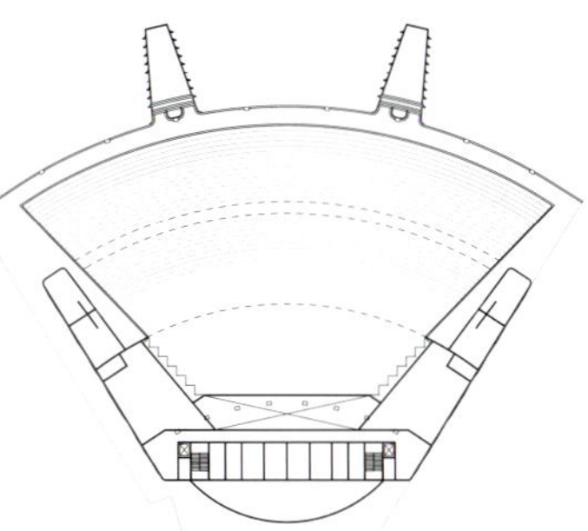

First-level floor plan

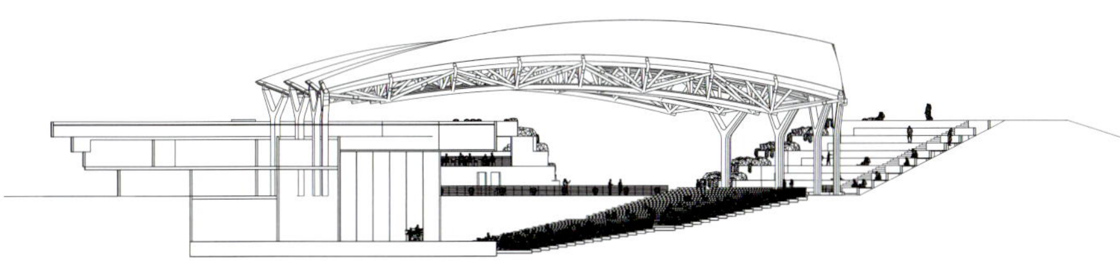

Section

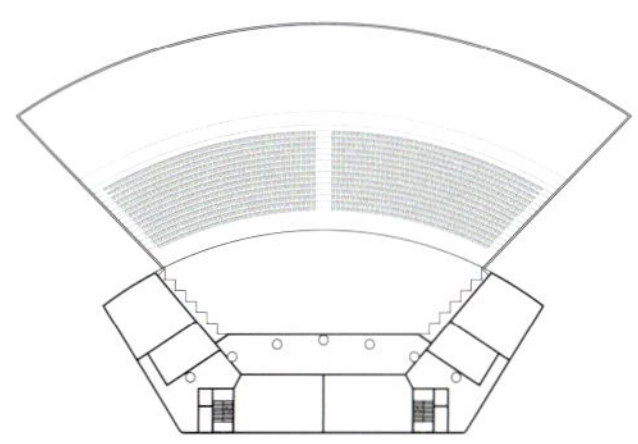

Stage-level floor plan

Seismic

This project was designed for a Louisiana-based company that was compelled to consolidate its headquarters in Houston, post–Hurricane Katrina. The decision to move was emotional and complicated for the owners and this complexity infused the design process.

The clients had influences and interests they wanted taken into consideration for the new headquarters, including a preference for the feel of the social scene of New Orleans. To be clear, they did not want to mimic the French Quarter stylistically so much as infuse the facility with the sense of buzz one finds there. Naturally, we had to begin with the architecture and distill from it the elements we could collectively agree contributed to the verve they felt they would miss. We were both compelled and awed by the idea of the building becoming an "exotic collage" of sorts. We were challenged to replicate a truly urban program to naturally sponsor the happy accident and complexity we expect in the city. A corporate headquarters certainly has program elements that, by analogy, can be construed as "urban" (work groups as neighborhoods and so on), but ultimately the notion of the building as a city has been employed time and time again to debatable effect. We felt we had to work at re-programming the program, combining functions with spaces in a way that mimicked the DNA of the New Orleans environment without the excitement of bars, buskers, and bums.

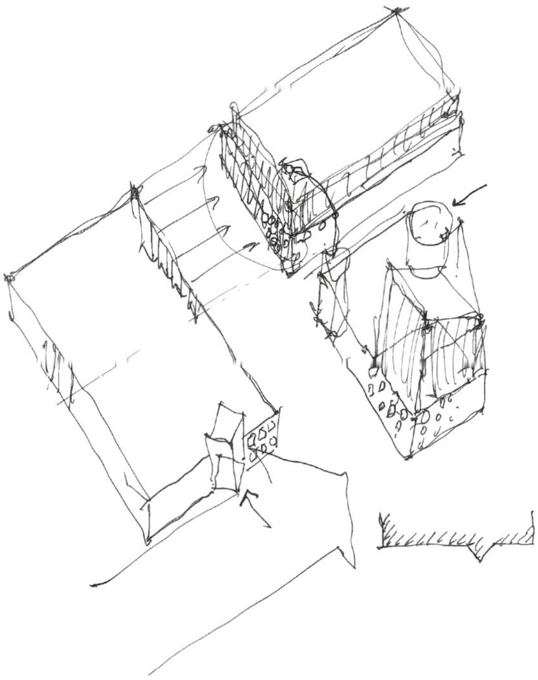

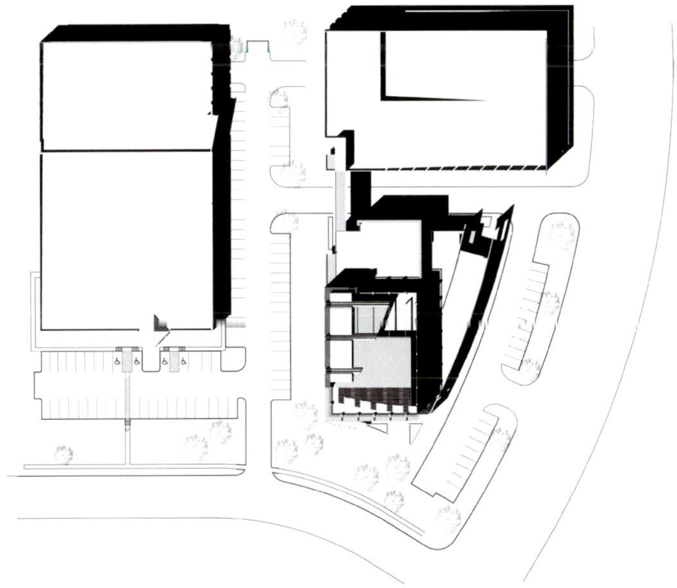

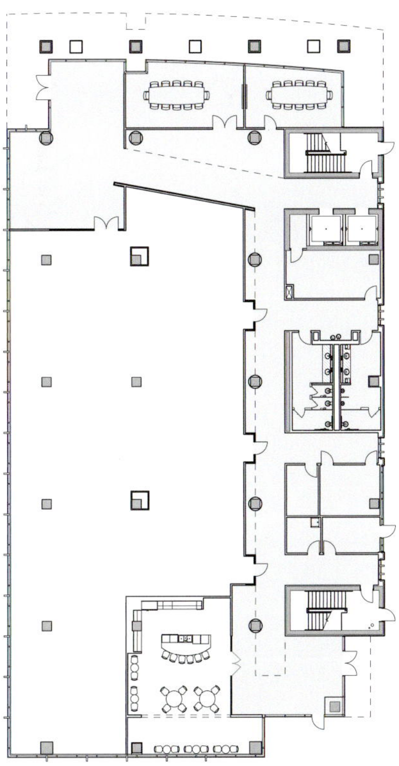

First-floor plan

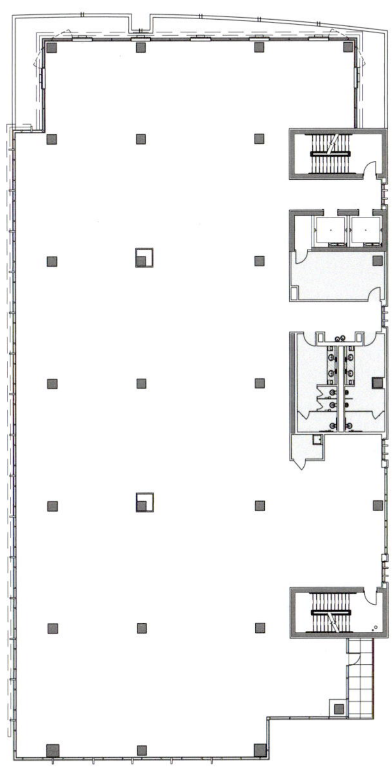

Second-floor plan

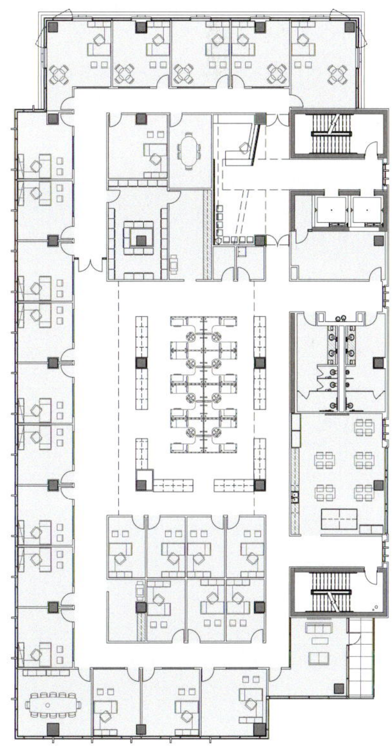

Third-floor plan

0 32 FT

In the same manner that private works rely upon a *perception* of experience that cannot be had by the public in general, public works must actually provide that experience. The old heuristic that architecture either tells a story or provides an experience *(is it possible that it is both?)* hedges its bets on providing experience in many cases that mainstream architecture encounters. Museums perhaps do both but many public buildings simply don't need to tell a story; it is often established many buildings prior among college campus architecture. In the projects exhibited in this section, Louis I. Kahn's servant and served maxim is transformed into servant becoming exhibited as part of served. Program in the fundamental sense is hard to overwrite in some campus buildings, like seeing the food being prepared in **Hillel**, or the athletic conference room overlooking the historic gym floor of the existing structure in the **Washington & Jefferson College** sports complex addition/renovation. All this, particularly in the context of the current, as of this writing, exploration of just how "public" is the college campus anyway. Using glazing as a metaphorical device for transparency in the design competition entry for **Sunnyside**, a historically black community neighborhood center, and creating a unique icon for the library rather than the football field for a Texas middle school in **Highlands** employ symbols in traditional yet blatant ways. The culture wars around access, the wealth divide, and class definition, continue to stress and redefine, if only from the outside, traditional understandings of the fundamental public–private binary.

Public

Washington, Pennsylvania | Recreational center | 120,925 square feet

W & J

This project proposes a new field house with a 656-foot track, meeting facilities, weight-training rooms, and health club amenities. The building will be located across South College Street—the traditional dividing line between campus and the Town of Washington, Pennsylvania. It is the first Town–Gown project in which the growing campus integrates closely into the established urban fabric.

Located at the corner of South College and East Chestnut Streets, the project will define the extension of an on-campus pedestrian circulation route called Pine Alley, across South College, on the south side of the new facility, and will terminate in a "shovel ready" stimulus-funded local transit stop and terminal. This alone will knit the campus building seamlessly into the urban building pattern yet maintain an allegiance to the campus structure and logic.

The 75,000-square-foot building is by program a large footprint structure and takes advantage of the steeply sloping grades to allow some program to be tucked away on grade at South College Street to minimize scale. The upper level contains the track and its event-driven required volume is enveloped in a skin that allows some natural light at strategic points above. The entry off Pine Alley includes an urban gesture of a grand staircase for access to the upper level through a visitor and lobby area as well as a traditional core. The fitness facility can be accessed at the lower level from the street or through the main core area.

The architecture of the building interprets the large footprint as a smaller series of volumes, each articulating a program element related to function or to quality—the skylights, for example. The purpose of the interlocking forms is to mitigate the scale of the building while not impinging upon its function. The goal is to portray a state-of-the-art facility in a manner respectful of its urban context.

JAMES DAVID ROSS FAMILY RECREATION CENTER

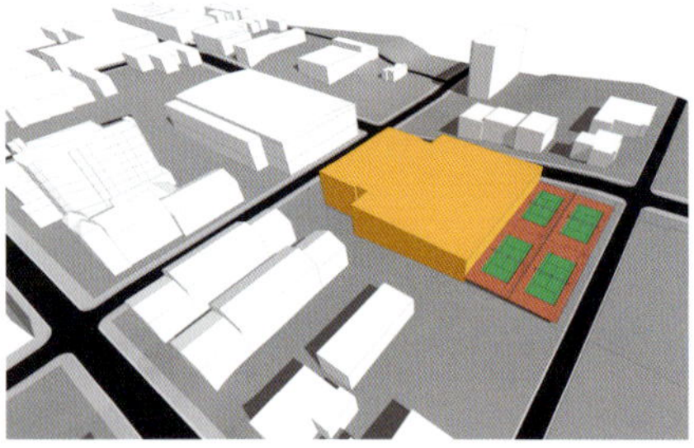

Existing site

- Adaptive reuse of existing tennis court hardscape
- Campus edge
- Urban setting

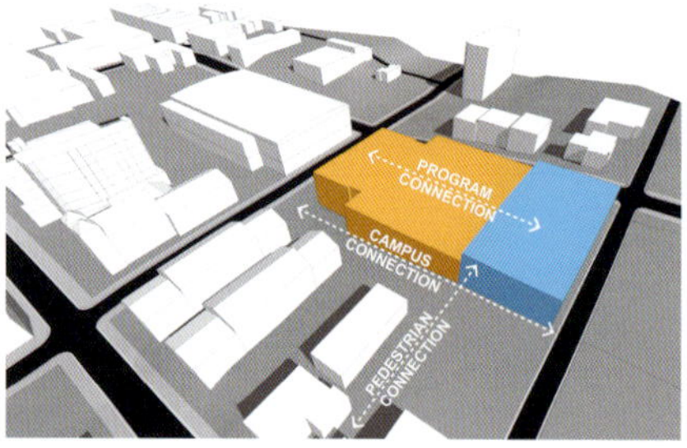

Connectivity

- Site orientation to maximize sunlight
- Response to campus proportions
- Campus to urban
- Pedestrian circulation
- Existing to new program

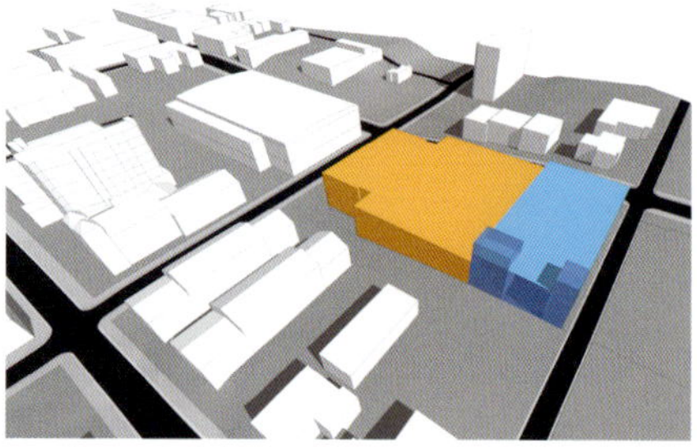

Building design strategies

- Building orientation
- Maximize sunlight
- Low-E glass
- Solar shades
- Visually articulated program volumes
- Response to existing urban fabric

JAMES DAVID ROSS FAMILY RECREATION CENTER

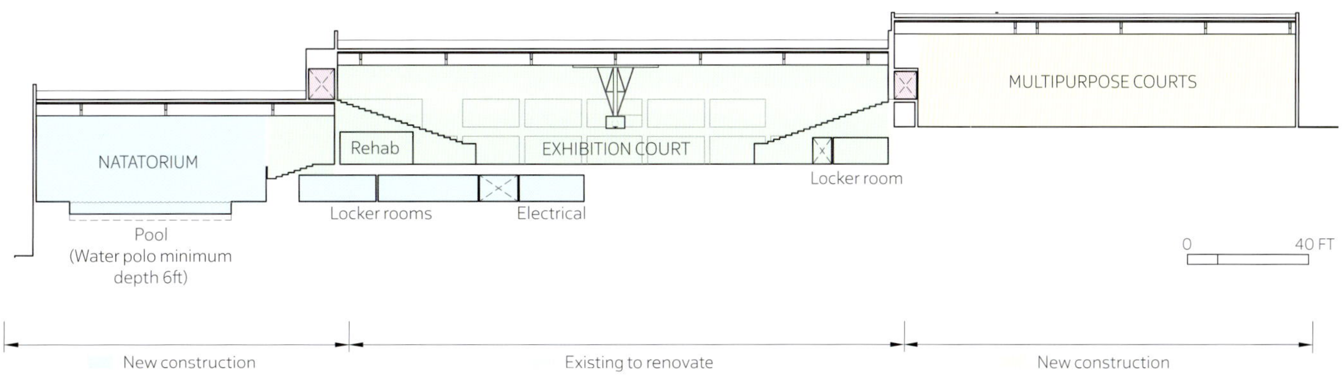
NATATORIUM
Pool
(Water polo minimum depth 6ft)
Rehab
EXHIBITION COURT
Locker rooms
Electrical
Locker room
MULTIPURPOSE COURTS
0
40 FT
New construction
Existing to renovate
New construction

JAMES DAVID ROSS FAMILY RECREATION CENTER

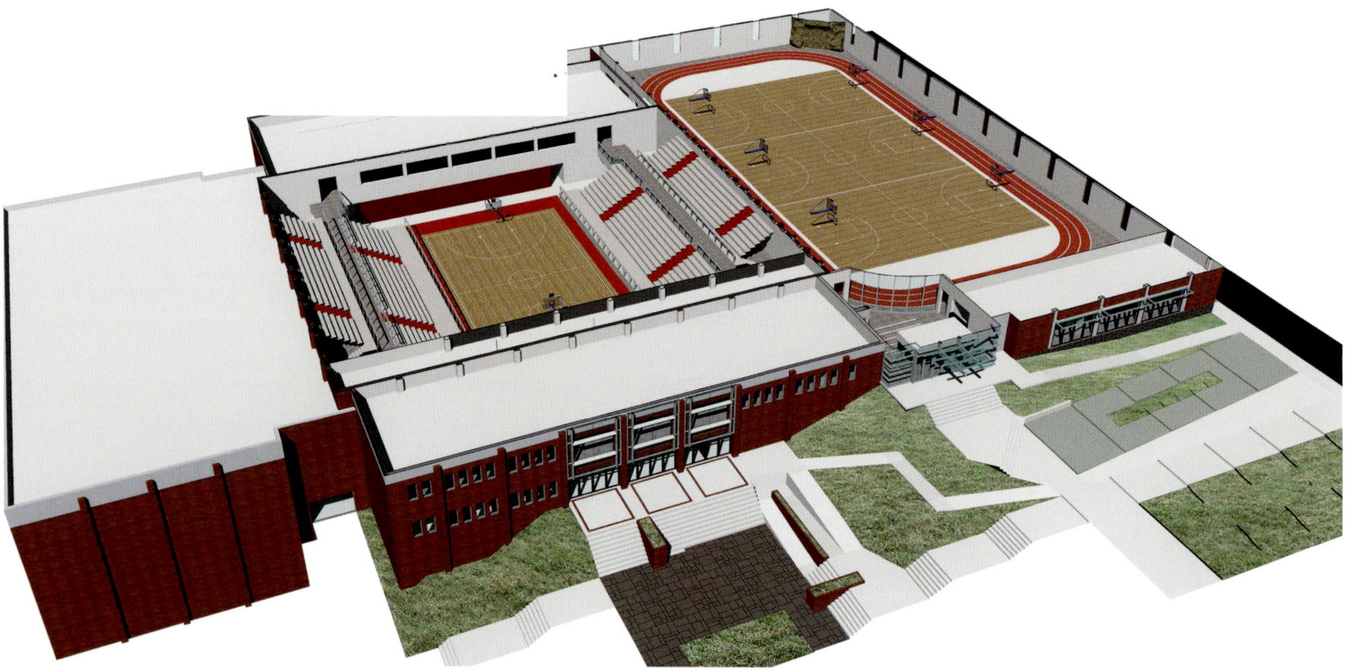

Sunnyside

We are often invited or shortlisted for projects that require a speculative design as part of the qualifications proposal. These efforts are typically unfunded yet play a crucial role in team selection. The effort we make in elaborating a design with no program beyond what we can surmise, no interaction with the end user and no sense of a budget, is a fraught endeavor. None more so than when the project is for a community center deep in the heart of a district with a large African American population, near one of the most challenged high schools in the region and with a very committed and active community willing to participate, albeit after the selection of the winning team.

This particular effort for the Sunnyside neighborhood proposed a ground-level community garden function to knit the site to the educational programs led by the local school to the general community as an invitation for consensus and cooperation. This garden theme extends onto the roof of the project as well. The building functions as a covered outdoor lecture space as the main stair has a dual function as seating. This outdoor "stairdatorium" also draws constituents deep into the heart of the building upon entry. Thus, they penetrate the core in a building many see as "bureaucratic" in administering to their needs. The building offers community space, various health services, and recreational support spaces.

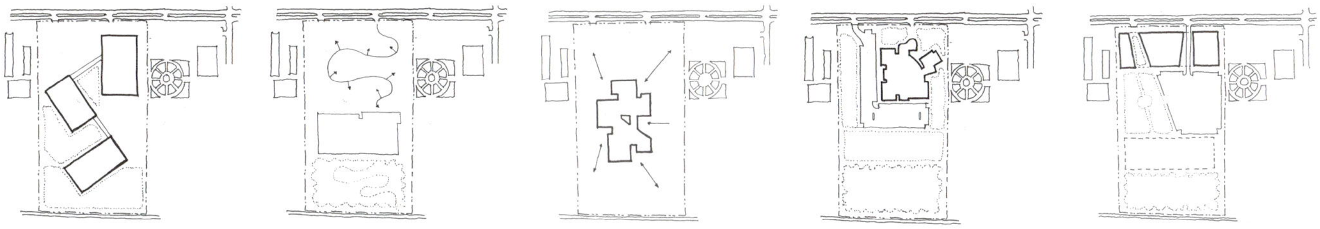

Site planning strategies

Hillel

The site for this Jewish student life center is located at the southwest corner of the intersection of 23rd Street and H Street, NW in Washington, D.C. The property consists of approximately 4,575 square feet of land and is located within George Washington University's Campus Plan Boundary.

The massing of the building design is one of simple moves, both literal and symbolic, where the strong base represents the history and the enduring commitment of the elders. The base once again contains the most formal spaces of the building. The upper floors represent Hillel's optimism for future generations and houses the day-to-day program spaces.

The design brings to life the vision of Hillel's new executive director. This vision includes creating a vibrant and dynamic environment in which the students can connect socially, culturally, and spiritually to their Judaic roots, while emboldening their own self-expression of their Jewishness. Hillel accommodates its program requirements in the strict footprint of the new building by integrating flexible elements into each of the program spaces.

The formal spaces stimulate a youthful enthusiasm through a logical convergence of both contemporary and modern design elements. Open ceilings and minimalistic finishes reminiscent of loft space combine with warm, textural materials to create a dynamic and welcoming atmosphere.

The design features an auditorium on the ground floor that accommodates worship services for the university's Jewish population (particularly during holidays) by expanding into the pre-function area through the innovative use of retractable partitions, allowing for the unification of the spaces. Folding glass doors, opening from the auditorium to the rear yard, provide additional space on temperate weather days. The lower level will house two kosher kitchens that will provide food services to Jewish students, and a dining area.

Site plan

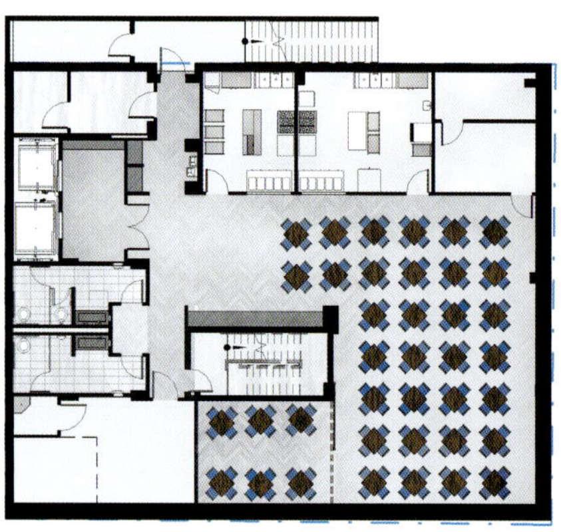

Lower-floor plan

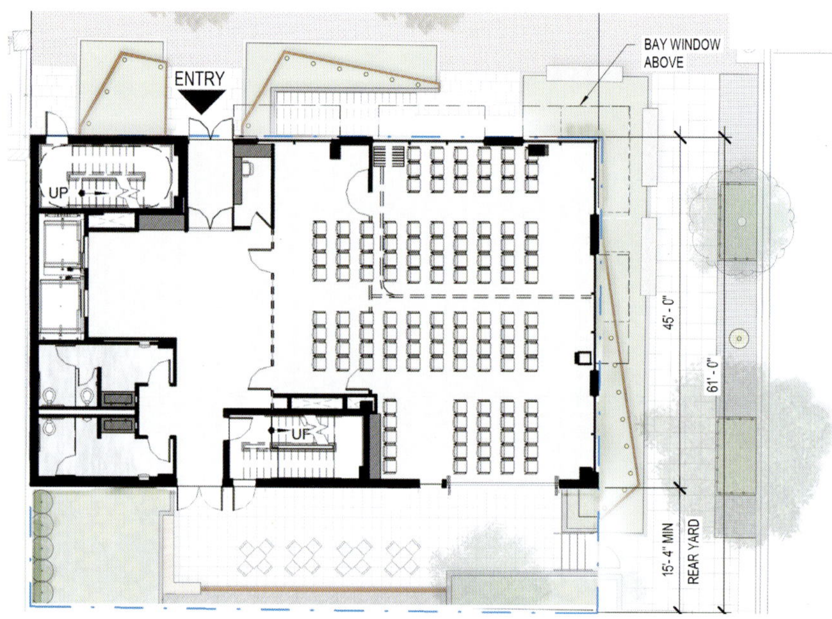

First-floor plan

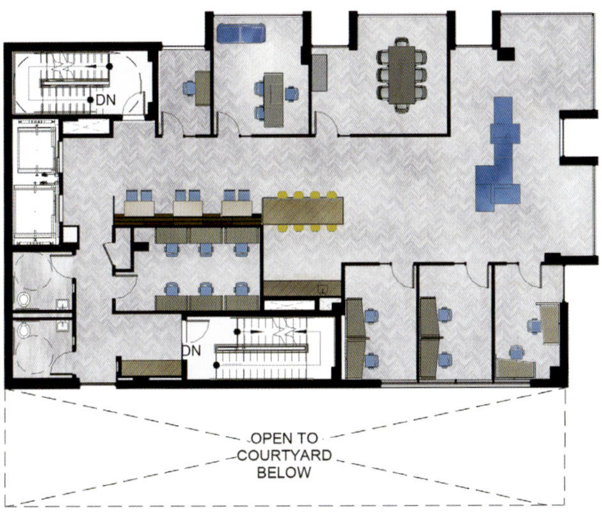

Second-floor plan

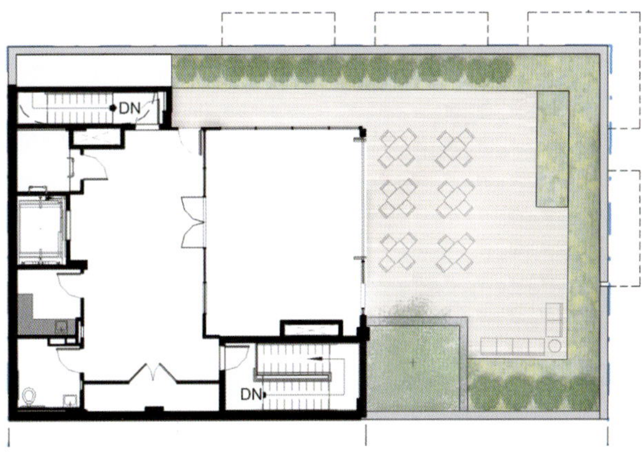

Penthouse floor plan

Bay projection study

- Bay window projections were studied to enhance the articulation of the façade.
- Incorporating the bay projections provides a connection to the architectural fabric of the city.

Single bay–no separation | Single bay–separation | Multiple bay–separation

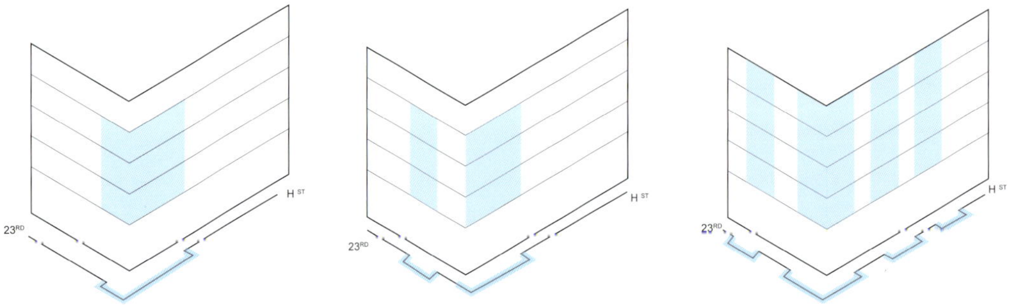

Hebrew alphabet | Character analysis | Character + bay-windows | Design interpretation

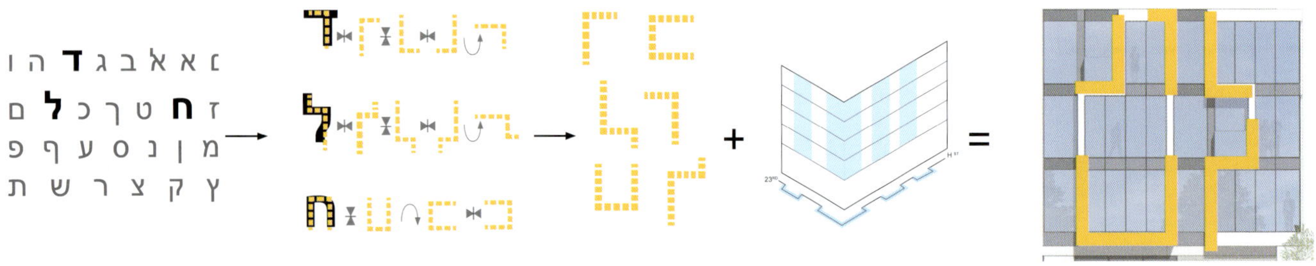

Highlands

The approach to the design of this 168,000-square-foot, 1,000-student middle school was undertaken in part as a critique of what amounts to a shocking dearth of invention in K–12 school design. Strategies rationalized over time as functional, defensive, secure, low maintenance and so on, have allowed a sense of complacency to substitute "bright color" in place of actual exploration of interesting and challenging environments for young adults to learn in.

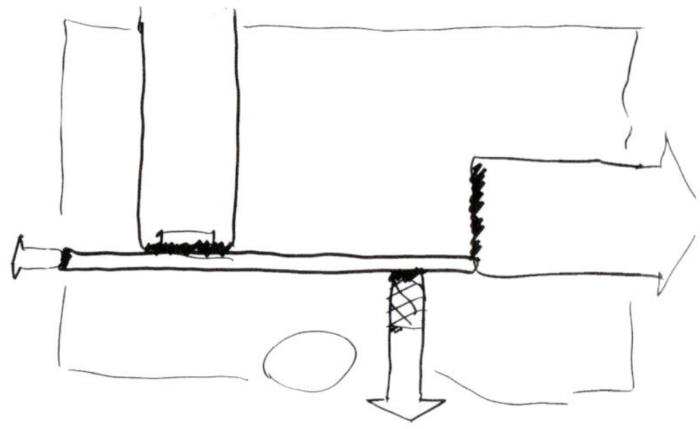

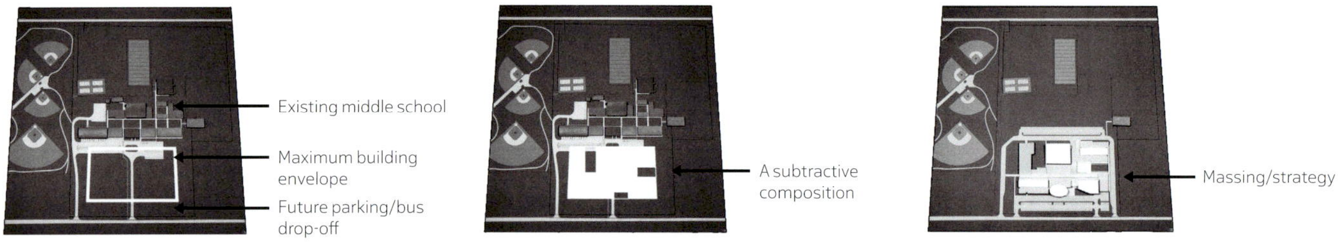

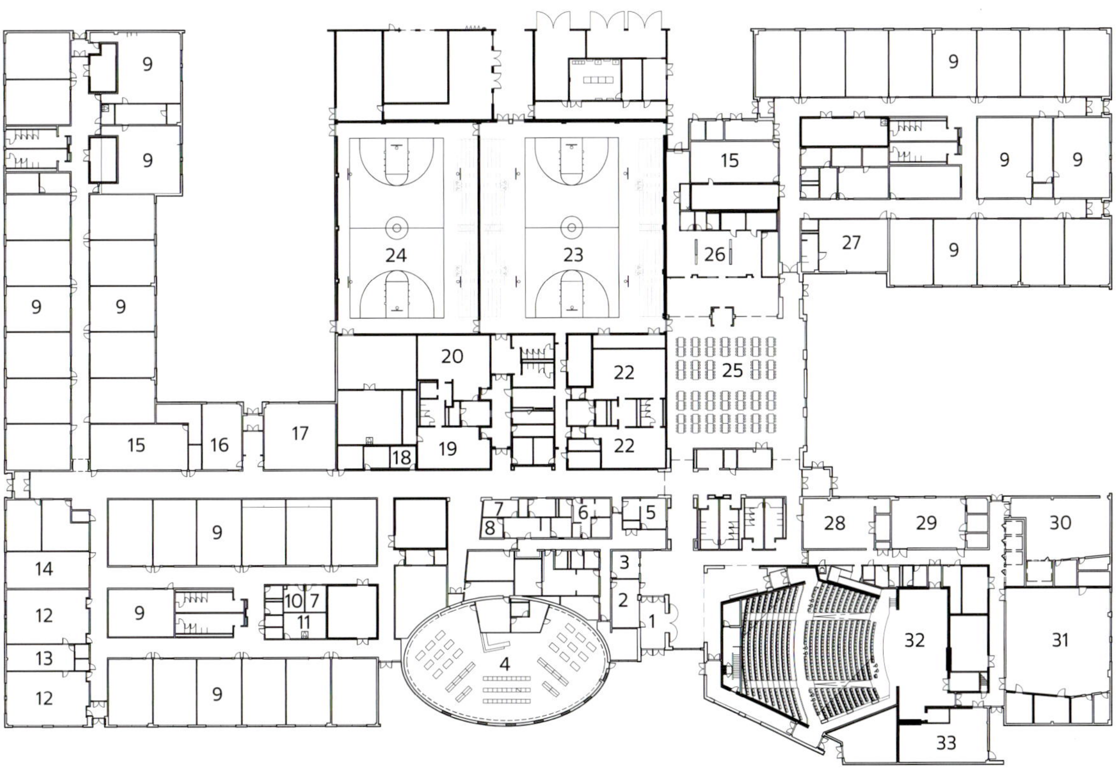

1 Main lobby
2 Reception area
3 Attendence office
4 Library
5 Principal's office
6 Clinic
7 Assistant principal's office
8 Psychology
9 Classroom
10 Counselor's office
11 Books storage
12 Science lab
13 Science storage
14 Special education
15 Computer room
16 Dyslexia/CM room
17 Computer room
18 Diagnostician office
19 Boys' PE locker room
20 Boys' athletic locker room
21 Girls' PE locker room
22 Girls' locker room
23 Competition gymnasium
24 Practice gymnasium
25 Cafeteria
26 Kitchen
27 Life skills room
28 Art department
29 Choir department
30 Orchestra department
31 Band
32 Auditorium
33 Drama department

Floor plan

0 240 FT

For starchitects, parking ain't what it used to be. The parking garage as spectacle in Miami, as cultural statement at Princeton University and many other projects have stretched the notion of parking. In particular, parking has evolved beyond simply a utilitarian building type. Books like Simon Henley's *The Architecture of Parking* helped to distort the apparent simplicity of the building type. Published in 2007 it used nonparking building types, many exploring the "continuous surface" proposals for libraries and museums in the late 1990s and early 2000s to predict and illustrate a path of possible evolution for idle cars. Cross-programming the garage as standalone building has been an interest of ours. In this we are inspired by Machado Silvetti's little garage on the Princeton campus—the best manifestation, of many examples of architectural style aside, of the potential beyond program, for the garage to take on urbanistic connotations. The functional requirements of parking as building have an astonishingly limited bandwidth so any urbanistic effect the type takes on is all the more impressive. In **Roy Kelly Multimodal** we cleave to this influential precedent with a building that functions first and foremost as an urban instrument, then as a garage. In **Galveston** we responded to the forces of The Strand's National Historical Monument status for context to achieve a cloaking of the functional without resort to mere "façadism." Finally, at **University of Houston—East Garage**, we contorted the form of the garage to the desires of a master plan that was at the "coming soon" stage, now built, and verifying the big move strategy of its initial form.

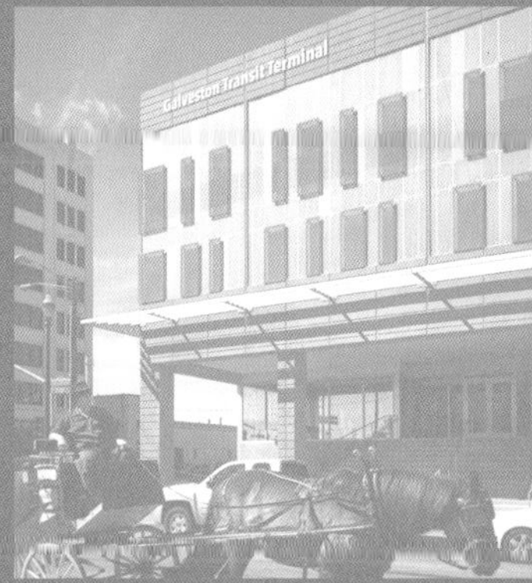

Park

Roy Kelly

The Roy Kelly Terminal and Parking Garage was commissioned by the Brazos Transit Authority in conjunction with the Brazos County Community Supervision Office and the Federal Transit Administration. The project program includes a 385,067-square-foot, three-story county office building housing the parole office; ground-floor retail; a 900-car garage that serves the county courts district employees and jury duty attendees; and a bus-to-bus/bus-to-car transit terminal serving regional travelers/commuters.

Our inspiration for the main organizing gesture of the project—the hyper-stair elevation on 27th Street—was from the extraordinary number of cast-iron fire stairs carefully preserved in the old downtown district. The overabundance of stairs on the facility draws parking customers to this façade then down to the connective corridor to the main street district. Alternately, visitors can cross from the new plaza formed at the juncture of office building and galleria connector to the historic Bryan Plaza in front of the courthouse. These stairs weave through a layered metal scrim system set up in bay formations that take their width and metering from the rhythm and cadence of the main street façades. Their diaphanous quality balances hiding the cars with the feeling of accessibility and safety.

The site was delineated in the Bryan Downtown Master Plan of 2001 as a transit location in accordance with its interface with the courthouse and connective possibility to the now revitalized North and South Main Street District one block west along 27th Street. The site is also strategically important in stitching together the courthouse with the large, converted church property now used as the main county offices one block to the south.

Existing site

Relocation of county office building

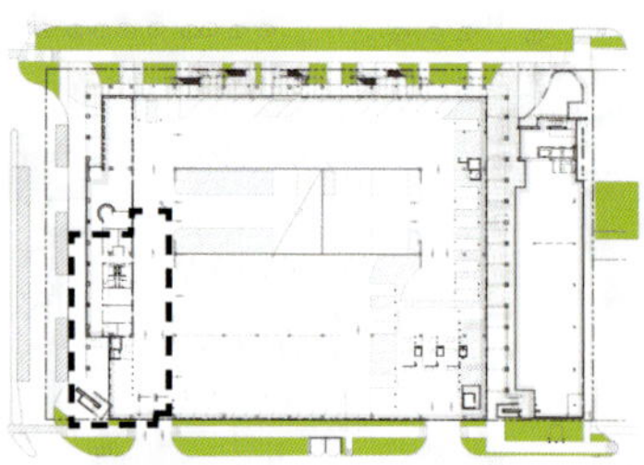

Proposed site plan

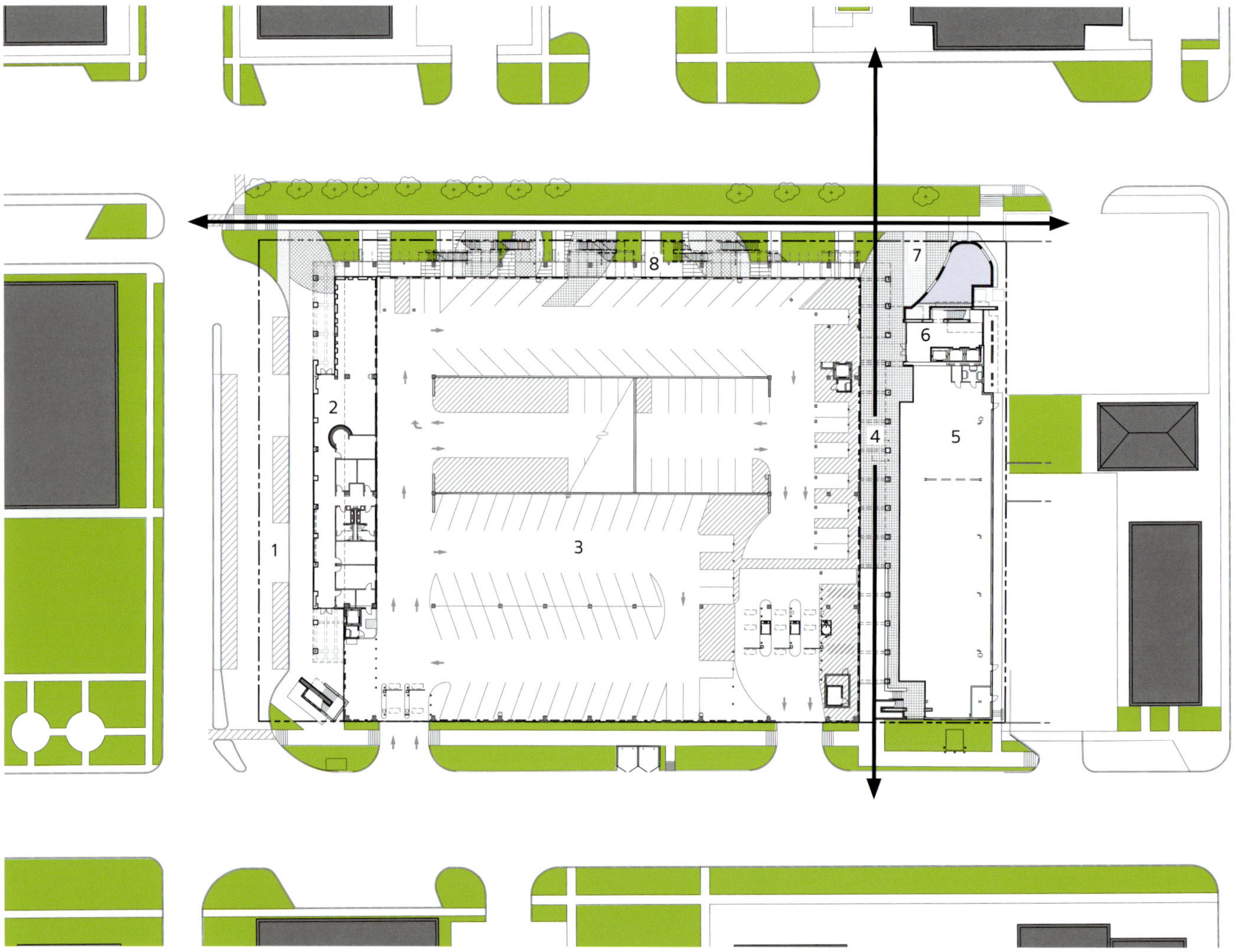

Ground-floor plan

1 Bus loading zone
2 Bus terminal
3 Five-level parking
4 Pedestrian zone
5 Ground floor retail
6 Office/garage core
7 Plaza
8 Garage vertical circulation/ pedestrian core

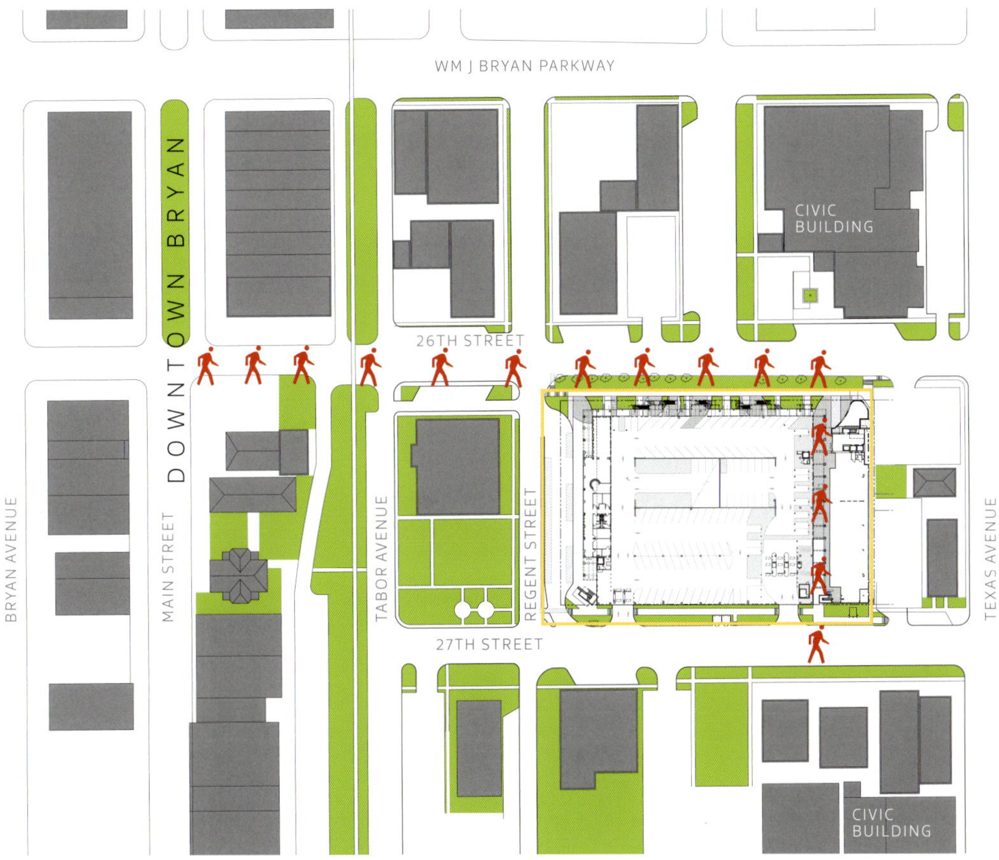

Pedestrian and green connection

Galveston

So, there we were, proposing a modern building for the last open parcel in a National Historic District and along what's known as the Strand. The Islanders, as they call themselves in Galveston, Texas, reacted as if we had just invaded their local surf spot and our big city yuppie architecture was not welcome there. It was the beginning of an aggressive process that ultimately resulted in a sensitive solution.

We met with state and local public entities, and local private entities over nearly 60 days and changed the design in some way after every meeting. We listened. We also stuck to our argument: the Strand is a complex narrative that is robust enough to accommodate our proposed building design; and, that reducing it to a Disneyland-like fragility of thin historic atmospherics would have simply been dishonest.

The solution was for a design carefully calibrated to be contextual on every level—from the selection of compatible materials, the alignment with adjacent façade and cornice height, the careful study of rhythm and cadence of the Strand's street walls, the incorporation of street-level retail and concomitant canopy, and finally the corner plaza that invests in the extension of the covered public realm of downtown.

In our process we committed early to the reality that the building would endure multiple floods throughout its lifetime. We elevated the ground floor to a safe level and designed a sectional condition that would still allow the storefronts to meet the ground. The solution addressed safety while allowing the adjacent street-level storefronts to remain unbroken and thus, urban.

The garage is clad with perforated anodized aluminum screens calibrated to allow the garage to vent naturally while providing a required vehicle screen.

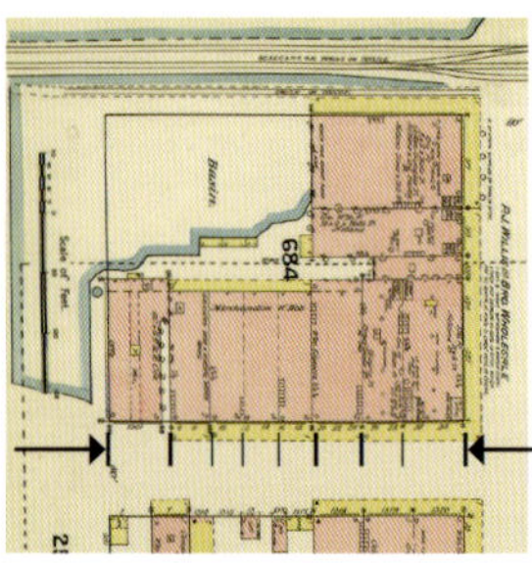

1889 (multiple building expression)

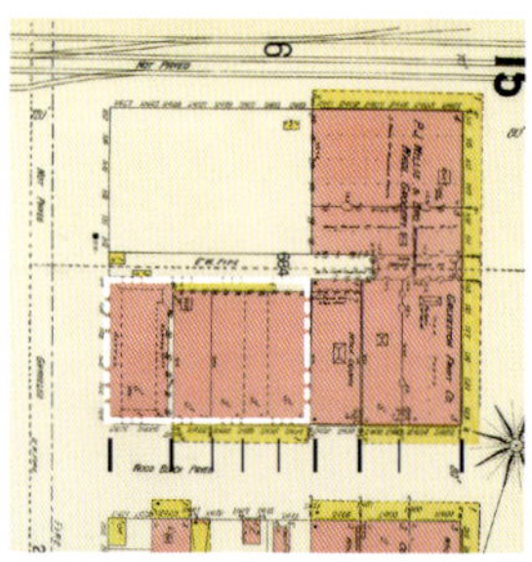

1899

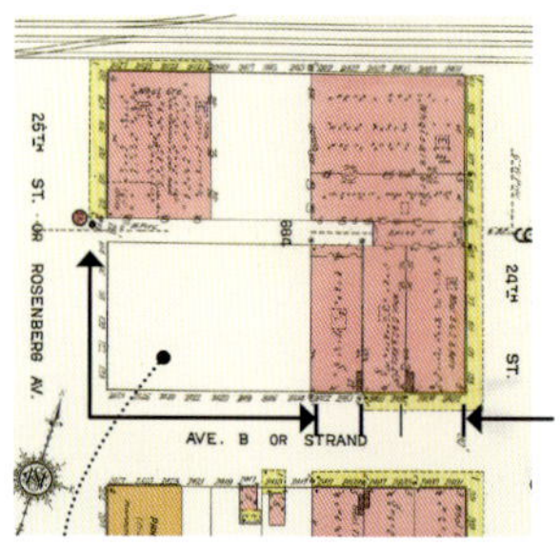

1912 empty corner site (unique condition in district)

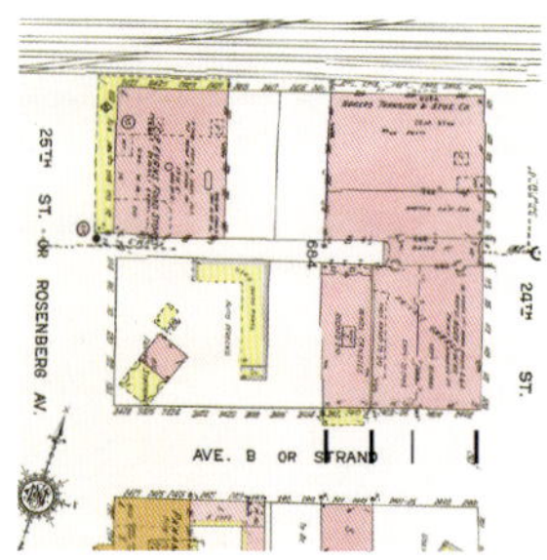

1947

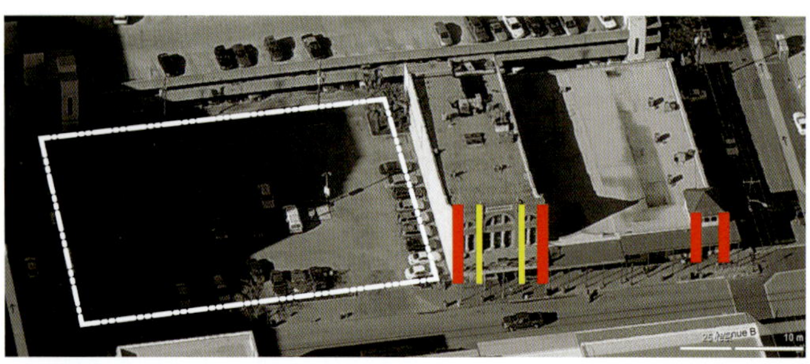

Existing site conditions (surface parking)

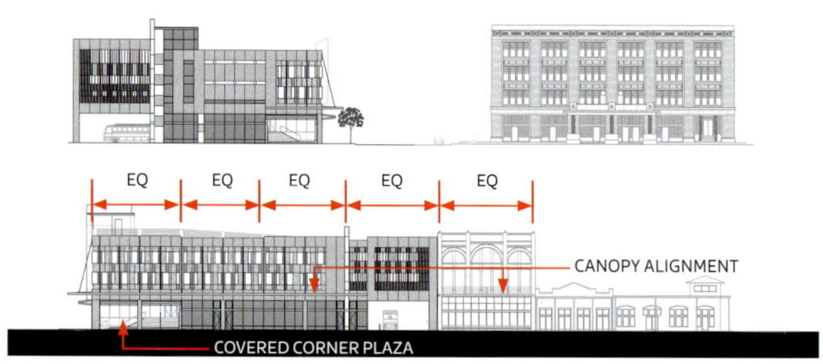

Stand elevation

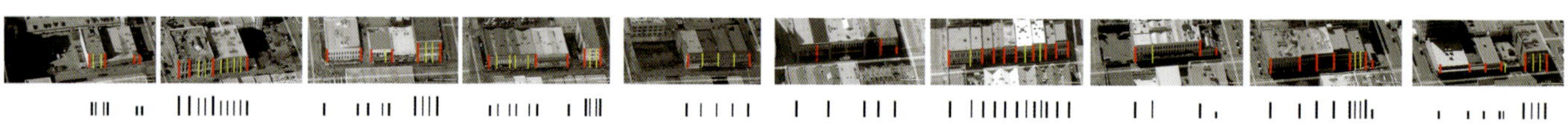

'DNA strand' concept

Public
Restroom
2418

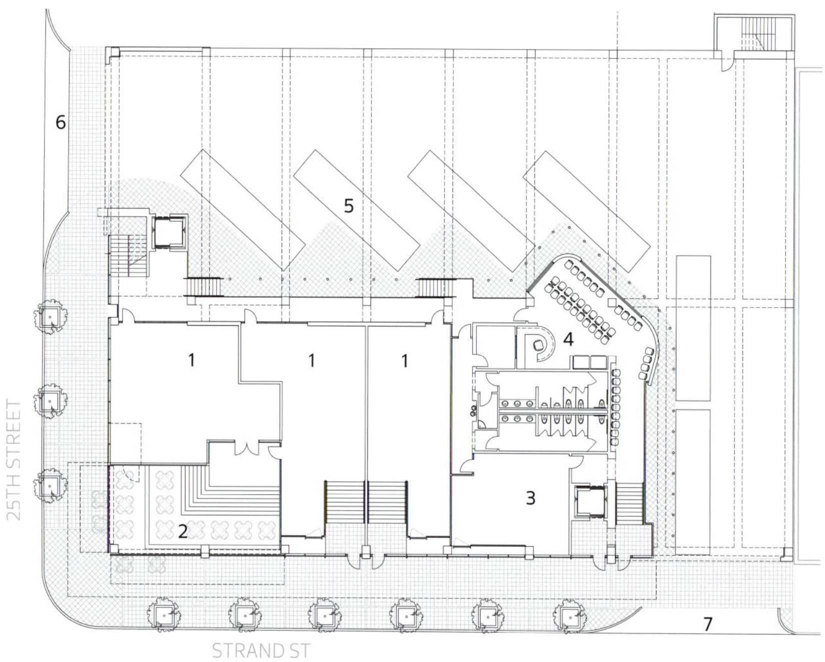

First-floor plan

1 Retail
2 Plaza
3 Visitor center
4 Waiting area
5 Bus parking
6 Bus entrance
7 Bus exit
8 Public restrooms

Strand street elevation

25th Street elevation

BUS EXIT
2 UTMB
LET US TAKE YOU THERE ISLAND TRANSIT

IV717
LET US TAKE YOU THERE
ISLAND TRANSIT

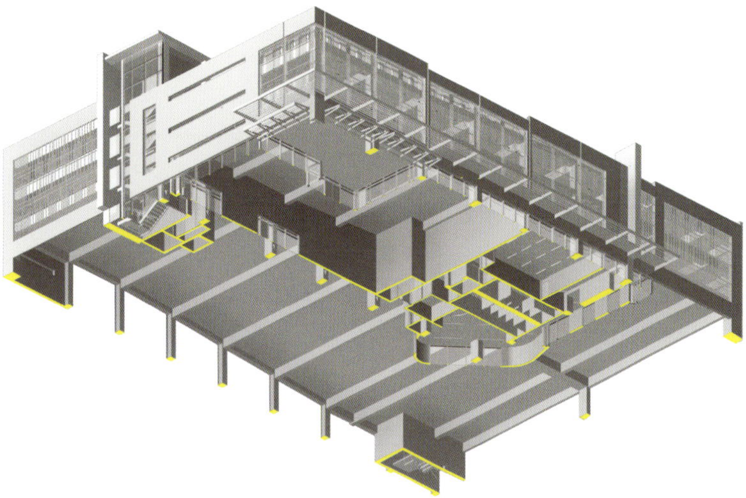

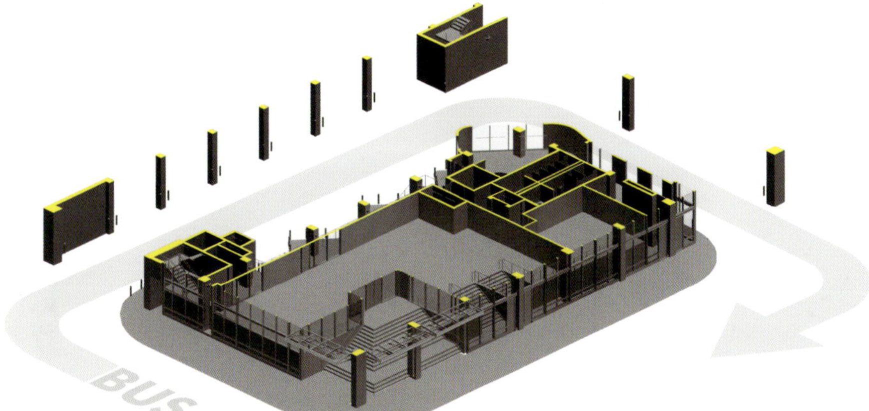
BUS

Galveston Transit Terminal

UHG

The East Garage at the University of Houston is the first of six proposed garages for the campus. This parking facility is strategically located at the main entry points to the campus between Calhoun Street and Spur 5. The structure has separate student and faculty entrances and houses parking for the Calhoun Lofts and the Bauer College of Business. The architectural addition to the garage was designed so that it could be utilized as a framework for signage and a video board.

The East Garage was by its very nature a "functional" project, procured through the Design–Build delivery method, with an emphasis on achieving an attractively low price. But this did not equate to abandoning a symbolic component. We observed several levels of symbolism at work in the campus morphology, choosing one appealing to the spiritual symbolisms as most appropriate for the garage.

Given the budget-driven delivery method, we could not foresee having enough "architecture" to camouflage the precast concrete, as we could not count on the quality of materials, given the limited budget, nor could we recode the DNA of the garage itself, thus the skin we used, composed of structural fiberglass members typically used for offshore oil-rig applications, acts as a kind of campus branding machine, more aligned with the campus's insignia/sense of spirit than with attempting to act as a garage in classroom building drag. Obtaining more to pattern than composition—a Mondrian-esque hierarchy still allows for basic wayfinding clarity and registration of campus-wide circulation cues.

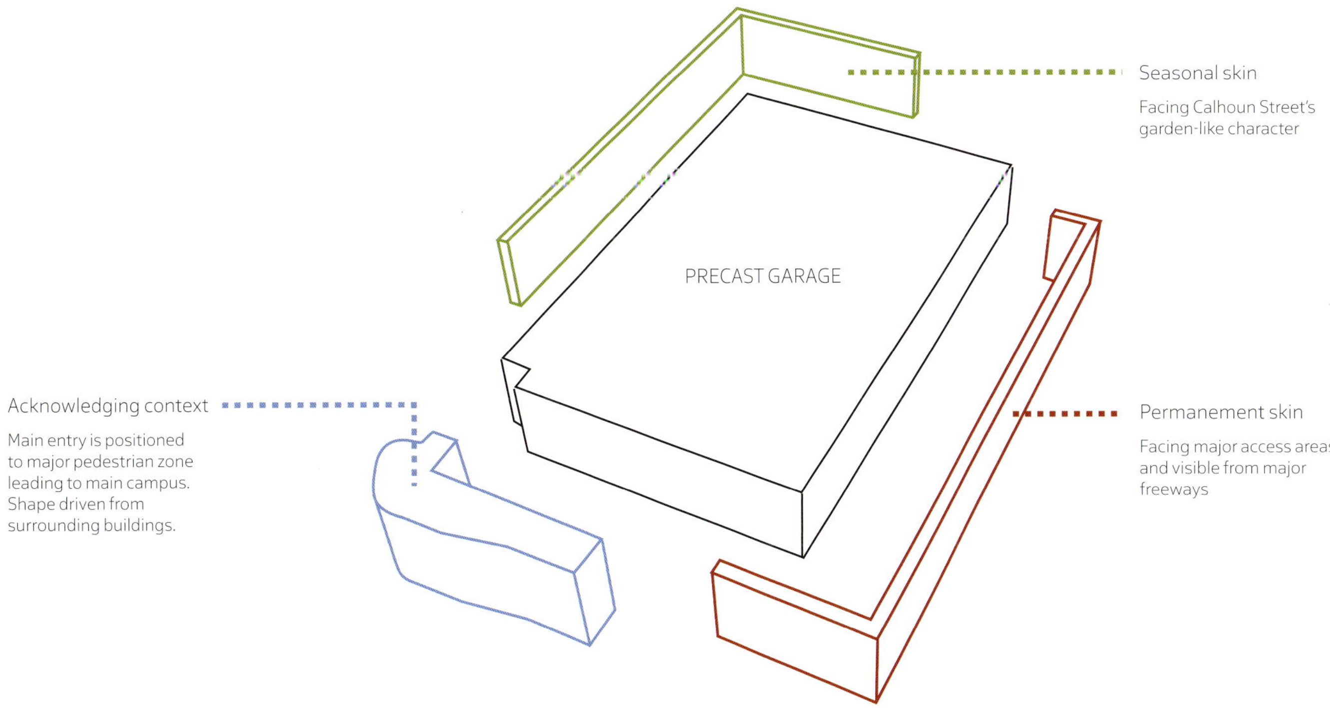
Seasonal skin
Facing Calhoun Street's garden-like character
PRECAST GARAGE
Acknowledging context
Main entry is positioned to major pedestrian zone leading to main campus. Shape driven from surrounding buildings.
Permanement skin
Facing major access areas and visible from major freeways

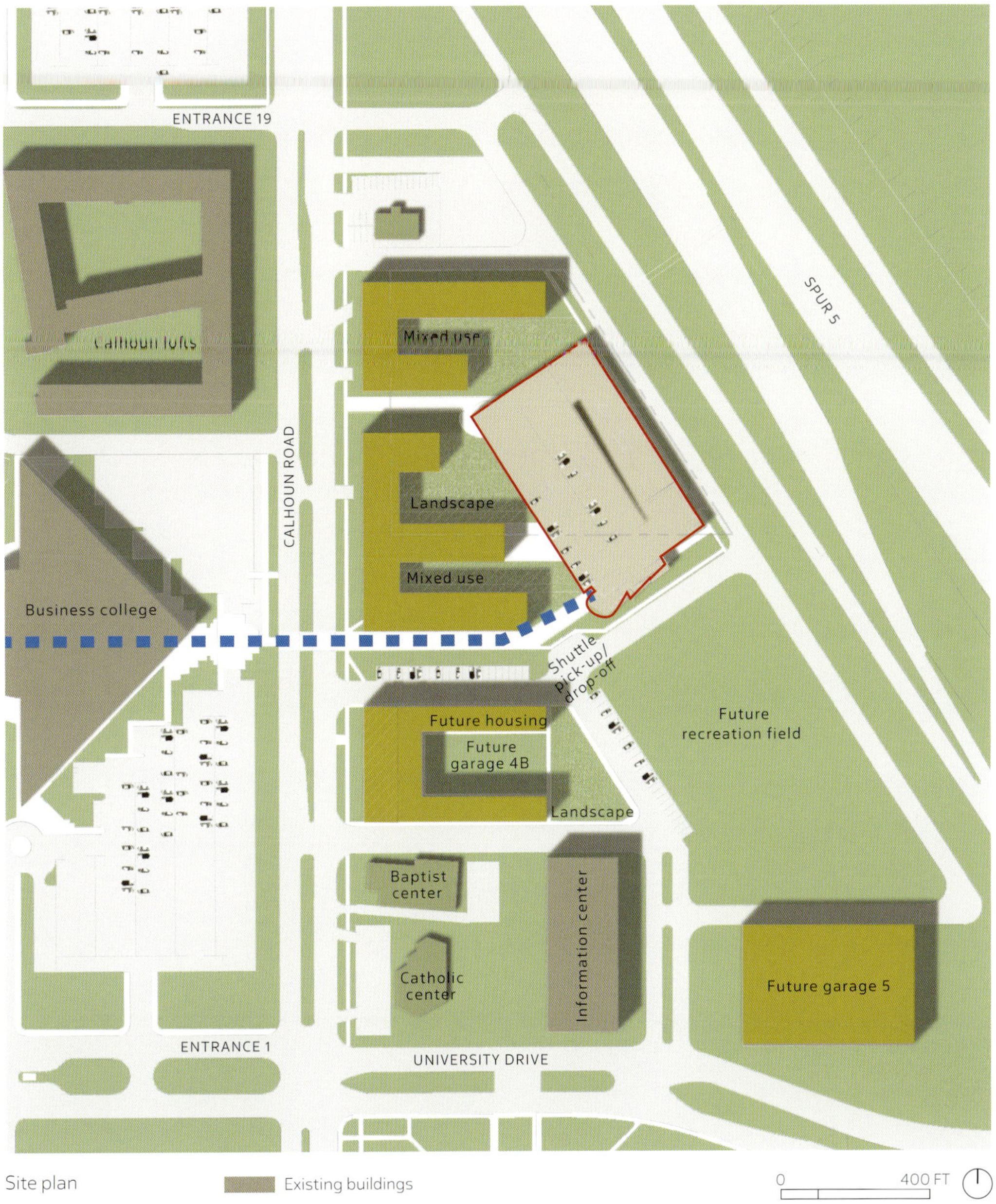

Site plan

Existing buildings

Planned buildings

Connection to campus

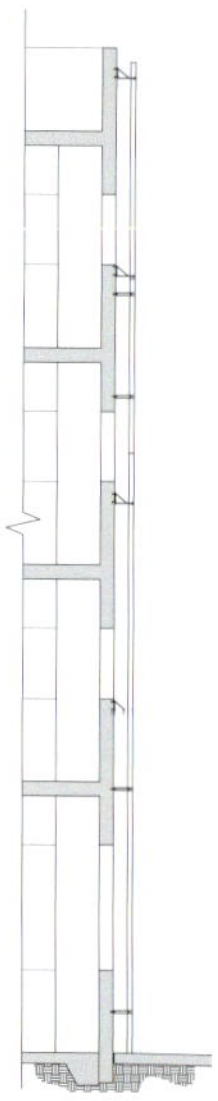

Stock item to pattern

Pattern is created using modular panel sizes and connections.

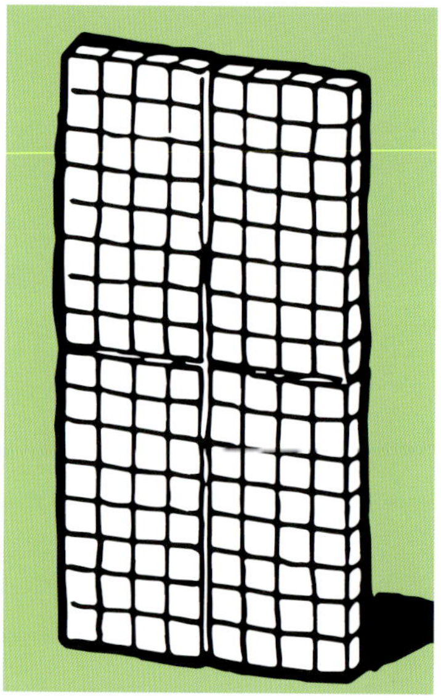

Modular trellising system

Three-dimensional, powder-coated, welded-wire trellising system is available in various panel sizes.

FIRE LANE NO PARKING

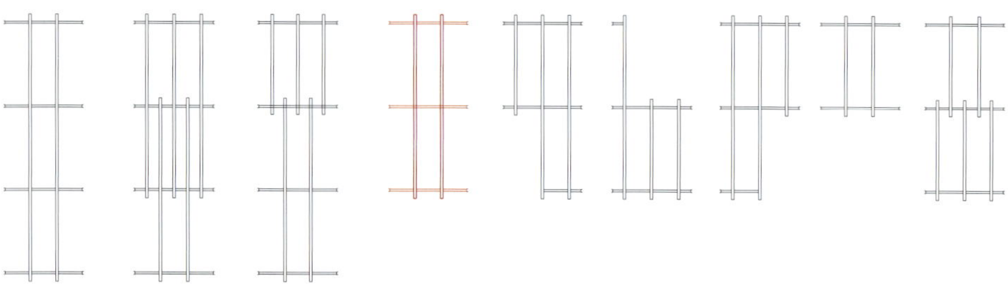

Nine modules

Module section mock-up

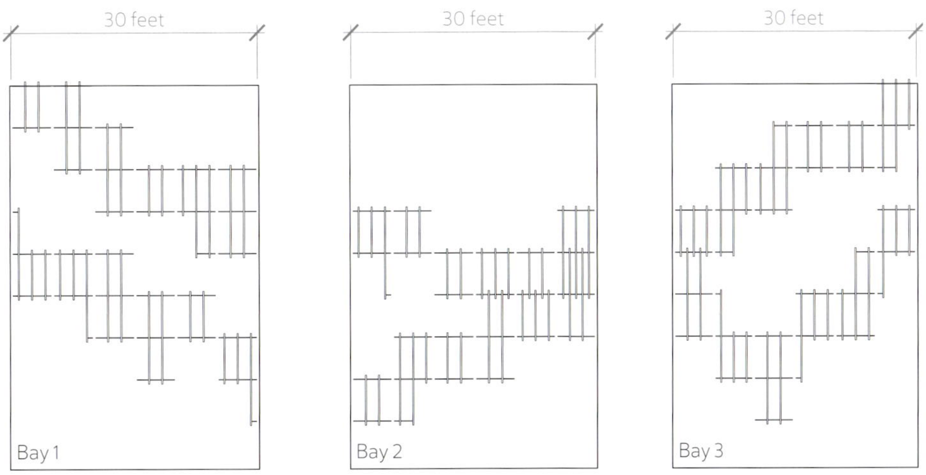

Three bays repeated

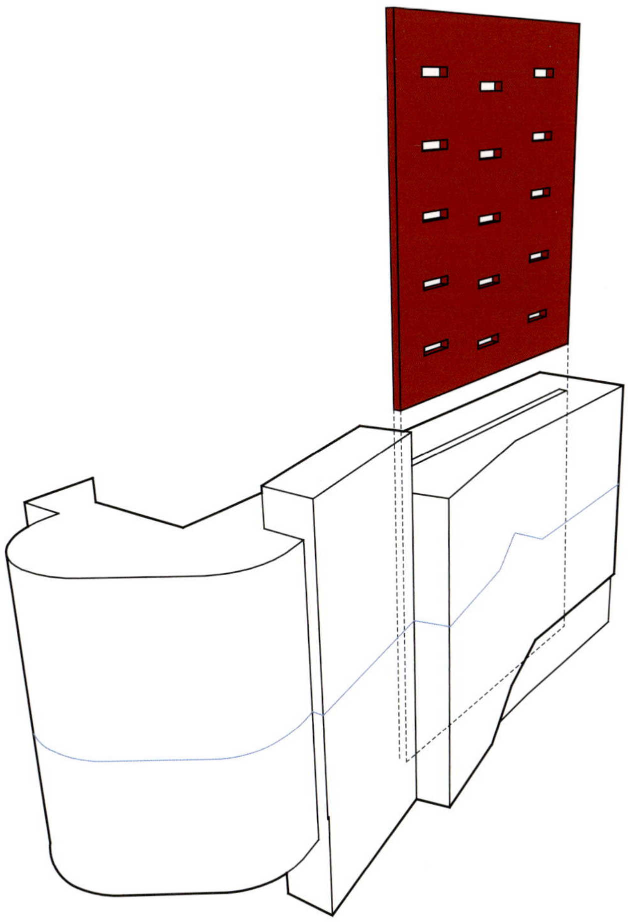

We have included three condominium projects under the title of "Home" as a provocation as much as anything aspiring to being categorically correct. The radical reduction of urbanity to the "Live Work Play" trope has exhausted its brand potency. It has been, at least in high-rise living, replaced by an equally aggressive campaign to create a brand around a building type that in the past regularly utilized its address for its "name." The effect of this brand syndrome at the mainstream level has been creating the building in coordination with, dare one say, inspired by the brand rather than from the architectural response to context, site forces, cultural inflections, and target market. Facilitating this backwards creative arrangement is the DNA of the type itself. High-rise condominiums are open to many formal possibilities, unlike office buildings about which it has been observed are really just "skin jobs" in that something like 80 percent of the key decisions are made prior to selection of the architect. Condominiums are robust with opportunities to change core arrangements, core-to-shell spans vary and many of the "set" elements of an office building are in play. At least in the mainstream market-based version of these typologies. In **Arabella** the brand was indexed to the demographic of one of the wealthiest zip codes in the United States, where, according to the client's research, women make the major decisions on "home." While this seemed anachronistic, scientific or not, **Marlowe** was branded with the urban/CBD dwelling early career and/or mid-career divorced lawyer as the prototype buyer. If these are examples of contextualism, **Innovation** is really an exercise in simple response to context in response to site, in particular a maximized façade surface gazing toward an infamous college football venue.

Home

Houston, Texas | High-rise condominium | 502,400 square feet

Arabella

The task, as described by our client was to create something "iconic." So, we approached the challenge as one of strategy rather than as a motif with ever more features. Our vision for this thirty-four-story tower was an ensemble of individually designed custom houses, not only all unique, but also identifiable—in other words, "architecturally iconic."

We experimented with rotating the floor plates about the core in an asymmetrical pattern and found that each shift in the floor plate became specific to the living spaces within. Local construction methods and structural restraints allowed for the cantilevering of the building slab to create balconies that would protrude from the living spaces. As a reversal of this logic, the living spaces are projected from the façade with terraces inboard. That is, a living room with multiple glass corners and three sides of exterior views could sponsor a terrace for a unit above and act as a shading device while overhanging the spaces below.

We then realized from our early site analysis that the building in its context, framed by surrounding tall buildings, would not allow for the perception of a singular sculptural form derivative of this perfect diagram. We decided instead to infuse the diagram with an architecture responding programmatically to the spaces within, resulting in an intentional juxtaposition of architectural elements. That is how we thought the building could be architecturally iconic. Strategized from the outside in and designed from the inside out, there are no typical floor plates; instead, ninety-nine unique homes of varying size and program are offered throughout a vertical neighborhood.

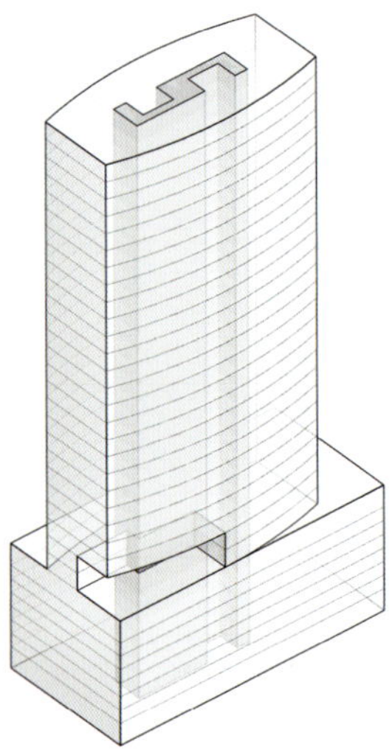

Etrude

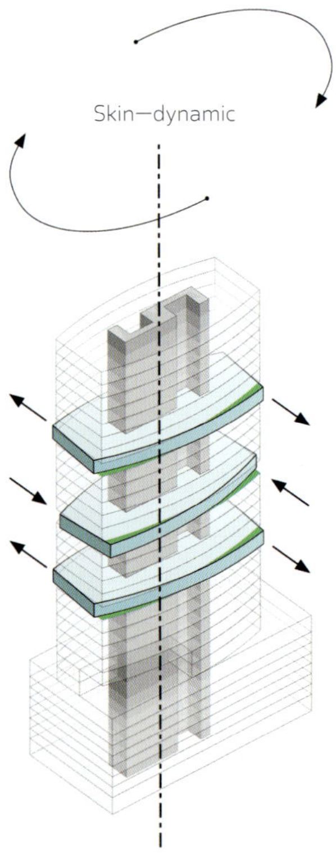

Building core—fixed

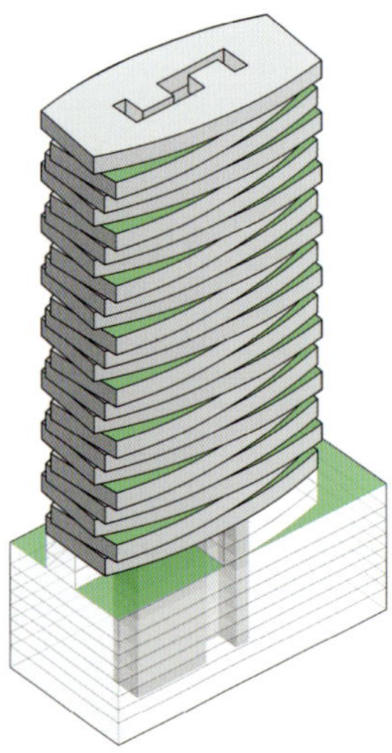

Strategy

Opportunity

Out of Arabella's ninety-nine units, seventy-nine have unique floor plans

Twenty-eighth-floor penthouse plan

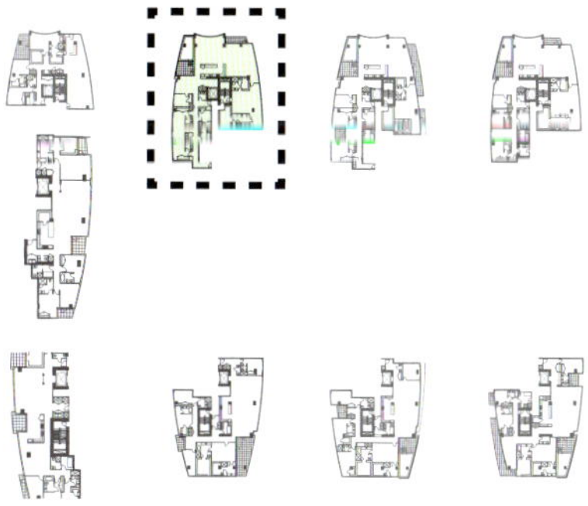

Twenty-seventh–thirtieth floors

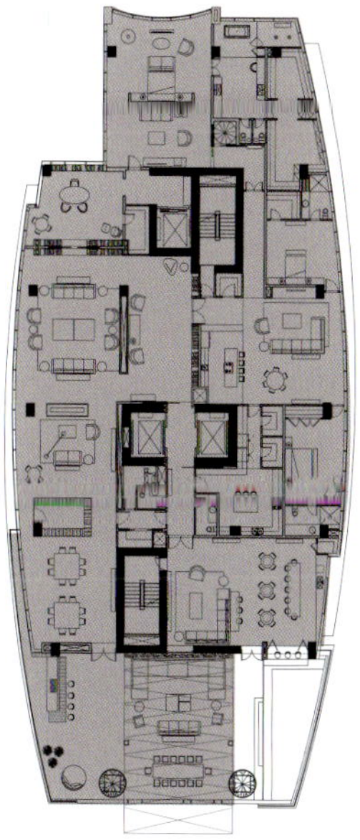

Thirty-third-floor penthouse plan

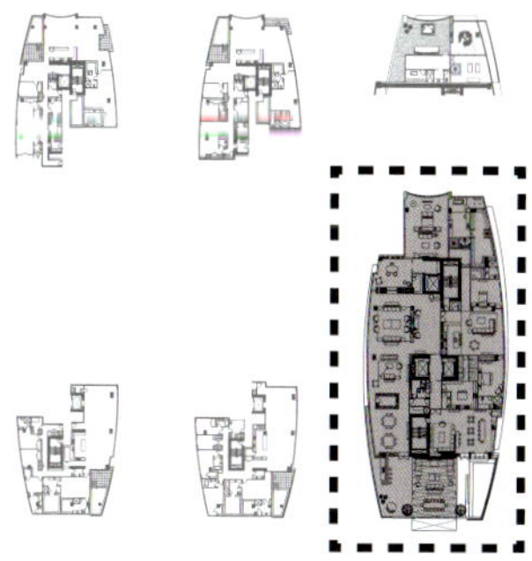

Thirty-first–thrty thrid floors

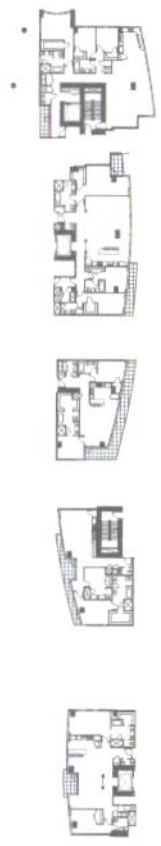

Tenth floor

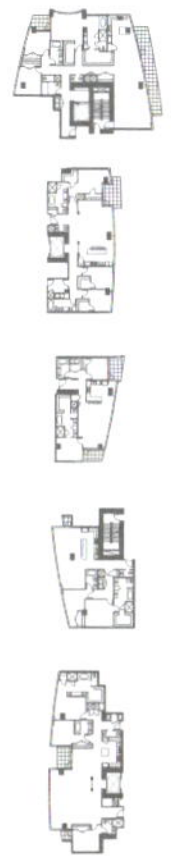

Eleventh and seventeenth floors

Twelfth and eighteenth floors

Thirteenth and nineteenth floors

Fourteenth and twentieth floors

Fifteenth floor

Sixteenth floor

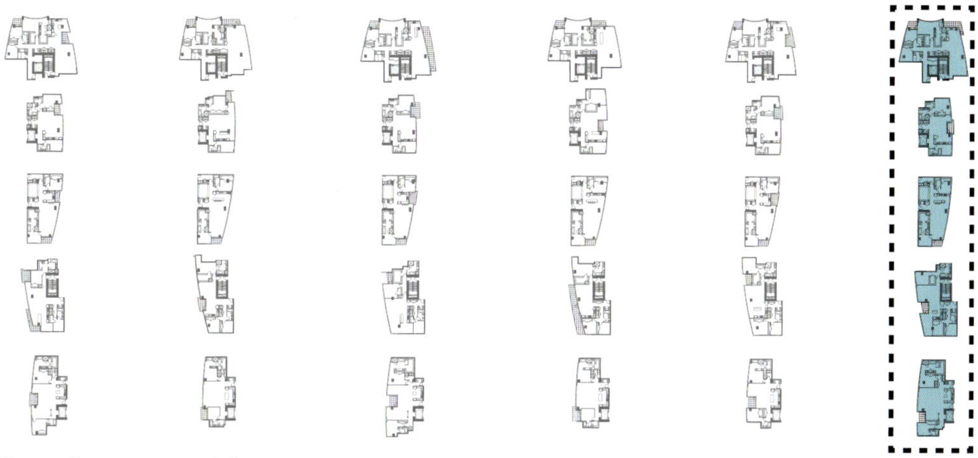

Twenty-first–twenty-sixth floors

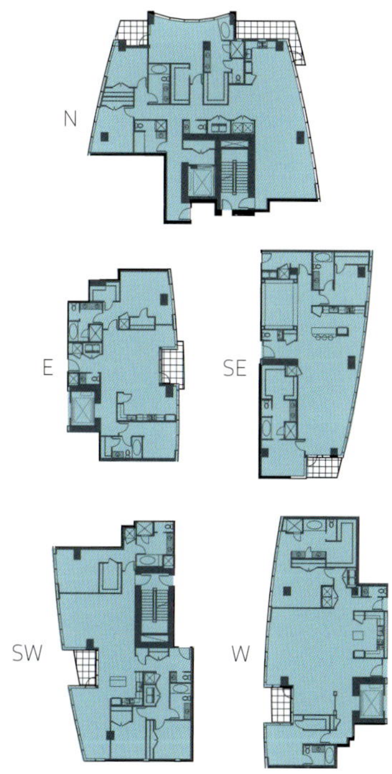

Twenty-sixth-floor unit plans

Cantilevered living rooms sponser terraces above.
Living rooms with panoramic views ...
... provide shade for terraces below.

ARABELLA

HOUSE

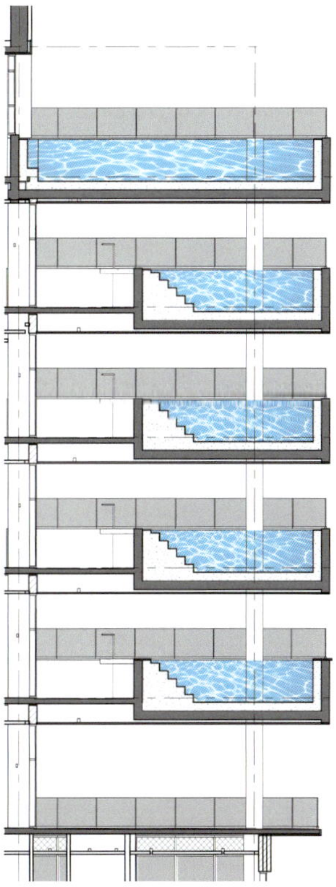

Sky pools section detail

Innovation

This uniquely rural condominium tower is located outside of a major college town yet has distant views of the Texas A&M University's famous football stadium, Kyle Field. The condo design takes its shape in a five-building master plan from its position at the extreme corner of the site as a diagonal bar with a curved face on the side looking toward the stadium. The approach was to maximize the surface area of the tower facing the important view; creating an arc on the view side of the bar floor plate allowed wedge-shaped floor plans with a grand curve supporting forty-five condominiums mostly set up for occupants to also enjoy the much-anticipated excitement of important game-day events held at the impressive stadium. The units feature strong social amenities such as grand living areas with open kitchen and bar features—for entertaining pre- and post-game or viewing distantly from the gracious balconies if not attending games in person. Units graduate in size, with 3,000-square-foot units on the ninth and tenth floors, and penthouse units above those. The building has secure parking and a pool deck with adjacent fitness amenities as well as on-site storage. The skin of the building features floor-to-floor fully glazed systems facing the southeast views with punched openings in the short ends and the northwest façades. Vertical living is usually associated with the need for density, but in this case, it is a case of creating an icon.

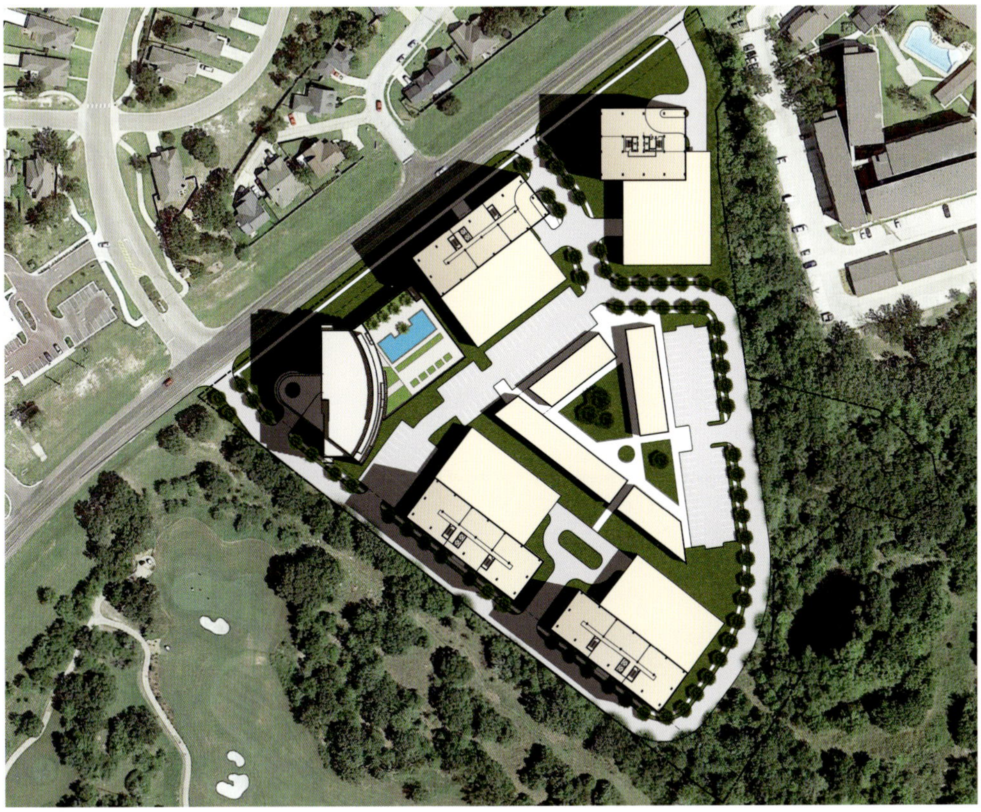

Elevation

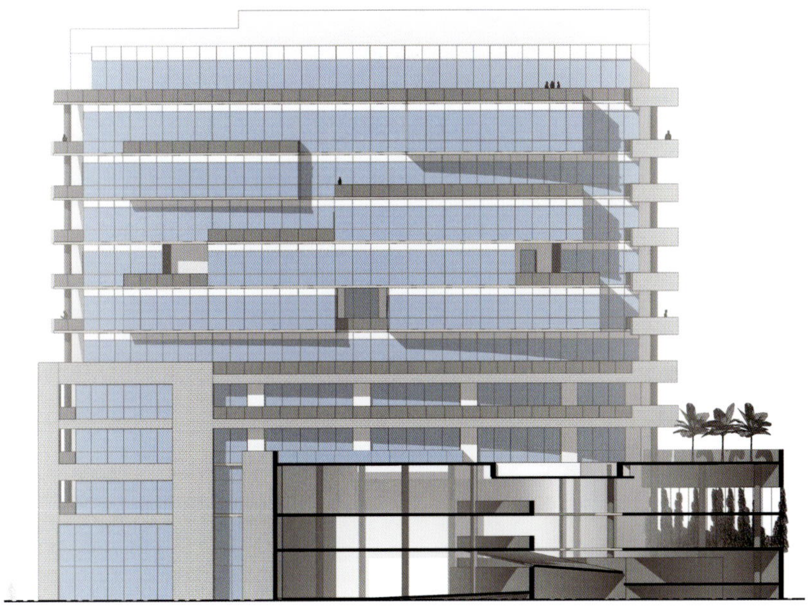

Elevation

Marlowe

The Marlowe is a twenty-story luxury condominium tower located within the entertainment-rich environment of Downtown Houston. The building form takes full advantage of its small footprint, completely occupying the 215,985-square-foot corner of Polk and Caroline Streets. This strategy of "maxing out" the site became the challenge for creating an innovative architectural form, as subtracting from this diagram would mean a certain loss of valuable floor area. As a solution, we performed a careful analysis of the surrounding views of and from the building to inform the locations of terraces and living spaces, creating an asymmetrical composition of glass, voids, and masses throughout the tower.

The living spaces are elevated and sit on top of a seven-level base containing 162 parking spaces and building service areas. An elevated pool deck is nested where the tower meets its base overlooking Green Street and takes advantage of the afternoon sun.

The architectural strategy of the base and 4,000-square-foot lobby indexes the House of Blues music venue across Caroline Street with an abstract pattern of "piano keys." We remained committed to this black-and-white detailing throughout the tower up to the glass box penthouse element. The interiors of the residences and our close attention to detail regarding kitchens, baths, and closets were paramount to the building's success. We organized the living/dining areas around an open kitchen, all rich with warm and inviting materials. Located in areas with preferred views, these spaces absorb the bulk of each home, intentionally compressing bedroom spaces that are permeated with natural light.

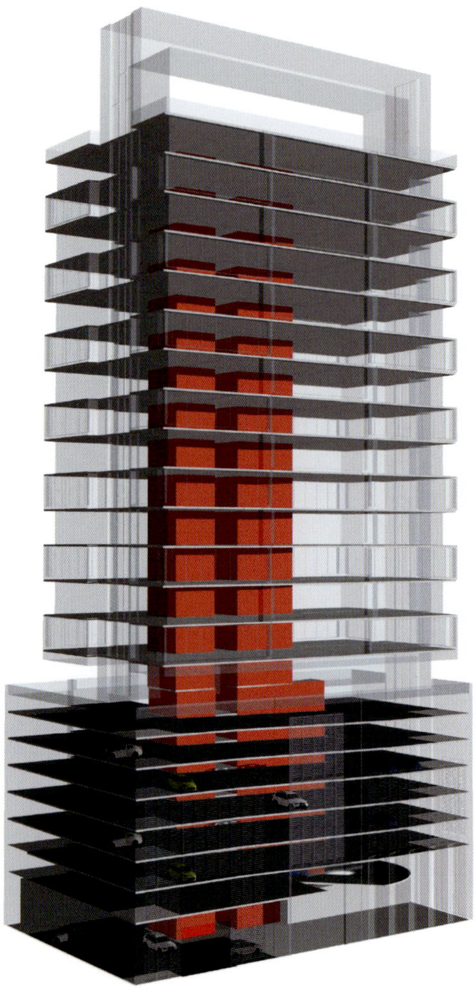

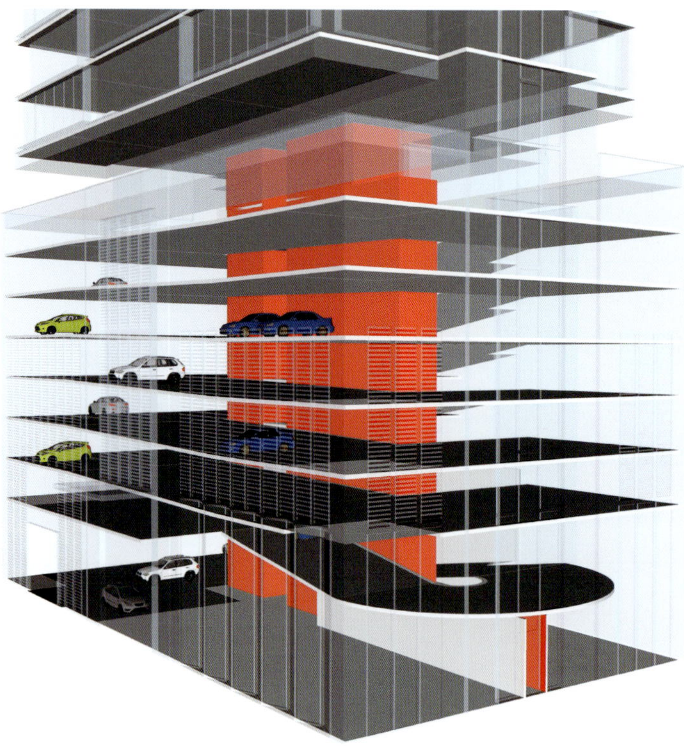

BOWL
MARRIOTT

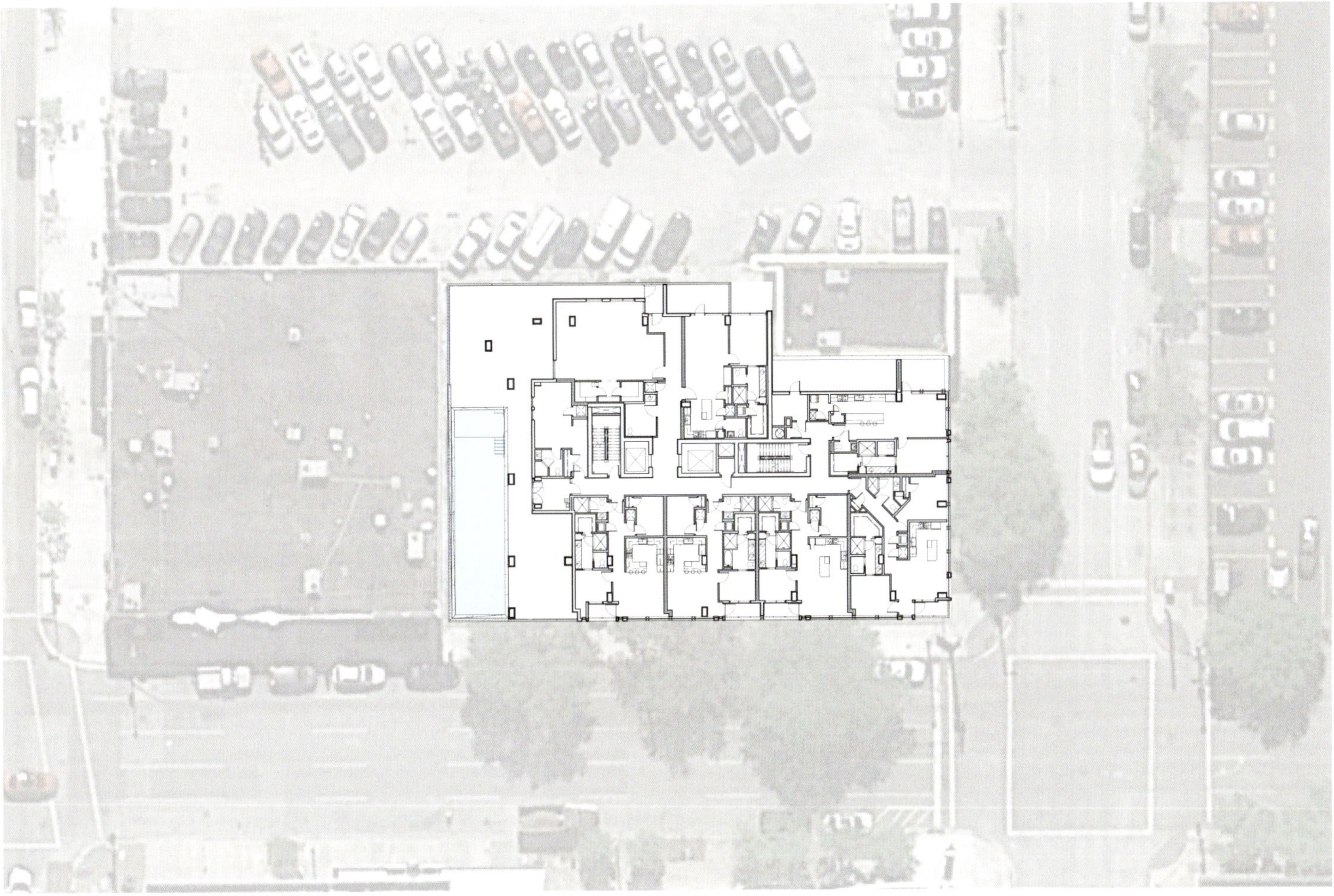

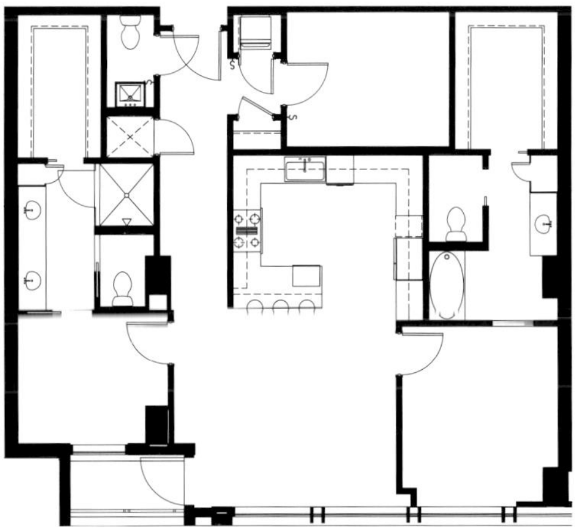
Stewart floor plan

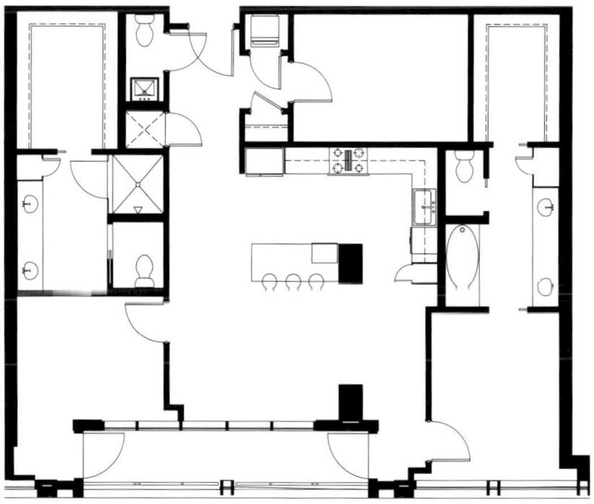
Stewart floor plan

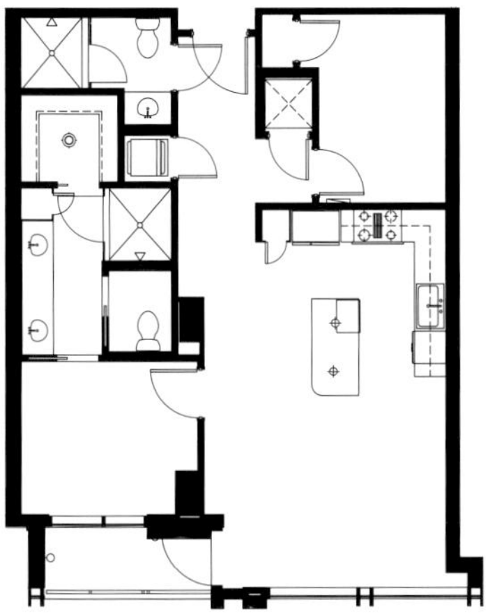
Sinatra floor plan

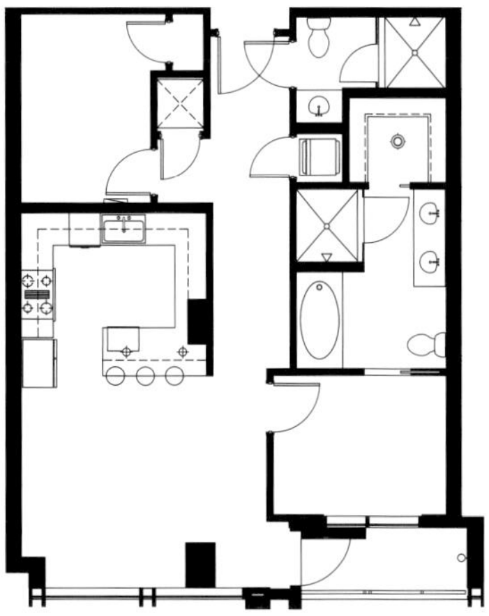
Sinatra floor plan

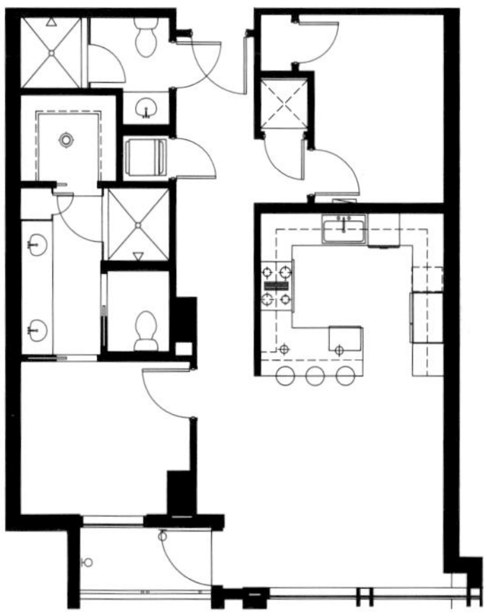
Sinatra floor plan

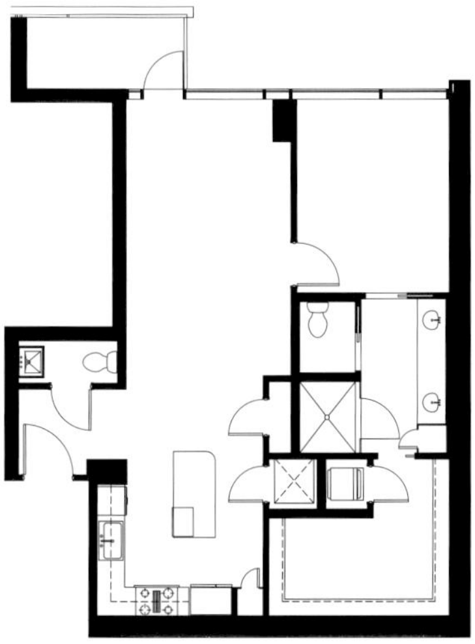
Brando floor plan

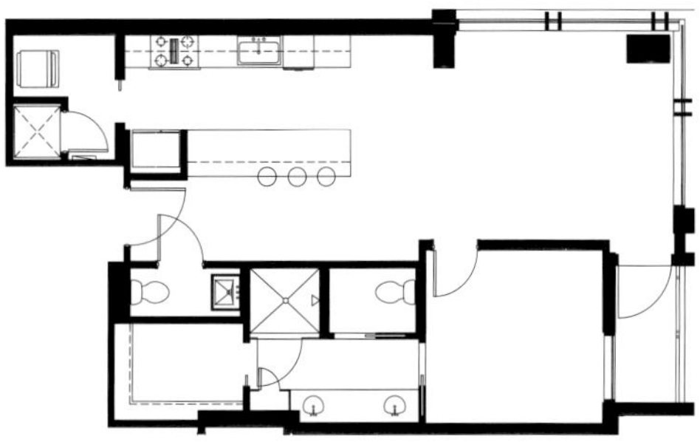
Brando floor plan

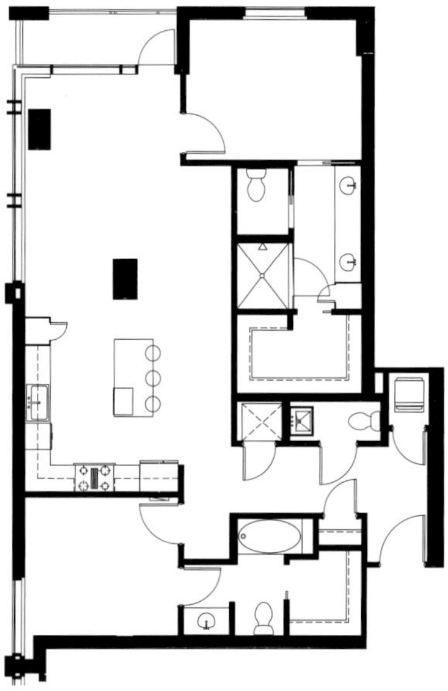
Newman floor plan

Façade glass concept modelling

BOWL
Hilton

The many definitions of "stay" in the English language are what perhaps kept the term out of the running from Live Work Play. Many of its forms are to secure something for a time, to stop things from going forward and, most usefully in noun form, a sojourn in a place. For us it seems to best describe our hospitality work, which is riven with experience-making. Every brand across the spectrum of hotels has an experience choreography that any other building type would envy. This experience characteristic has a tendency to mire design efforts in a kind of interiority vacuum. **Hemisfair** and **Breeze** are attempts to tightly constrain the "experience programs" to the interior of the form as a composition of spaces along a plot-based approach—things lead up to bigger things, better experiences via compilations of formal variability. This can wreak havoc on the skin of the building where there are many competing program elements trying to capitalize on the inside/outside reciprocity architects learn as their first trick in the design studio. Big space, big window, or really emphatically small window. These two buildings create a conceptual membrane that leverages the outside forces as a datum for the various interior itineraries. Both Breeze and Hemisfair are destination hotels situated in well-known, tourist-driven urban environments; that is , they are not in theme parks but their close cousin. Each utilizes a "big form" response to the exterior. **Thompson**, one of the most well-known hotel brands does the opposite. Located on the San Antono River Walk and adjacent to the only major performing arts facility in town just across the river, it combines the branding approach of condominiums with clear exterior communication. The massing steps to scale for the intimacy of the River Walk infrastructure expresses the difference in the hotel elements and the condominium zone, all in a tightly controlled fractured slab.

Stay

San Antonio, Texas | Conventon hotel |185,000 square feet

Hemisfair

The Hemisfair district in downtown San Antonio was established during the 1968 World's Fair (HemisFair '68) hosted by the city. Various attempts to reinvigorate the area have been recently consolidated in coordination with park planners, residential and hospitality developers, and the city itself.

This project represents 250 hotel rooms adjacent to the newly redesigned park space across from the convention center entrance and an existing historic modern pre-fabricated hotel across the street. Our team was involved with the hospitality developer who is also the contractor who built the prefab hotel in the 1960s. They had a vested interest in "relating" somehow to the original structure's brutalist façade. We chose a counterpoint scheme that established the object nature of our skinny tower using the older hotel as a backdrop while not cutting off the view to it from the park, thus integrating them as an urban composition. We also wanted to record the importance of the world-famous River Walk that is adjacent to the site.

The point tower floor plate sits atop a two-story base with retail on the first level along with various and discreetly placed service elements to the south. The entry on the north street side combines a lobby with a restaurant entrance, allowing the dining area to open out to the new parkscape immediately adjacent to the east side of the base. This arrangement also activates the lobby zone with pedestrians and walk-in traffic. The second level has a small conference center convertible to a small exhibition space to complement the convention center. The tower itself draws upon the fair theme as it "spins" in a spiral to the rooftop bar. The rotating floor plates graduate the movement of the balconies on each level, creating a band of outdoor space with planters at the balcony edges carrying the park theme vertically.

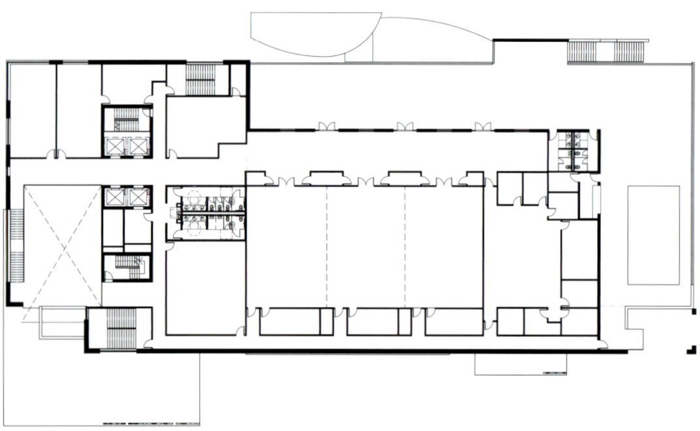

Second-floor plan

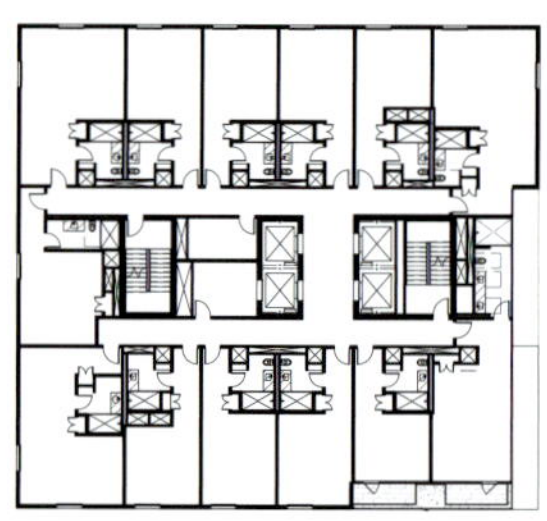

Eighteenth-floor plan

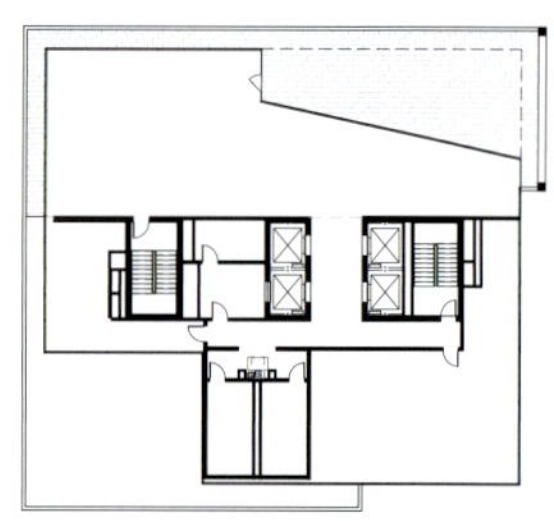

Nineteenth-floor plan (rooftop bar)

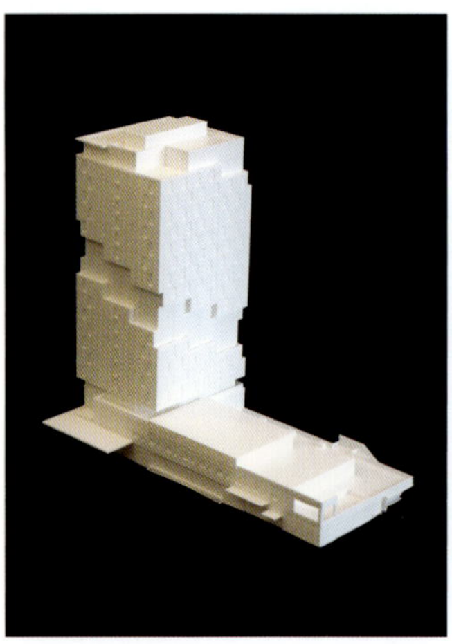

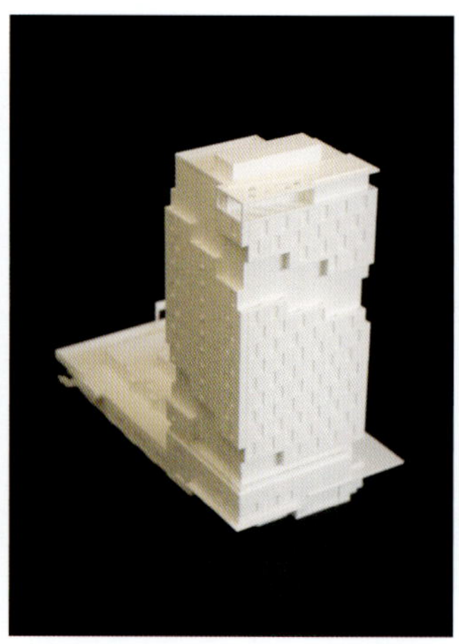

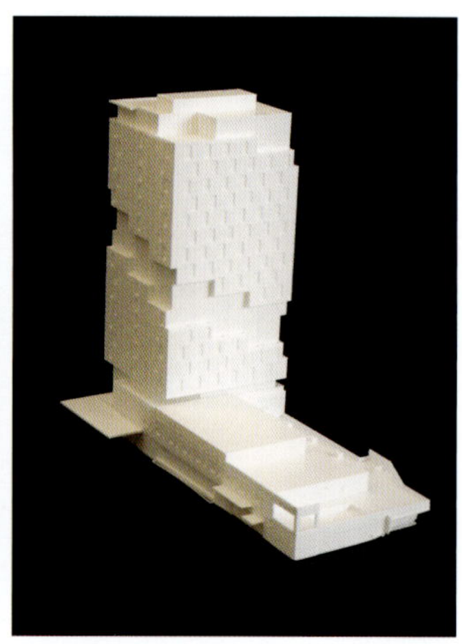

San Antonio, Texas | Hotel and high-rise condominium | 372,654 square feet

Thompson

The Thompson Hotel & Arts Residences consists of twenty stories with sixty-two condominiums atop of 152 hotel rooms directly above a series of base levels containing a new chef-driven restaurant, lobby ballrooms/meeting area, pool and spa, accompanied on the first four levels by parking. Adjacent to the historic River Walk in San Antonio, we had a rich series of forces to navigate in the building's design approach.

We conceived of the building as a base that could extend the urban logic of the context with a complex constellation of volumes and planes resting on it and comprising the tower. The entire ensemble negotiates the opportunities of its urban locality and the obligation to the city skyline that a twenty-story building in downtown San Antonio has.

Given the extreme site constraints, the tower was forced into the most formidable urban trope: the slab. Our approach was to articulate the program elements of condo, public spaces, and the hotels sub-components to deconstruct the slab using formal "cleaving" operations. Cleaving is a separation and a holding together of things simultaneously.

The first cleaving of the slab is a vertical sliding of both "halves" of the double-loaded corridor north and south to the limitation of the base, creating empty corners that we occupied with sloped conical volumes—one expanding downward to the street locating the entry of private condo owners, and the second along the riverfront, rising from the bottom to top toward the urban core views.

The second cleaving is a horizontal zoning of the hotel on the lower floors from the condo units on the upper floors; done by separating them physically at the top level of the hotel program of the special suite units that was at exactly mid-tower. This facilitates a successful sense of wholeness at numerous scales without sacrificing its overall place on the skyline.

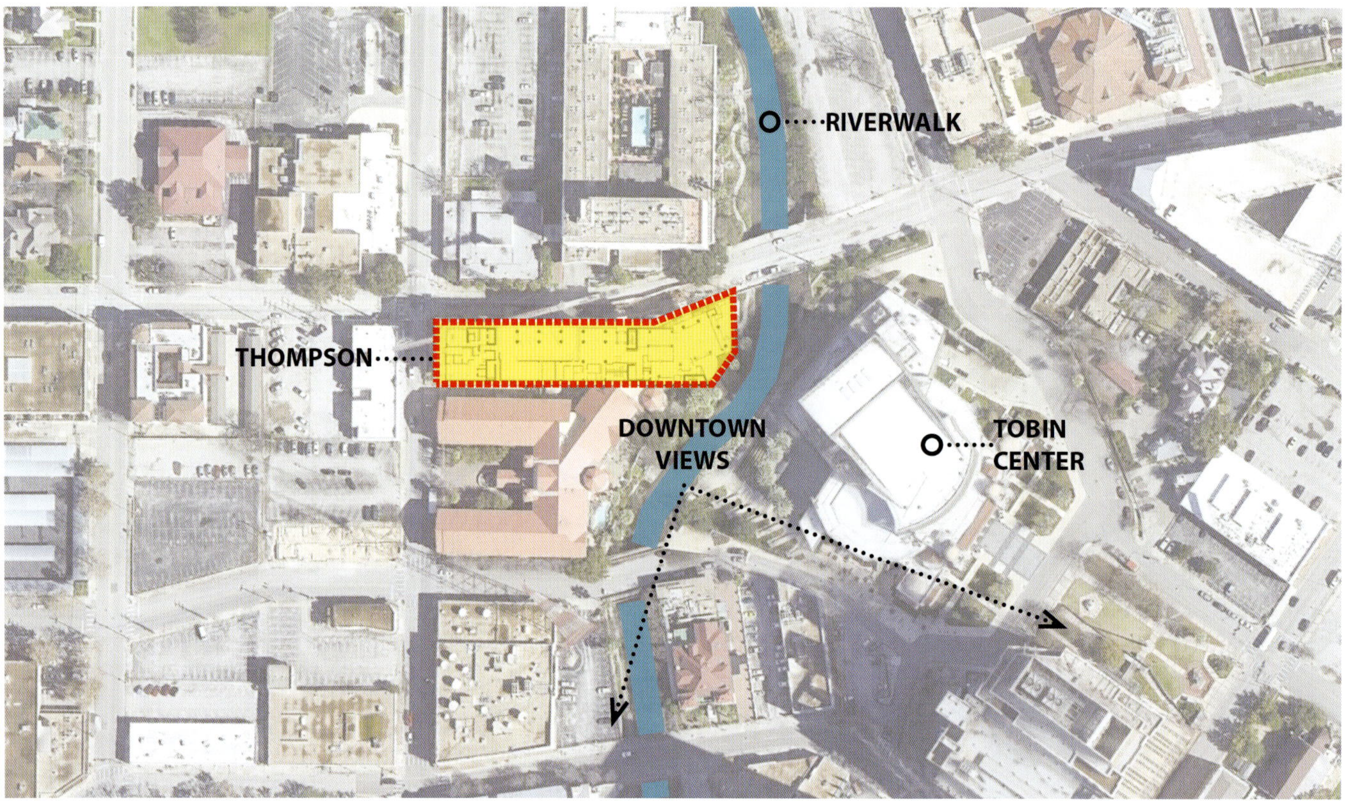

Site plan

CADILLAC LOFTS

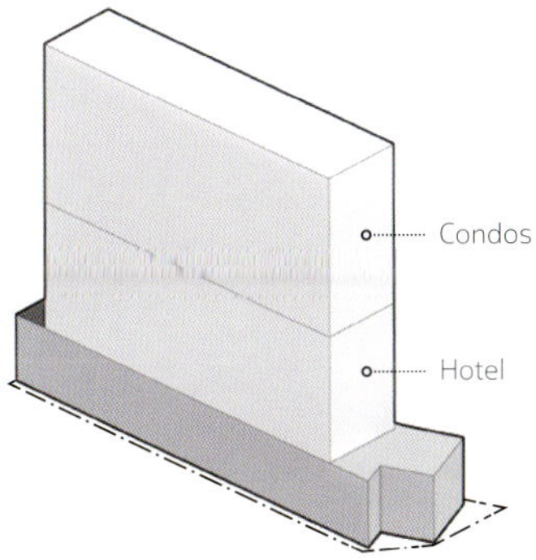

Tower program stacked on base

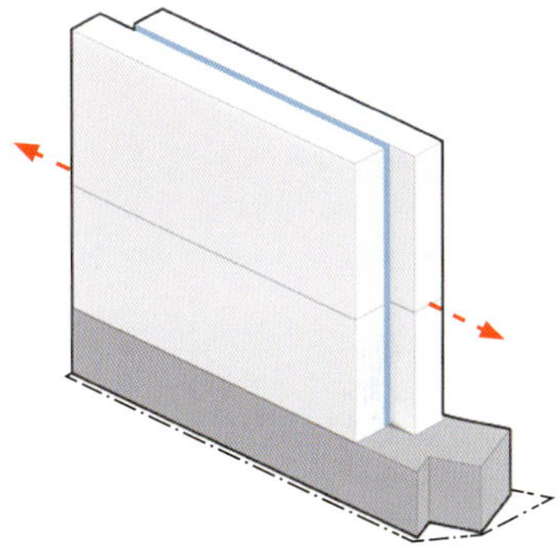
Horizontal "cleaving" of tower program

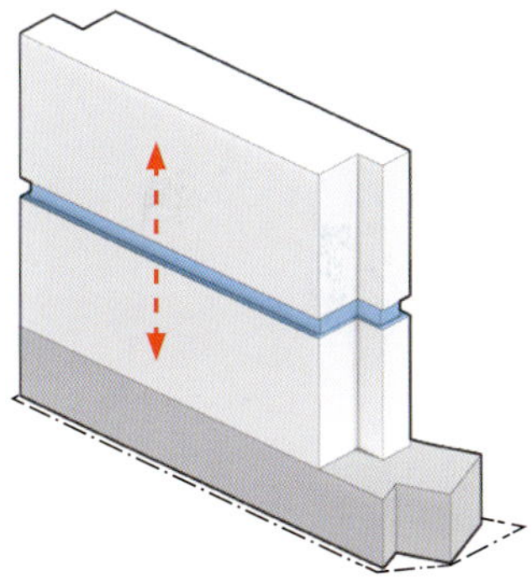
Vertical 'cleaving' of tower program

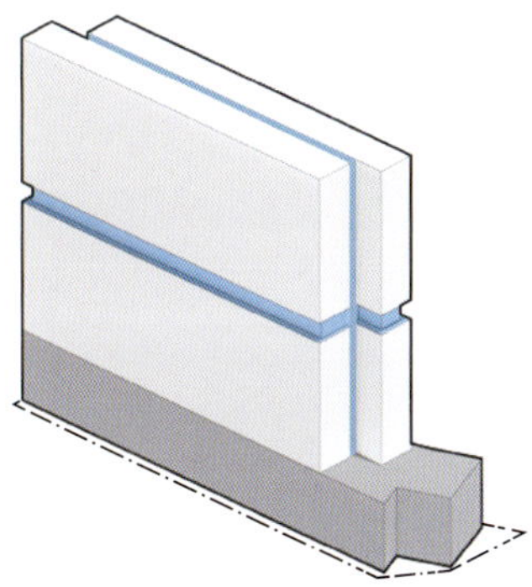
Seperation and holding together
of things simultaneously

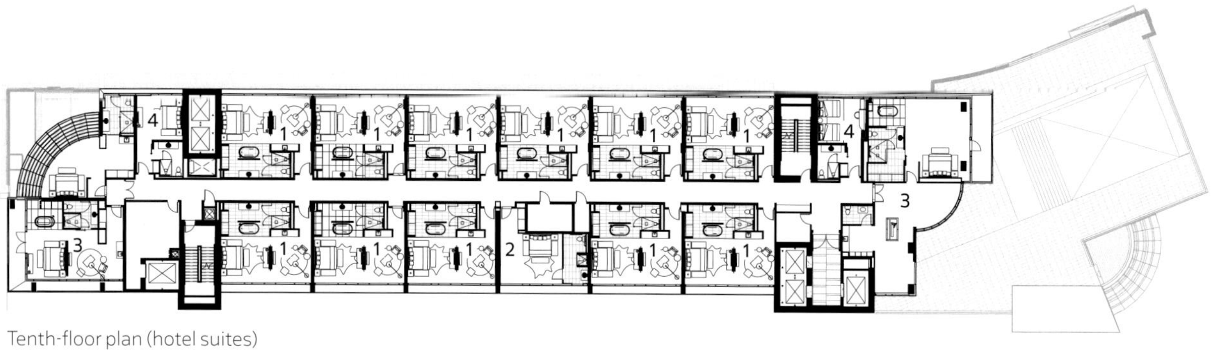

Tenth-floor plan (hotel suites)

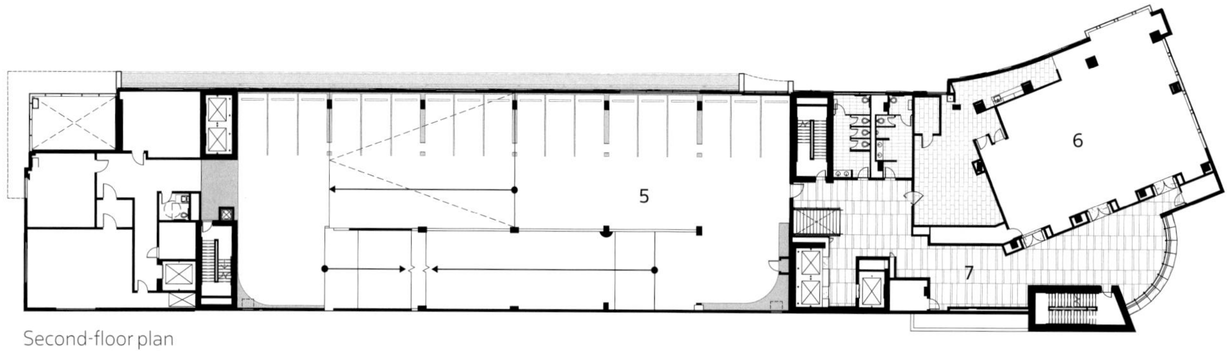

Second-floor plan

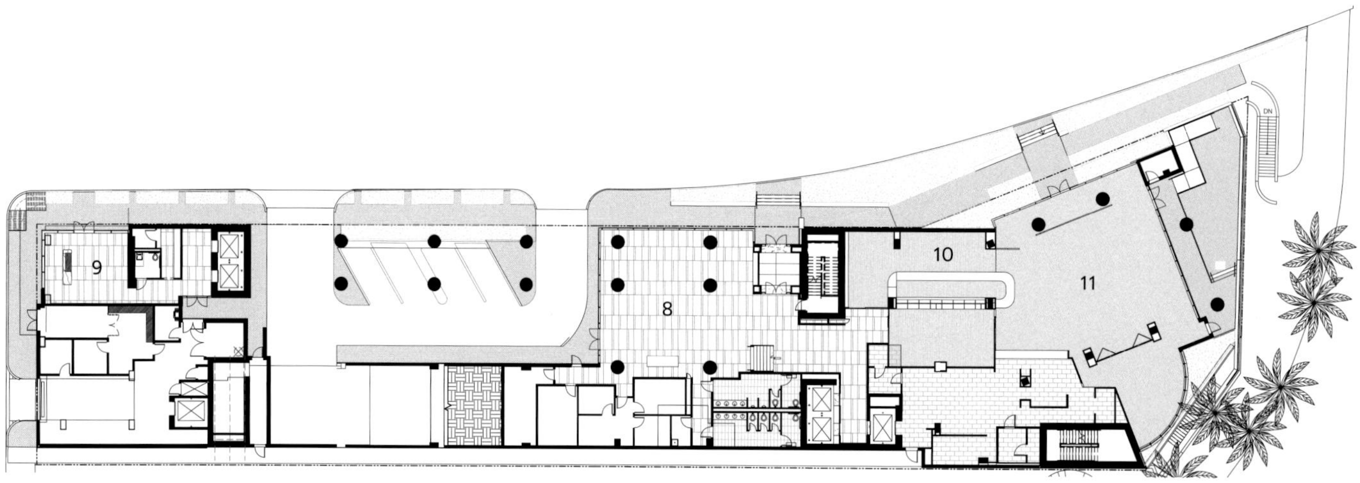

First-floor plan

1 Suite
2 Accessible suite
3 Thompson suite
4 Standard room
5 Garage
6 Ballroom
7 Prefunction
8 Hotel lobby
9 Condo lobby
10 Bar
11 Restaraunt

0 45 FT

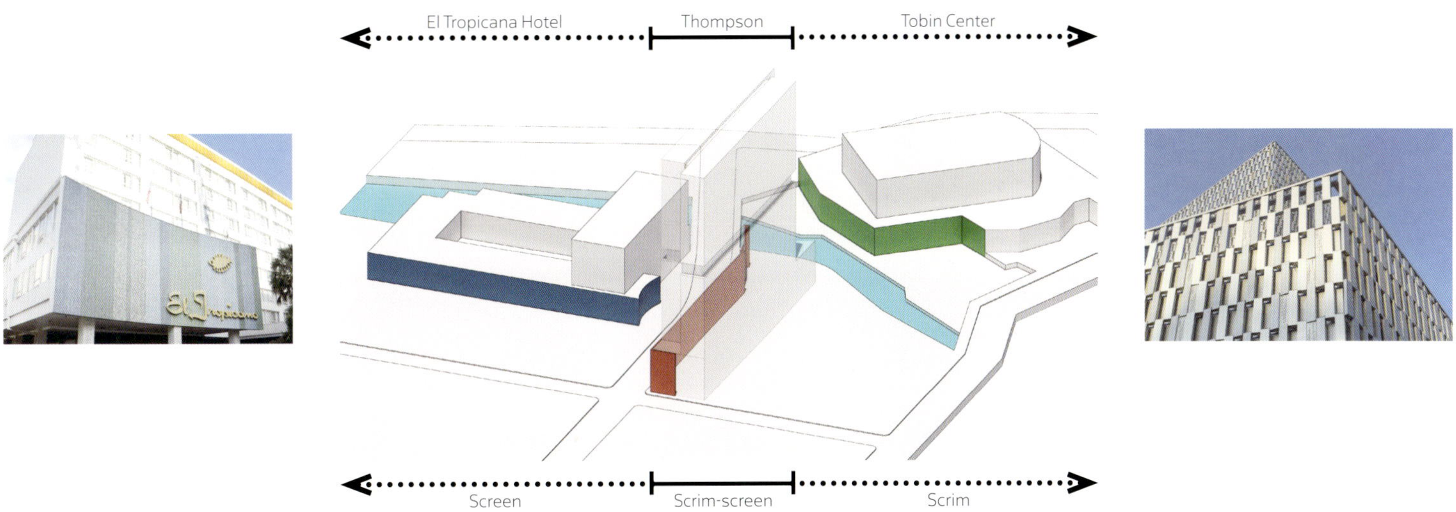

Façade cladding concept

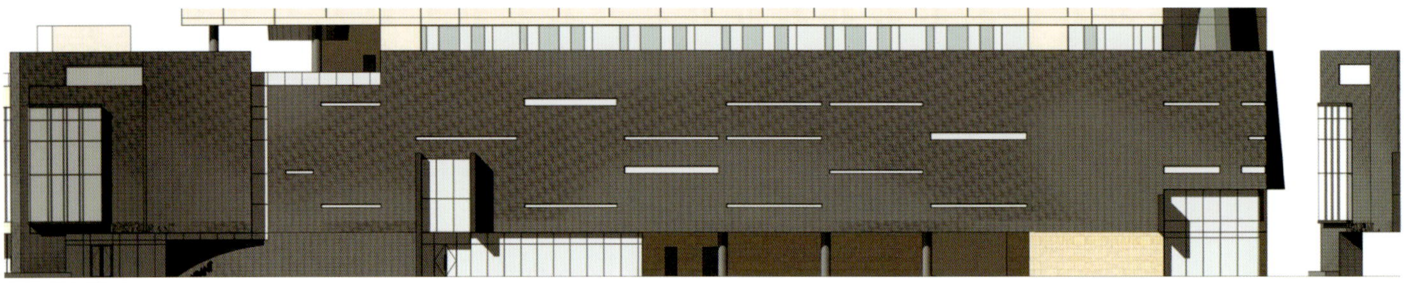

River flow pattern on metal screen façade

Breeze

Nestled near the intersection of a historic avenue and a major historic boulevard parallel to the seafront, the Breeze hotel serves as a new placemaker for residents and visitors. The tower's design pays homage to the very spirit of Galveston—the sea.

Inspired by the sails of vessels as they react with concave and convex geometries to the coastal breeze, the tower's façade is a dynamic display of undulating forms as each curve evokes the fluidity of sails in motion. The result is a striking visual presence that seamlessly blends with the city's maritime heritage.

The project's location as the only hotel on the island to be situated on the seaward side of the main seafront drive presented challenges as well as unique opportunities. Without the protection of the seawall, the occupiable spaces of the project were required to be lifted above the base flood elevation, which allowed the lower floors of the project to become parking. The "ground" level of the hotel is elevated 23 feet above the beach and contains a large ballroom and meeting spaces. The restaurant and bar are located on the east side of the project to take advantage of the views and provide direct access to the beach for both guests and the public. Located on top of the tower's podium are the outdoor amenities, including a bar, sundeck, and infinity-edge pool that offers unobstructed views overlooking the local beach. The tower's design maximizes these views for guests, with each room positioned to frame the natural beauty of the sea.

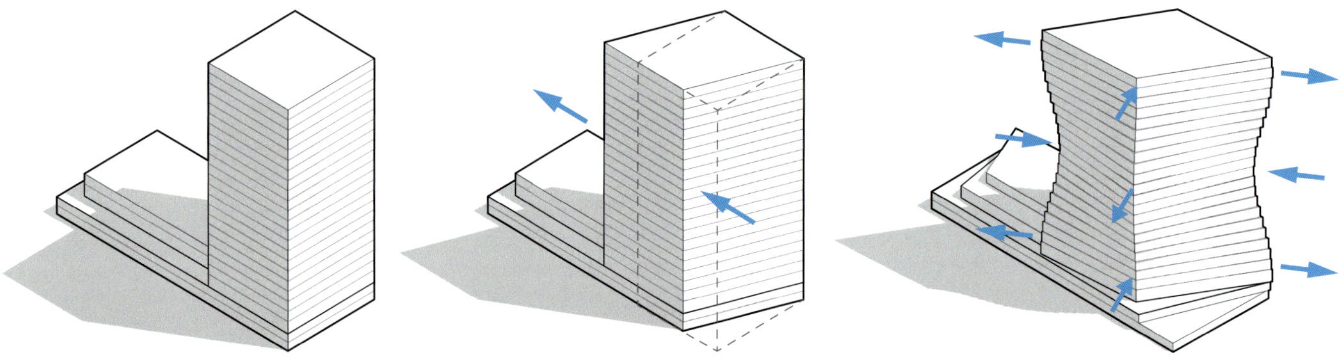

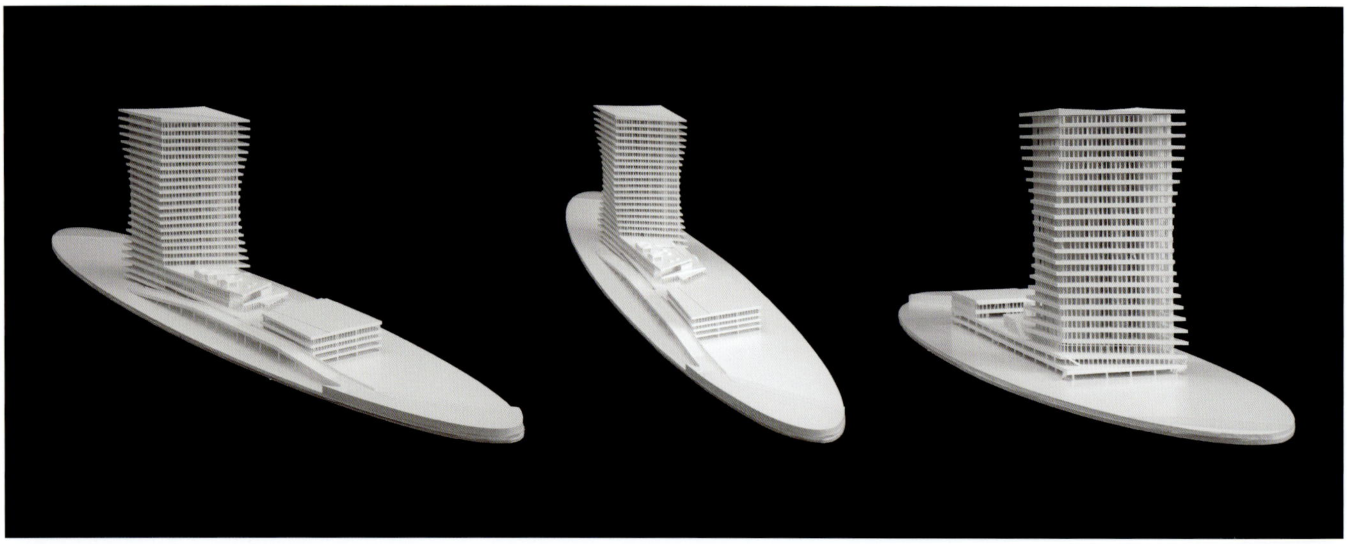

SEAWALL BLVD

Our practice has always adhered to the concept and philosophy of sustainably in its many guises. Starting our practice in 1999 put us on the rising arc of LEED, Green Globes, and numerous organizations that put forth schemes and lists for what is objectively quantifiable as good for the environment across spectrums of low-impact materials, systems that work optimally with energy sources and community impact. There has always been a skepticism around the aesthetics of sustainability. Should the building look ecologically appropriate; should it code into its form its hidden aspects? The lists were not much help in determining aesthetics. And trends emerged where criticism worked against doing the "right thing" as it was too expensive. Sauerbruch and Hutton observed, in an essay on what sustainability should look like, quoting guidelines from German local government regulations stated, "buildings are temporary depots for future building waste." We are not sure things have come much further since then, but with the rise of organizations like Phius, there has been a more integrated emphasis on performance over the performative, which has inspired us to begin new projects from the basis that our design will be carbon neutral within current means and the client can, if she chooses, to opt out of it. In **POST** we had the great fortune to be collaborating architects with OMA (led by Jason Long) in the adaptive reuse of a 500,000-square-foot post office, built in stages starting in 1936. Our role in sustainable research on the project was integrated with the design process led by OMA into a seamless merging of the possible and the beautiful. In **Stratford** we encountered a common challenge in the transformation of dead big box buildings into new programs. Challenges like inducing natural light in huge floor plates and solving code changes are common in big box reformation but the result reduces carbon footprint and the waste stream. While POST also intersected the Federal Historic Tax credit process, other projects like **Red Gap** fall under Historic Structures protection. Here, the age-old debate about how the old and new invade and accommodate one another is at play.

Recycle

Stratford

Stratford University is a private educational institution offering programs in fields such as information technology, hospitality, culinary arts, business administration, and healthcare. Stratford University is growing, with additional campuses throughout the state of Virginia. This 52,000-square-foot project for the Richmond campus occupies a remodeled and altered third-generation warehouse space in a local business park. The first bay of the 65,000-square-foot footprint was demolished to account for required additional parking and an enhanced entry image. The "new" section of this renovation comprises an expressed corner element housing the library and a small urban courtyard to provide outdoor gathering space for the students. The general interior scheme is a double-loaded corridor lined with all of the classroom and teaching labs and cooking spaces. The corridor is punctuated by small courtyards with integrated seating and laptop standing spaces and wi-fi. Another layer of hierarchy overlaps with the corridor social space: the collective spaces made by the cafeteria and the lobby to the main auditorium. All of these spaces are lit with skylights and articulated with high-finish materials, and have enhanced ceiling height. These are "slow spaces" on a corridor that is kinetic by nature. The main administration area is immediately across from the library forming the entry way at the corner of the main circulation system. The classrooms are organized by discipline, with tech clusters and health clusters interspersed with general skills classrooms. Ultimately, the strategy was one of urbanizing a derelict big box space; the pressure the program effciency places on the public circulation is the catalyst for the synergy that gives the inherently interior scheme the campus feel.

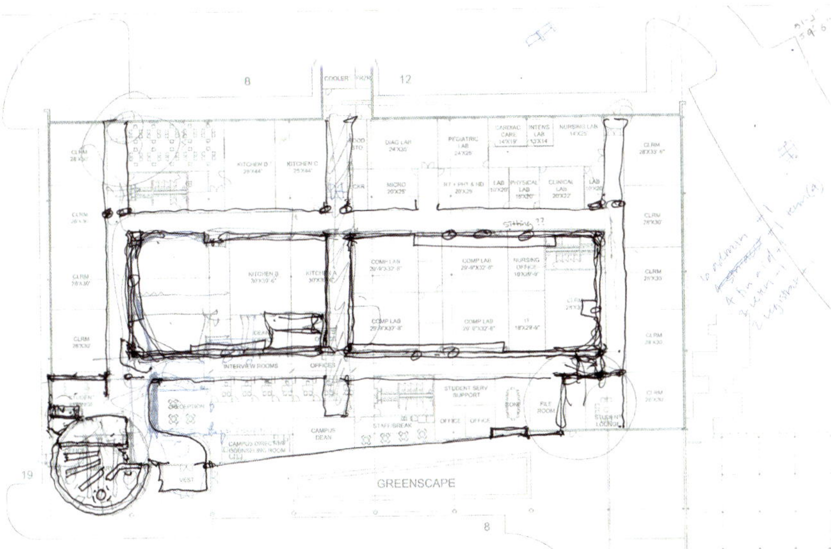
GREENSCAPE

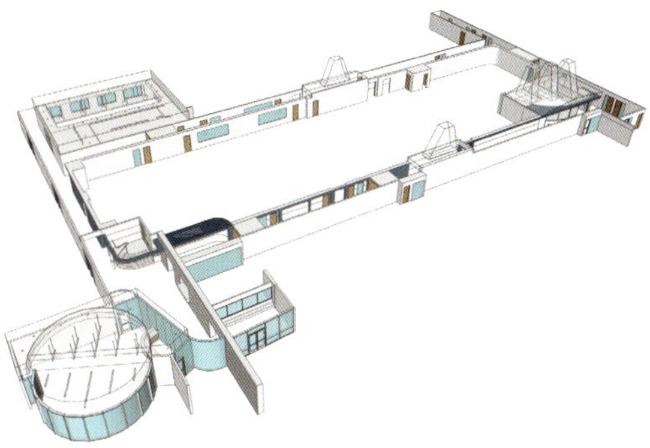

STRATFORD
UNIVERSITY

Fort Worth, Texas | Tech headquarters | 5,000 square feet

Red Gap

Red Gap is a VOIP service company that wanted to remain in the Sundance Square District of downtown Fort Worth, Texas. They chose to renovate the 5,000-square-foot second floor of the historically designated Jarvis Building constructed in 1874. The space is unique in that after an internal fire in 1968, an African American theatrical performance company renovated the lower floor and removed the columns for the stage by employing an upturned truss. The truss at the second floor rendered the space as storage until our renovation. It is located in the geographic center of the space and we used that to organize all of the company's functions. Emanating from the truss is an oval-shaped wall that slopes from its first, more open appearance at the entry to enclose the more private functions along its path. Splayed walls that fill in the poché between the oval and the existing box walls form the offices. We worked to detail the space in a manner that would not compete with the bolted tectonics of the truss but rather complement its obvious uniqueness. Transparency and strategic cutting of the oval wall allow the truss to frame many of the experiences of the space.

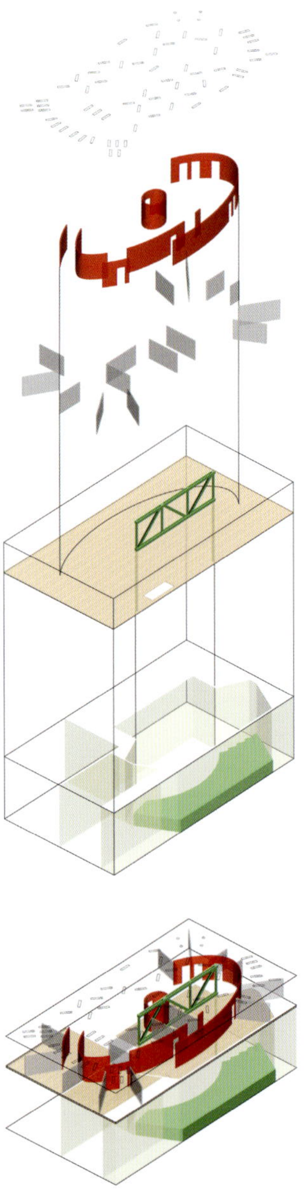

POST

The adaptive reuse of POST was dedicated to the idea of sustainability from the beginning—reuse itself intersects with sustainability in the most powerful manner. The building achieved LEED Gold in 2022 under LEED v4 of the rating system. It takes a special building in a densely populated area to achieve that level of certification, but POST really is a special building at the heart of the Houston metropolis. Apart from certification, we see three key achievements at POST as the key vectors of sustainability for this project: daylighting, water, and life cycle.

Daylighting

Daylighting enhances occupant well-being by providing a connection to the natural environment, reduces stress, and improves mood and productivity. It significantly reduces energy consumption by reducing artificial lighting required during daylight hours, leading to lower operational costs and reduced environmental impact. Daylighting isn't just a design choice; it's a multifaceted strategy that aligns environmental responsibility, energy efficiency, and human delight in architecture.

The transformation from an almost windowless two-story warehouse to the buzzing cultural center POST is today, was predicated on how daylight was to enter the building. Before POST was constructed, the building was famous for how voluminous and dark it was. In the years between its function as the Barbara Jordan Post Office and its new life as POST, it was home to an annual visual and music festival. Concert-goers meandered through light and sound installations in an otherwise black cavern of concrete columns. It was a beautiful use of architecture, but for only a few days of the year.

Natural light was the first, and perhaps most critical, "feature" that the architecture had to establish. The logical questions were how many apertures and how big? The integrated project delivery facilitated the necessary feedback loop between cost, structural integrity, and of course, design. However, the key objective check and balance came from daylight simulations run in-house as changes were iterated upon. In addition, an independent feedback loop was running, driven by input from the historical side. OMA produced the original design intent to cut three atriums and some series of other skylights on the roof. Early skylights were square and arranged in linear forms. Eventually the approach became softer in nature, a more appropriate reflection of the lush green-roof environment designed by Hoerr Schaudt. Thus, large circular skylights of varying sizes and angles were able to better distribute light throughout the building. The large spans of the final atrium design were achieved using ETFE plastics with incredible strength-to-weight ratios.

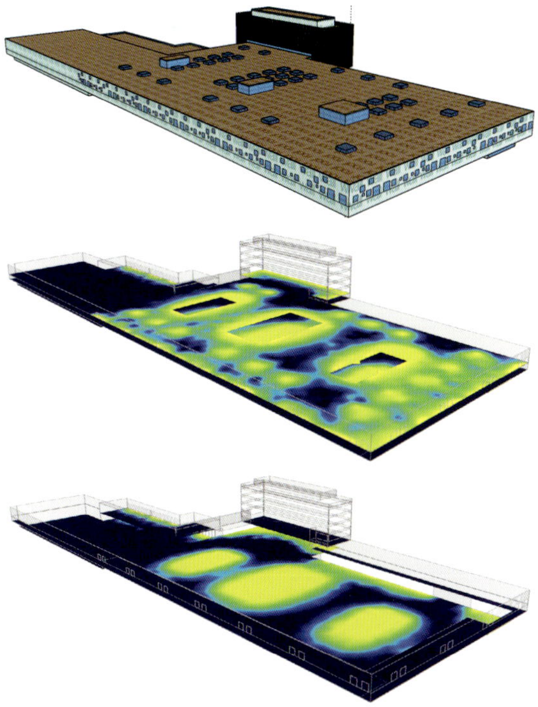

Daylight penetration analysis

Water

The project's size, location, and program ensure that it will consistently be highly occupied for its entire second useful life. Roughly 500,000 square feet comprises the concert venue, dining hall, offices, retail, outdoor rooftop park, and indoor gathering spaces. This left the project team with an incredible opportunity; any percentage reduction in resource use would have outweighed absolute reduction potential. Water, in this case, was the biggest opportunity for outsized savings.

Conserving water in commercial buildings is paramount for several compelling reasons. First, it reduces operational costs, saving money on water bills and lowering the burden on municipal wastewater treatment. Water scarcity is also a growing global concern, and responsible water management is essential to mitigate this crisis. Moreover, water-saving measures often go hand-in-hand with energy efficiency, as pumping and heating water require energy. Therefore, reducing water usage also lowers a building's overall energy consumption, reducing its carbon footprint and environmental impact. Furthermore, embracing water-saving technologies and practices can enhance a commercial building's reputation, attracting environmentally conscious tenants and customers.

Typically, indoor water savings are tackled through public fixtures. Indeed, the result conservatively saves over 1.3 million gallons of water per year through careful fixture selections. Further savings are then typically driven through outdoor plant selections and water delivery methods; again, POST conservatively saved an additional 1.5 million gallons of water per year through reduction of use and evaporation. However, the greatest source of water reduction came through improved process.

The team collectively settled on a cooling tower for the air-conditioning needs. Cooling towers use the evaporative properties of water to efficiently cool air. However, the process is fraught with maintenance and consumes industrial quantities of fresh water. The team identified a technology to send an electric signal to the water supply, which prevents minerals from adhering to surfaces. This elegant solution reduces risk of corrosion and micro-organism growth, ensuring it operates at peak efficiency. Reliance on chemical additives was also greatly reduced. This also allows the towers to operate longer with higher concentrations of minerals as water is lost to evaporation. A staggering 6.5 million gallons of additional fresh water is saved per year with the addition of this technology. The project also gained back what would have been additional maintenance room space and avoided a full-time maintenance person. Savings to the owner over twenty years is expected to be over $3 million.

Ultimately, saving water at POST became a win-win strategy, benefiting the bottom line, the environment, and the broader community.

Life Cycle

POST could have been demolished and replaced with skyscrapers. In fact, that was the more likely outcome for a building of this vintage in a metropolitan downtown area. Bold vision matched with historic tax credits allowed the project's transformation to take place. But beyond the financial case are the cultural and environmental values in saving a building. Today simply citing "embodied energy" has become a green building trope. That's because we have incredible data and quantifiable metrics to better judge our actions in the business of buildings.

Life cycle assessments (LCAs) are an analysis technique to help design professionals assess the comparative environmental impacts associated with different building components and design options. The impacts studied typically include acidification potential, eutrophication potential, global warming potential, ozone depletion potential, smog formation potential, and primary energy demand with a full cradle-to-grave or cradle-to-cradle scope. The application of LCA software within a detailed architectural model first requires the accurate assignment of material specifications to all building components. This then outputs specific material quantities and allows the LCA software to extrapolate those quantities to the large body of research about the environmental impacts.

Material quantities are also a critical component in assessing the environmental impacts of embodied carbon in our buildings. The project team took the outputs from the completed LCA and integrated them into a triple bottom line–cost benefit analysis. Design valuation software allowed the project team to financially quantify the environmental, social, and economic costs and savings of different design options for this adaptive reuse project.

Financial benefits of improving the building were from direct paybacks. The lifetime net present value (NPV) of water and energy savings came to $1.8 million. However, the marriage of these two analyses specifically allowed for the calculation of the social cost of carbon by leveraging the body of empirical economic research on the subject. Core and shell reuse constituted 12 percent wood, 99 percent concrete, 60 percent steel, 3 percent glass, 100 percent brick, and 2 percent drywall. The results concluded that an estimated lifetime NPV of $2.3 million of negative social externalities due to carbon emissions alone were effectively avoided by keeping the building intact.

Beyond carbon, the social and environmental impacts of the green roof were assessed. The community recreation from the rooftop park for the next twenty-five years resulted in a NPV at $15.6 million. And the air and water and urban heat island effects mitigated had an additional NPV of $929,000. The combined social, financial, and environmental value of the design totaled over $24 million.

This section is titled "systems" when it may well be titled "urban design." Somehow for us, systems and the two projects we include here sum up our response via architecture and our practice format to the pandemic. Architecture has had an on-again, off-again relationship to the city in the guise of urban design. As of this writing we are in a valley regarding urbanism and city planning, and we seem to have abandoned the city for the very big building more often that not. Looking through our academic resources we also see less writing about cities and more about technologies. Perhaps this will swing again to the large scale of experiences, as it is in the nature of architects to be interested in the entirety of the built environment. Which is why from time to time architects get involved in systems. Systems seem to outrun notions like composition but not escape the gravity of "design." European work on the EU logo by OMA and the Rhine Ruhr region forum in Germany involving MVRDV are examples of contemporary systems efforts—there are many others. It is the unique education of architects that makes us so prone to things not architectural but involving a great deal of strategy on an analogical scale. **MEDDNet**™ is a pure system. It involves the logistical planning for surge capacity for medical services in times of emergency. It was inspired by the dreadful environments created within convention centers and hospital parking lots with makeshift shelters and leftover equipment. During the early days of the pandemic, we collaborated with medical specialist architects, engineers, logistics planners, and the largest industrial developer in the world to propose a system run by the government in cooperation with the private sector. It has been presented to the likes of Federal Emergency Management System (FEMA) and the army corps of engineers. **Mall** is a different approach to using system thinking and it's an architectural building type born out of the pandemics, surely permanent programmatic desiccation of the shopping mall. It describes grafting market-based distribution warehouse typologies onto the dead "anchor" appendages of nearly every American mall.

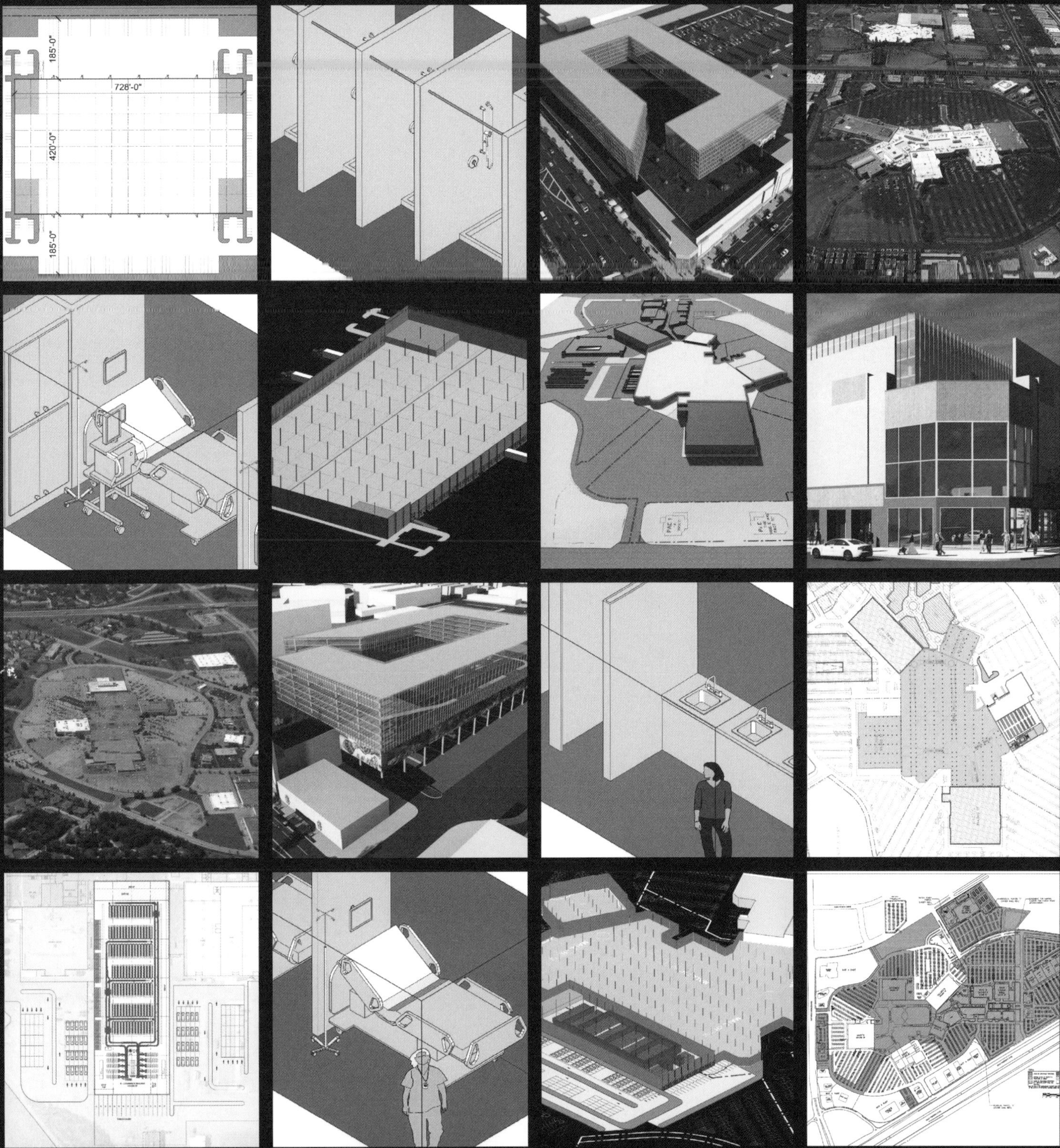

Systems

MEDDNet™

The MEDDNet™ proposal solves the problem of the surge need for regional disaster relief. It is based on a proposed combination of a public/private partnership procurement, an existing national warehouse inventory, the logistics of the trucking and train industries for distribution to the required destination/s, and the government's ability to develop and manage a simple asset for distribution over this network.

MEDDNet™ (Medical Emergency Disaster Distribution Network) is a disaster distribution system strategy. MEDDNet™ proposes the utilization of existing private sector commercial real estate networks to distribute "plug and play" medical pods (i.e., shipping container pod systems). The pods would be stored in climate-controlled regional warehouses, ready for distribution within a day's radius through regional real estate networks, to become temporary medical crisis centers in national disasters. It combines existing infrastructure and widely available shipping strategies into a federal-scaled network that harnesses the potential of existing public/private cooperating resources. Existing resources currently being developed in the United States can be easily adapted to varying disaster conditions and types, such as hurricanes, flooding, earthquakes, and pandemics. That is, a private-sector solution for real-time response to the distribution of medical services in the form of climate-controlled temporary crisis hospitals in national disasters. It proposes a strategy of storing ready-to-go shipping container medical pods in regional warehouses for distribution to destinations in less than a single day's trucking distance (approximately 600 miles).

Most current medical and disaster solutions for temporary emergency rooms and bed accommodation rely upon many elements coming from multiple sources. The MEDDNet™ proposal is consolidated—the "plug and play" solution would be coming from a single source and arriving at a source predetermined for easy deployment.

The pods would adhere to the dimensions of a standard forty-foot shipping container. Shipping containers are the ideal solution. Currently there are between six and 14 million unused shipping containers globally, so 1) they are readily available; 2) they are indexed to transporation infrastructure; and 3) there's in-built functional flexibility, i.e., they are sized to readily accommodate multiple functions, such as retail, office, medical, and hospitality use.

Trucks and trains are the most common transport modes of shipping containers. Warehouses are commonly specified to market sizes, and volumes are designed to store a simple forty-foot shipping container. Within a seven- to ten-day timeframe, hundreds of beds could be put in place in the required regional center on effectively zero notice from order issued to last pod off the truck at the destination.

Thus, transporting shipping container pods modified for medical use using existing truck and train routes from regional storage to local deployment is a radically simple, low-cost, ready to implement solution to surge bed deployment.

MEDDNet™

Powers Brown Architecture
LJB Inc.
Leo A Daly

The following is a proposal for a business plan that solves the problem of the surge need for regional disaster relief. It is based upon a proposed combination of a public/private partnership procurement, an existing national real estate network/inventory, the logistics of the trucking industry for distribution to the real estate inventory, and the governments ability to develop and manage a simple asset for distribution over this network.

It combines existing infrastructure and widely available existing shipping strategies into a federal scaled network that harnesses the potential of combining public and private resources…

…to provide solutions in the United States easily adapted to varying disaster conditions and types.

MEDDNet is a disaster distribution systems strategy.

Medical **E**mergency **D**isaster **D**istribution **Net**work

=

MEDDNet

www.meddnetwork.com

MEDDNet Components:

1) Individual pod system
2) Distribution network strategy
3) Real estate strategy

Powers Brown Architecture MEDDNet LEO A DALY

Disasters such as:

Hurricanes
Flooding
Earthquakes
Pandemics

Current Methods for Temporary Emergency Medical Rooms

Most current medical and disaster solutions for bed accommodation rely upon many elements coming from multiple sources.

Why Shipping Containers?

They are:

- Readily available
- Indexed to transportation infrastructure
- Sized to readily accommodate multiple functions.

Powers Brown Architecture MEDDNet LEO A DALY

Available

Millions unused

MEDDnet proposes the utilization of existing private sector commercial real estate networks to distribute "Plug & Play" pods to local warehouses, becoming temporary crisis centers in national disasters.

Powers Brown Architecture MEDDNet LEO A DALY

Infrastructure

Flexible use

Pods designed to these forty-foot container dimensions already exist as proposals and actually in production.

Flexible use

They are also designed to house retail, office, housing, hospitality, etc.

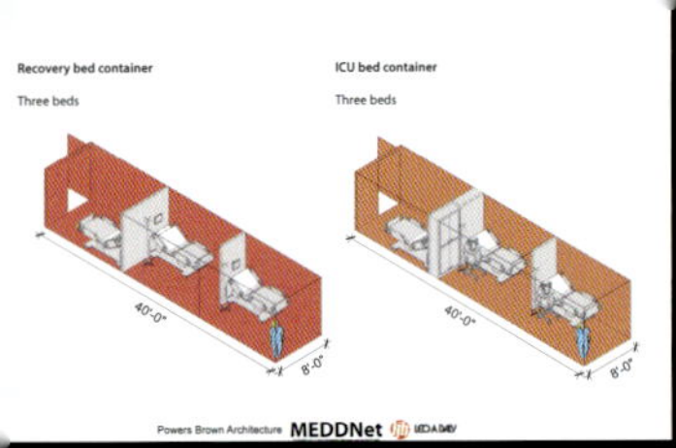

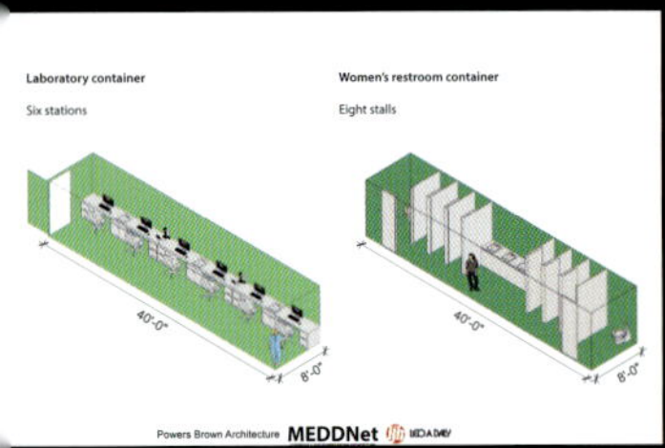

MEDDNet Facility Strategy

The MEDDNet strategy assumes, in combination with government, either through a Design Build Lease Back procurement or the provision of land for the government to build through its own outside competitive procurement process, that the developer would manage a **Regional Storage Facility** containing the medical pods which then would be distributed to a **Local Warehouse Facility** or vacant space in existing facilities in that developers network.

Powers Brown Architecture MEDDNet LEO A DALY

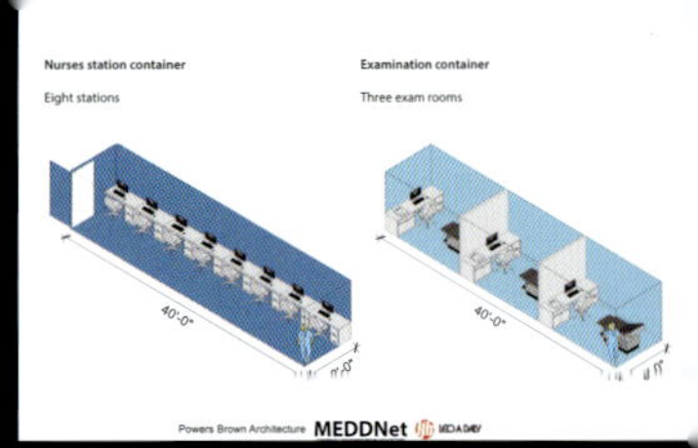

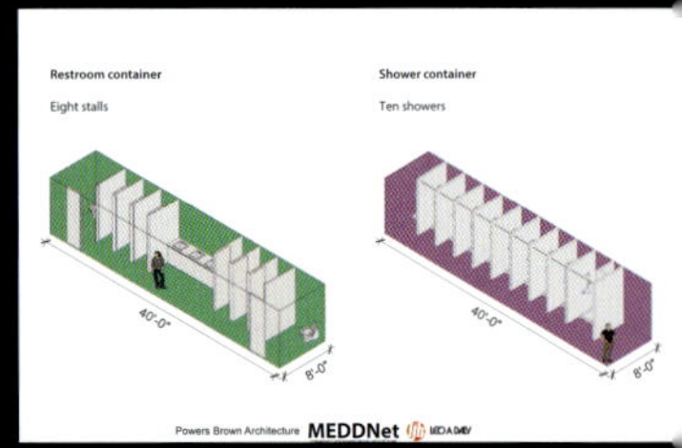

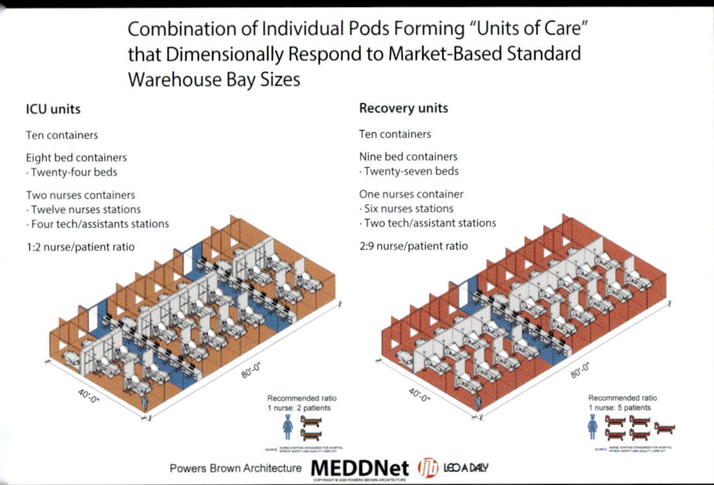

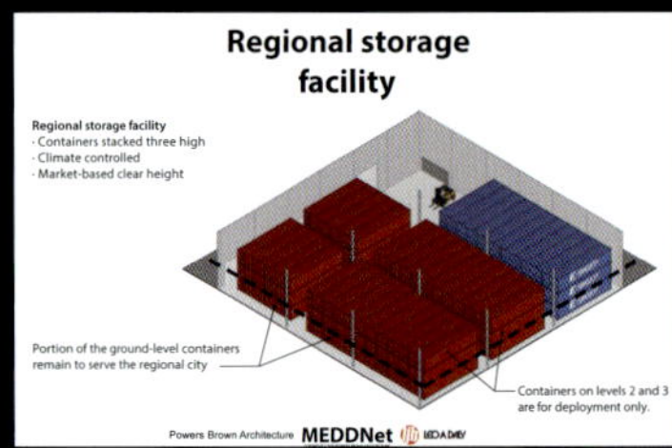

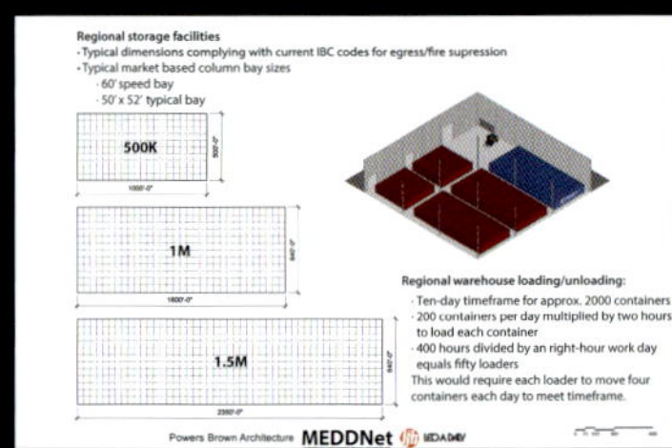

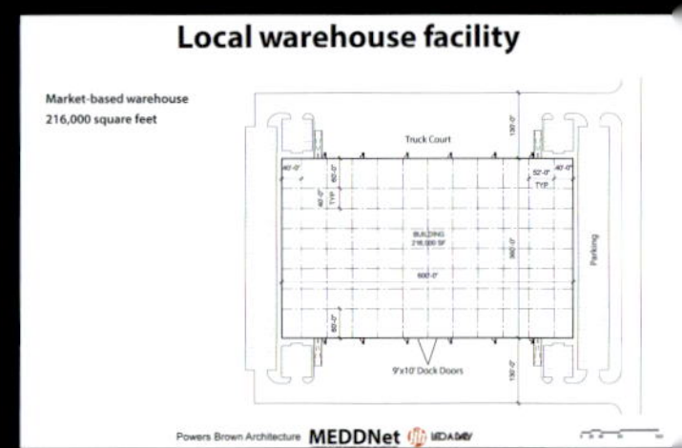

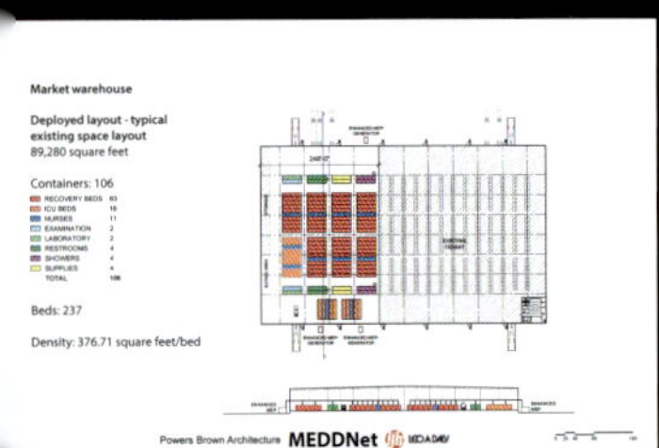

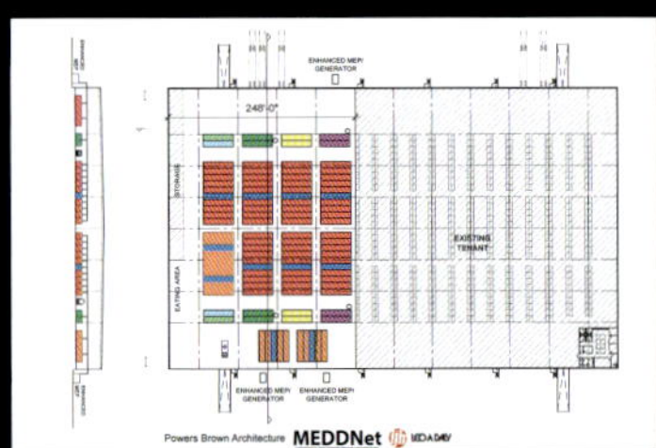

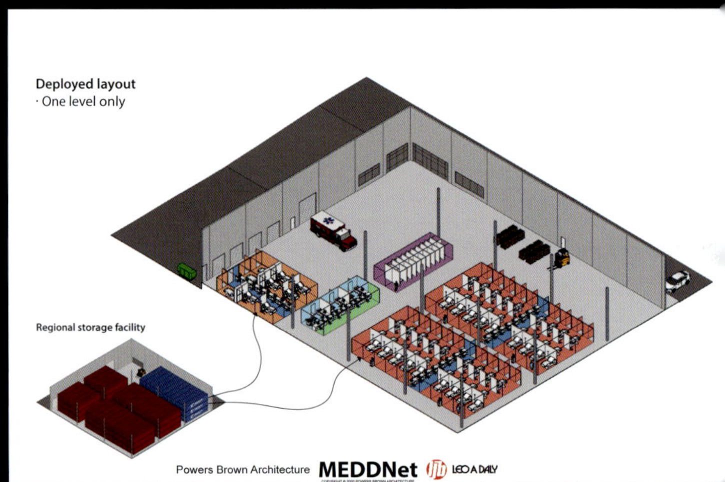

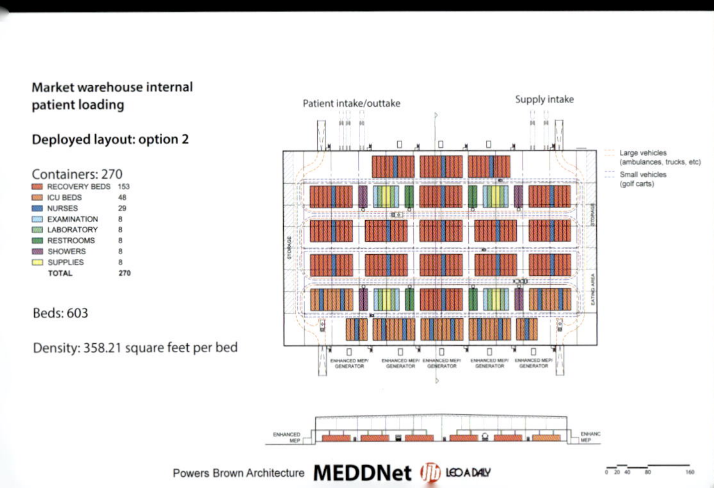

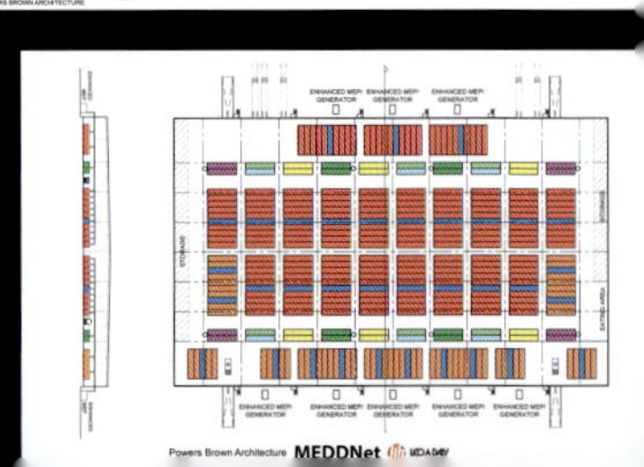

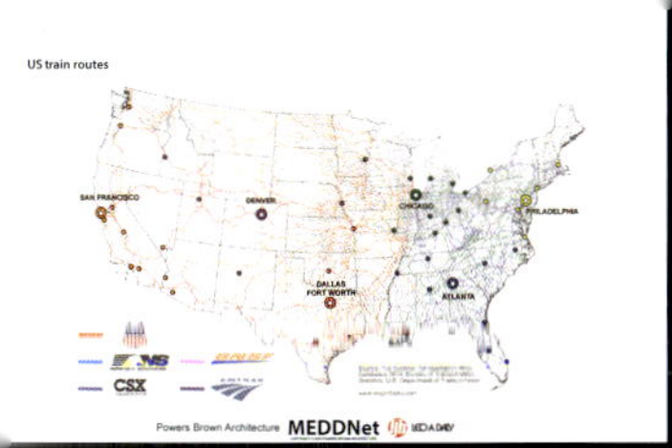

Distribution network strategy

Warehouses

This illustration of the strategy uses the tactic of mapping distribution onto a single commercial real estate developers existing network of inventory

It would also provide real-time ongoing management of the vacancies in its existing facilities in cities recieving the medical pods distributed to from the regional warehouse.

In a seven- to ten-day timeframe, hundreds of beds could be put in place in vacant facilities on effectively zero notice, from order issues to last pod off the truck at the destination.

Powers Brown Architecture **MEDDNet** LEO A DALY

Regional distribution cities | 173,374,680 people served | 95,077 beds

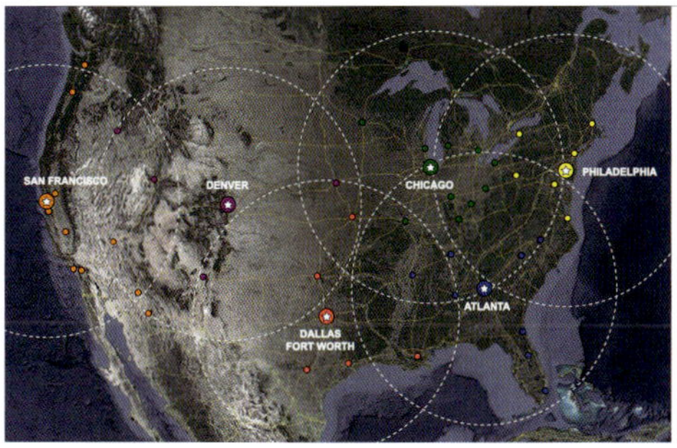

Atlanta
Serves 24,752,978 people
1 m storage facility
Capacity: 14,829beds

Philadelphia
Serves 44,486,659 people
1.5 m storage facility
Capacity: 21,767 beds

Dallas Fort Worth
Serves 22,027,707 people
1 m storage facility
Capacity: 14,829 beds

Chicago
Serves 32,605,561 people
1 m storage facility
Capacity: 14,829 beds

Denver
Serves 6,816,597 people
500k storage facility
Capacity: 7,056 beds

San francisco
Serves 42,685,178 people
1.5 m storage facility
Capacity: 21,767 beds

Powers Brown Architecture **MEDDNet** LEO A DALY

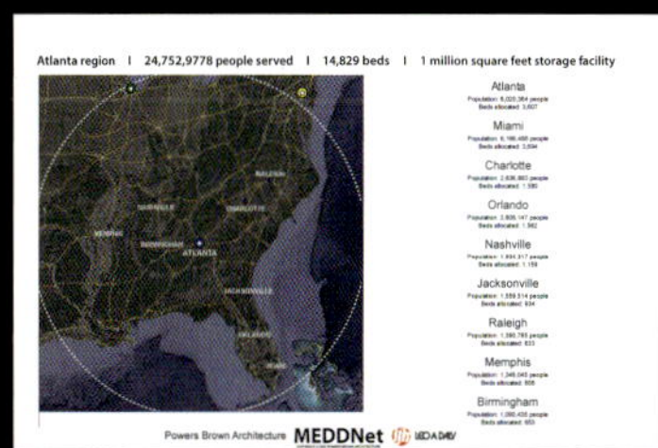

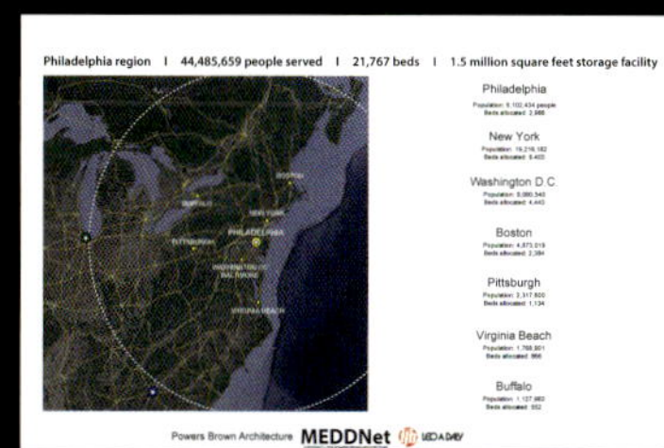

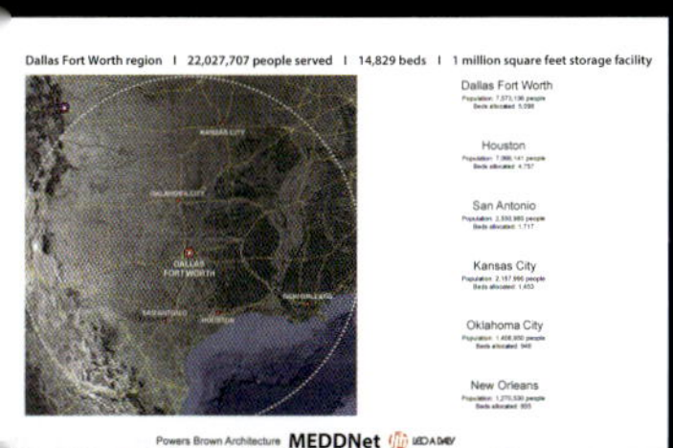

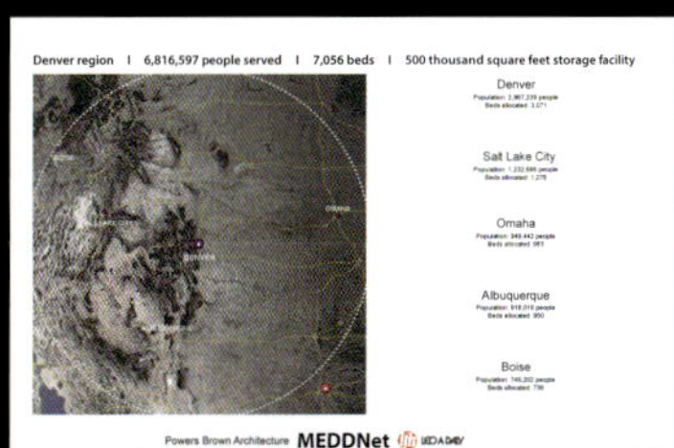

Nashville | 250 miles from Atlanta | 3 hours, 42 minutes drive

Population of city
1,934,317

Population percentage of region
(City population divided by region population)
7.81%

Beds allocated
(Proportional to population)
1,159

Approximate area needed
(Based on squre feet per bed of deployed layout)
340,539 sf

4 partial warehouses

or

1 vacant warehouse

Vacancy area
(Open industrial space in city)
6,550,199

Vacancy utilization
(Area needed divided by vacancy area)
5.20%

Powers Brown Architecture **MEDDNet** LEO A DALY

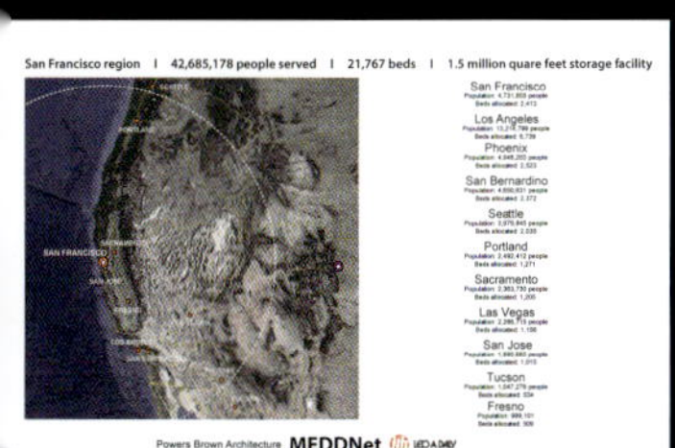

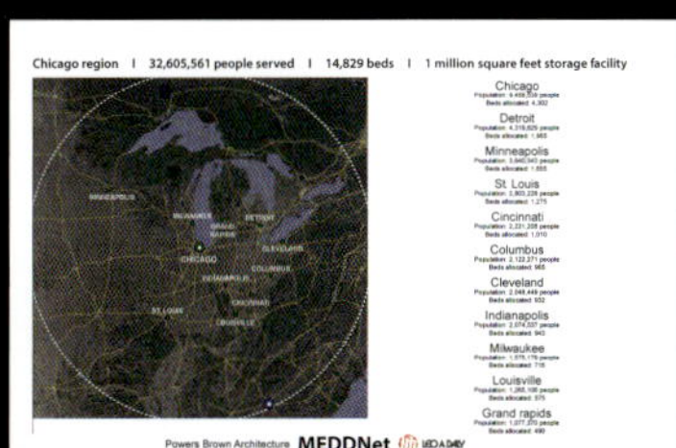

Real estate strategy
Developers and investors

Strategy A

Government
↓
Single industrial developer
Largest industrial developer in the world | Owner and operator

Confirmed facilites by single developer in these markets

PHI	ATL	CHI	DFW	SF	DEN
NYC	MIA	CIN	HOU	LA	
DC	CHA	COL	SA	PHO	
	ORL	CLE		RIV	
	NSH	IND		SEA	
				POR	
				SAC	
				LV	
				SJ	

Possible partner developer(s) in these markets

Powers Brown Architecture **MEDDNet** LEO A DALY

MEDDNet

A single national warehouse developer was used for purposes of consolidated inventory numbers. There are numerous alternative manifestations of a program that could exploit this robust, existing distribution.

The government could

- contract with multiple developers by region
- team with a single source capital management group to procure developers per region for both the regional storage facility and its local network
- team with a single source capital management group to develop/build/manage the regional facility and single source multiple developers in the distributed to cities
- manage or outsource the program to third-party broker or manager.

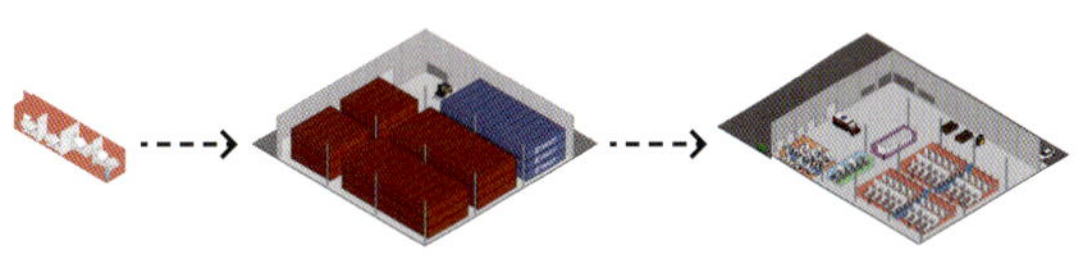

= **MEDDNet**

Powers Brown Architecture **MEDDNet** LEO A DALY

Strategy B

In this scenario a company such as USAA would develop and invest in the development of others to secure the required network of space.

Government
↓
Single investment management real estate company
Invests, finances, develops and manages real estate

PHI	ATL	CHI	DFW	SF	DEN
NYC	MIA	DET	HOU	LA	SLC
DC	CHA	MIN	SA	PHO	OMA
BOS	ORL	STL	KC	RIV	ALB
PITT	NSH	CIN	OKC	SEA	BOI
VB	JAC	COL	NOLA	POR	
BUF	BAL	CLE		SAC	
	MEM	IND		LV	
	BIR	MIL		SJ	
		LOU		TUC	
		GR		FRE	

Powers Brown Architecture **MEDDNet** LEO A DALY

Strategy C

In this scenario master developers selected by regional capabilities would require terms and conditions very similar to Strategy A

Government
↓
Master developer in each regional market

Developer 1	Developer 2	Developer 3	Developer 4	Developer 5	Developer 6
PHI	ATL	CHI	DFW	SF	DEN
NYC	MIA	DET	HOU	LA	SLC
DC	CHA	MIN	SA	PHO	OMA
BOS	ORL	STL	KC	RIV	ALB
PITT	NSH	CIN	OKC	SEA	BOI
VB	JAC	COL	NOLA	POR	
BUF	BAL	CLE		SAC	
	MEM	IND		LV	
	BIR	MIL		SJ	
		LOU		TUC	
		GR		FRE	

Powers Brown Architecture **MEDDNet** LEO A DALY

Strategy D

Government
↓
GSA

PHI	ATL	CHI	DFW	SF	DEN
NYC	MIA	DET	HOU	LA	SLC
DC	CHA	MIN	SA	PHO	OMA
BOS	ORL	STL	KC	RIV	ALB
PITT	NSH	CIN	OKC	SEA	BOI
VB	JAC	COL	NOLA	POR	
BUF	BAL	CLE		SAC	
	MEM	IND		LV	
	BIR	MIL		SJ	
		LOU		TUC	
		GR		FRE	

Powers Brown Architecture **MEDDNet** LEO A DALY

Mall

The purpose of this research is to explore the mall typology; understand why it has been considered somewhat of a dying building type (when defined as America's retail apocalypse, as reflected in continuing record levels of store closures); and to conclude that adaptive reuse could be the most successful contemporary typology.

As communities across the country have been struggling to find new uses for shuttered shopping malls, real estate professionals have been converting them into industrial facilities or a blend of retail and industrial. We wanted to define a more interesting speculation about how to imagine the future of industrial facilities that was different from what was seen as "vertical." We found that the future of industrial building types (as well as distribution and e-commerce–related building types) is the adaptive reuse of the shopping mall—by converting it to last mile, especially where malls have a great connection and catchment area, with the latter being critical in bringing "last mile" closer to population centers.

Malls have evolved along a common spatial arc since the 1950s, and new forms began to evolve from the 1990s. The general geometry and configuration of the mall is based upon two fundamental and simple layouts that were driven by retail needs/metrics of the era: 1) single- and two-story forms, with an empty center (the atrium); and 2) a triple-loaded center lease space, also with an atrium. The first of these is considered the composite form, derived from an aggregated building type due to architectural responses to market forces over time). The second is called a linear form that evolves through organic growth, i.e., the center expands by just adding another link (or wing). In each instance, the mall zone—the central atrium—is surrounded by anchor stores. What has occurred in some instances is the demolishing of the mall (and some anchor space) to accommodate market-defined warehouse prototypes.

Adaptive reuse, however, has more potential than the demolition of the entire existing building. We believe that adaptive reuse is a better option as it attempts to preserve the mall by modifying it to accommodate warehouse needs while saving investment dollars (a possible 25 to 40 percent saving on construction costs, including construction time savings of up to four months) and increasing mall synergy. By adding e-commerce or market-based commercial/industrial building types to these pre-1990s malls as expressed in the geometry and adjacencies of components—anchors (dead or alive); adaptation of weird-shaped mall zones; different parking configurations; suitable clear height for different transporation needs; and structural bay spacing—most malls are suitable to adaptive reuse to successful last mile.

Summary and history;

Several circumstances converged on influencing us to create a story line about warehouses and malls that we could consolidate and share with our clients.

The first circumstance was clients. Namely the brokers who transact in the industrial market. Brokers always need an edge, and some of the most competitive brokers we work with were mentioning the same phenomenon in different ways: Amazon was buying malls. Amazon was "renovating malls, malls were the next big Amazon play."

Of course the demise of the mall was, at least in terms of the speed of the market and the times, old news.

But what Amazon was doing with malls was a rumor based upon perhaps one project in the very early days of these musings. We wanted to understand the "phenomenon" better and define it relative to industrial: why is it important that Amazon, who was warping warehousing typologies via e-commerce needs was interested in malls?

And frankly we were tired of all of the prognostications that the future of industrial was vertical. That story-line had been out for over seven years and had lost its purchase on the term "future" let alone its false premise that it would be something new to vertical warehouses. Many making this "prediction" have not been to Chicago as best we could tell. We wanted to define a more interesting speculation about how to imagine the future of industrial.

E X C U R S U S

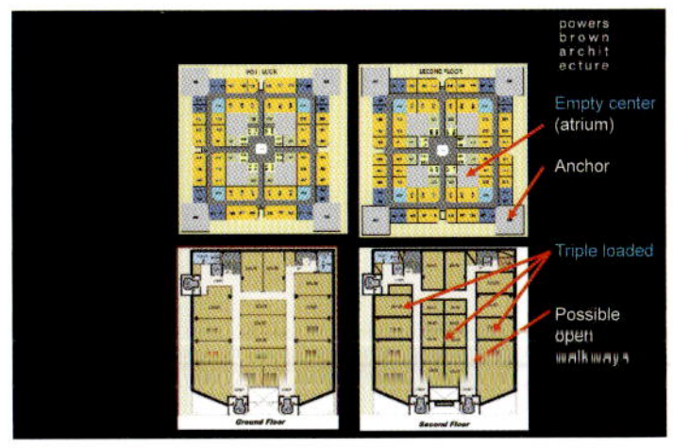

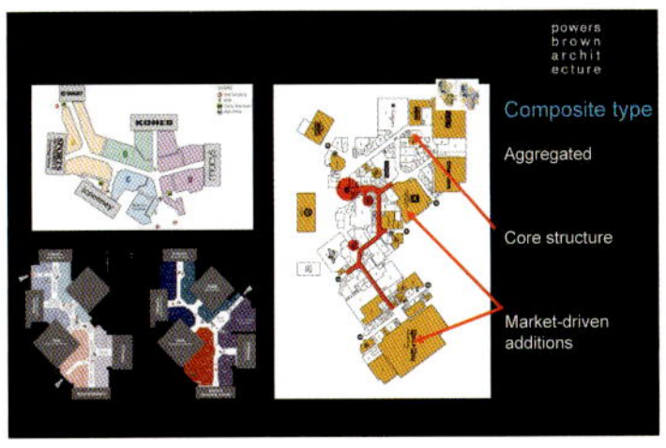

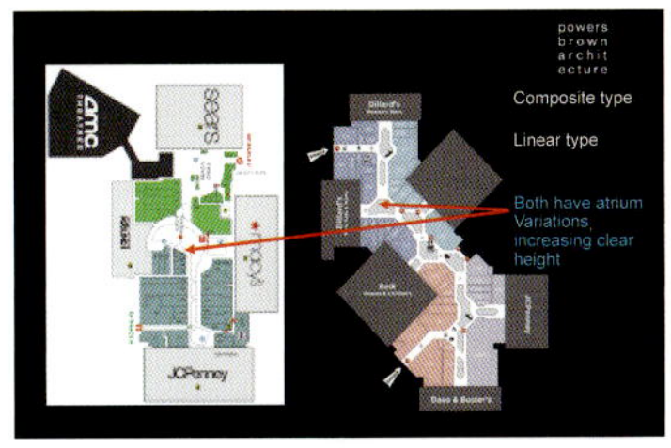

The big idea

Adaptive reuse is a better option for malls being converted to last mile. Malls in the right demographic spots were too expensive to buy and demolish. And the building types that accommodate last mile needs don't need excessive land bays in most cases, as well as having some positive vitality potential for what would be left of the mall: the employees of Amazon.

E X C U R S U S

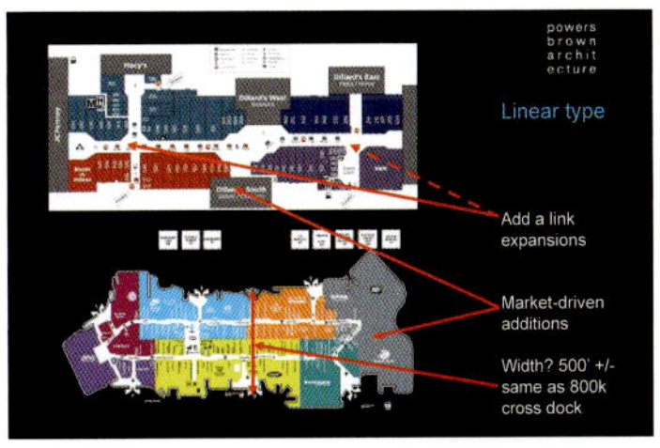

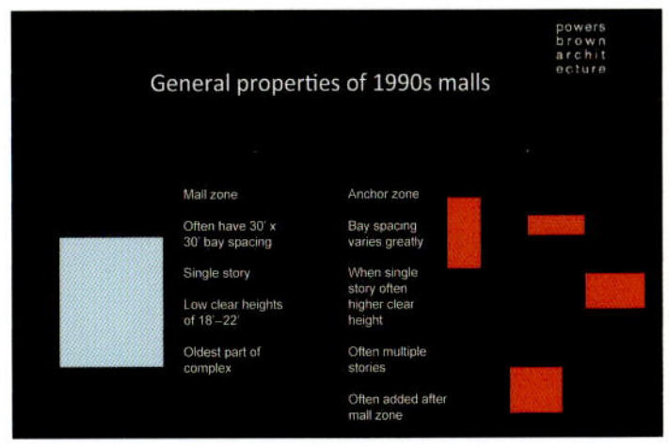

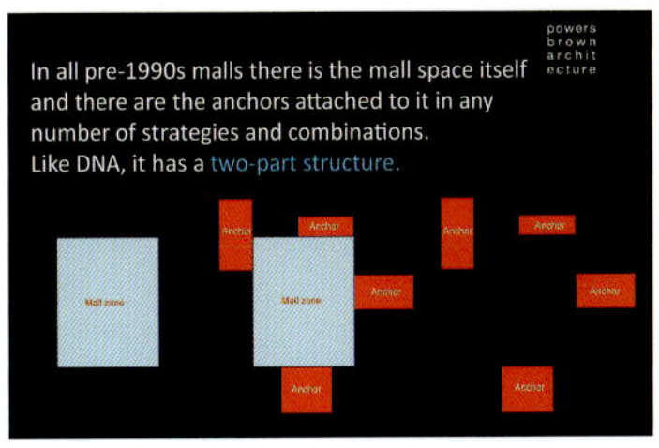

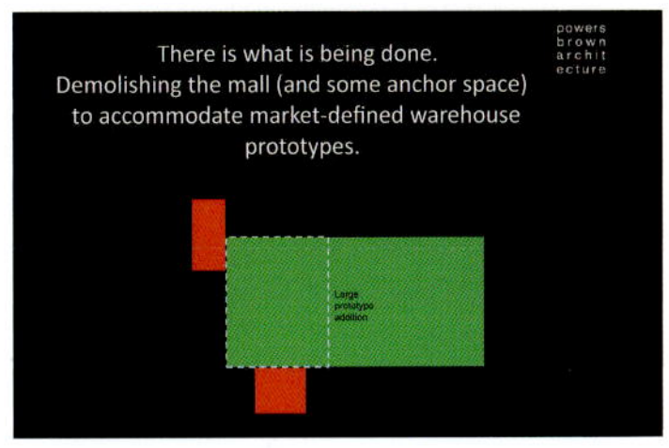

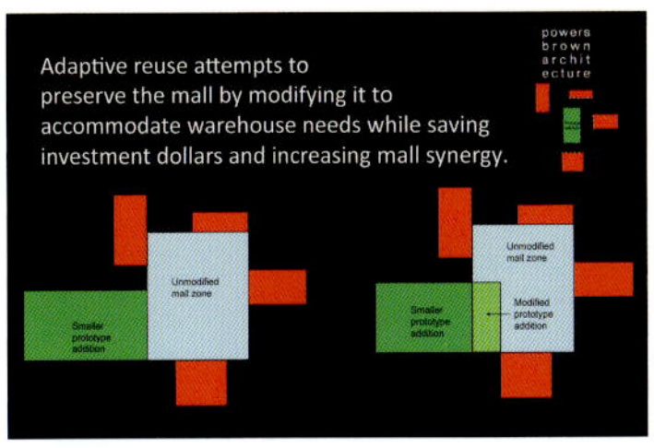

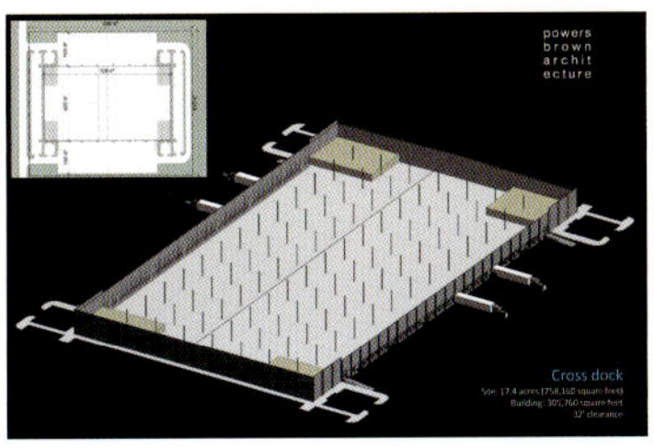

Explainer

Understanding the origin of the mall—why its wide and fat and empty at the middle—helps us to understand where it intersects with the contemporary industrial typologies.

Understanding why it is a dying building type points out what to get rid of, and what, with some intervention, could still thrive.

E X C U R S U S

Explainer

Here we pivot to the reasons why adaptive reuse has more potential than demolition of the entire existing building.

Adaptive reuse: How to start strategizing what to use and what to demolish

E X C U R S U S

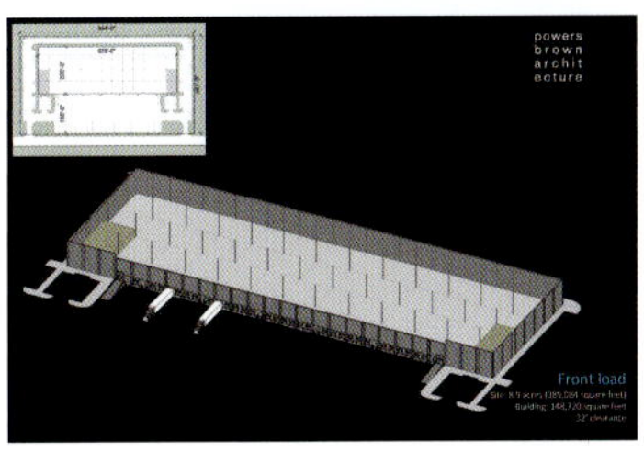

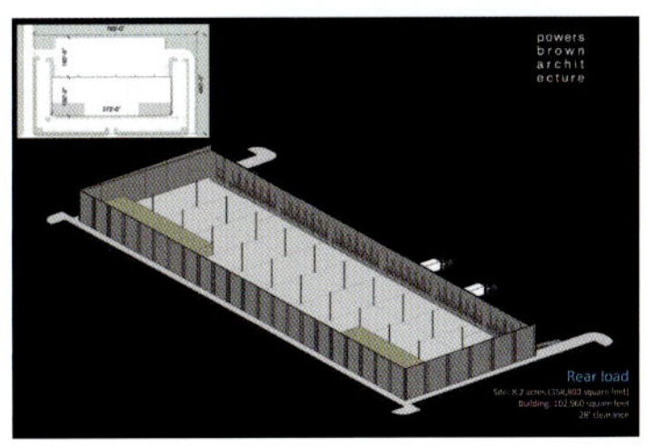

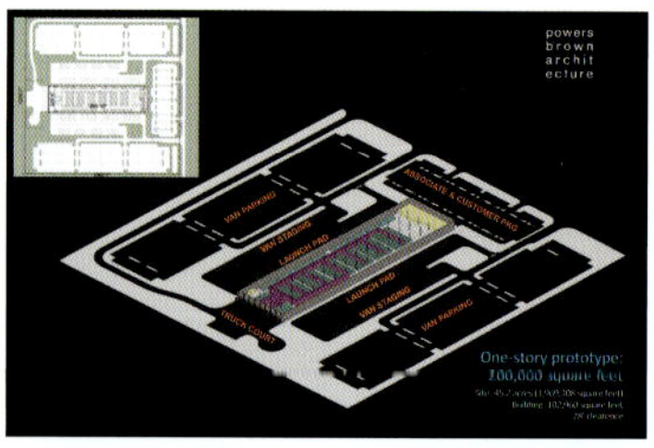

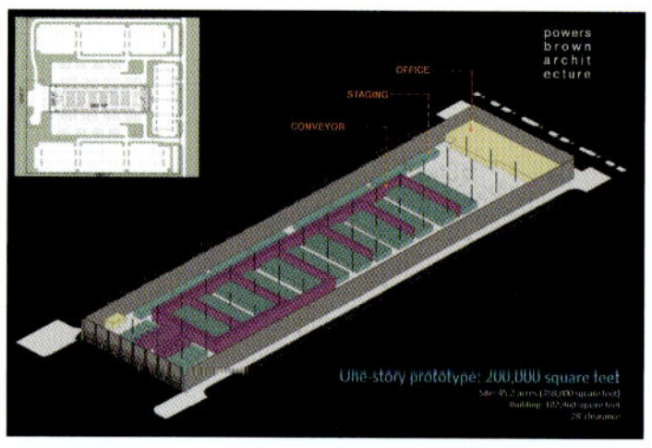

Explainer

In understanding why malls are wide and fat and empty at the middle are a couple of quick asides that some people have already speculated about malls and e-commerce in different ways and some seem to have a different opinion as to why and how this could work.

There are also some side issues.

E X C U R S U S

Explainer

The following set out the kit of parts we have defined that will fit most often with minimal demolition and minimum distortion of key market-based dimensions and parking/truck court needs.

Building types and functions to be applied to mall transformations

This will be our **kit of parts** in assessing the viability of mall conversions.

Speculative distribution protypes compatible with common mall building and site sizes:

· cross dock
· front load
· rear load

E X C U R S U S

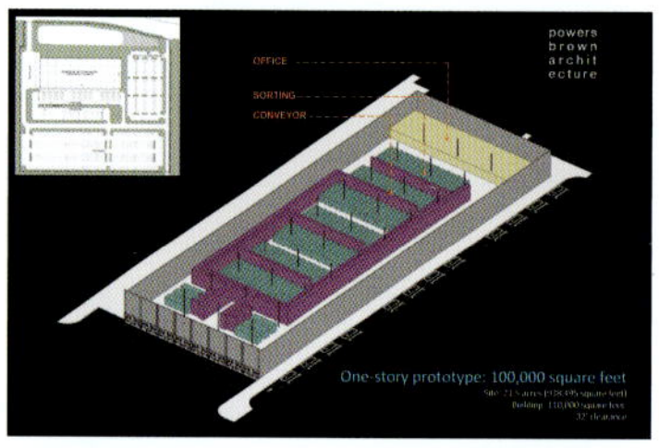

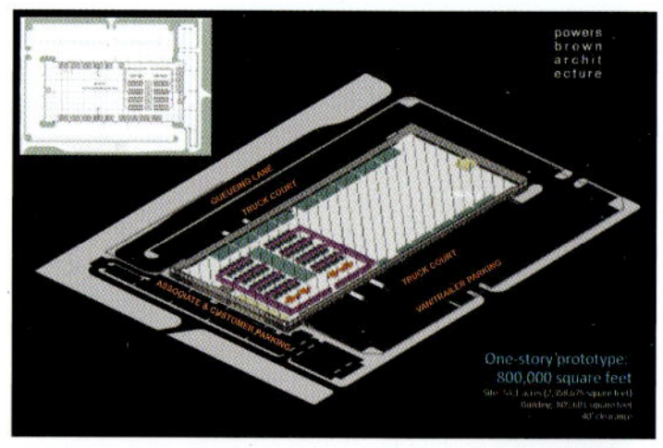

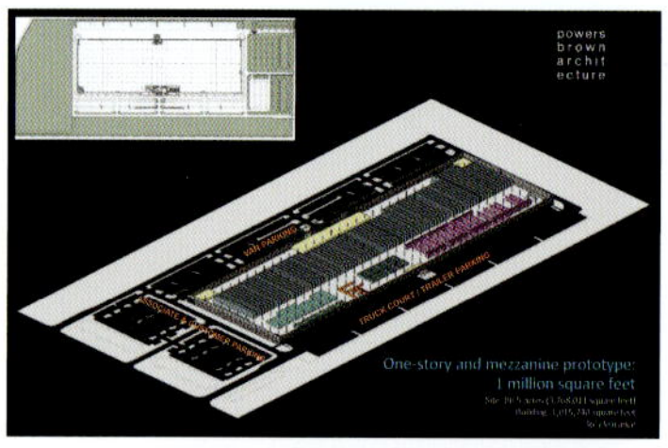

Explainer

A quick but important note: the malls have varying but typically lower than market clear heights and the fact that many e-commerce building don't use the clear heights they are provided with.

E X C U R S U S

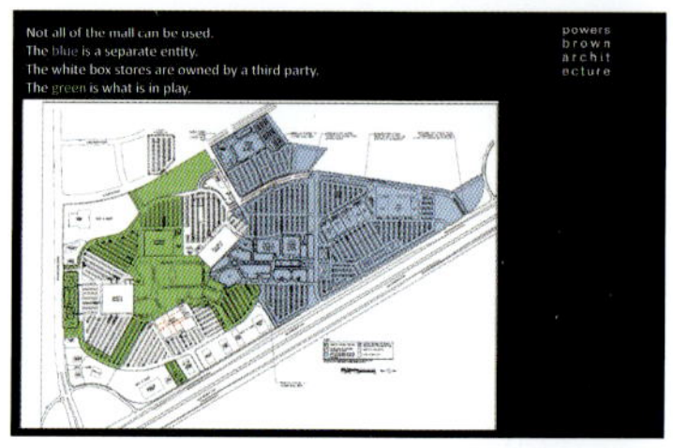

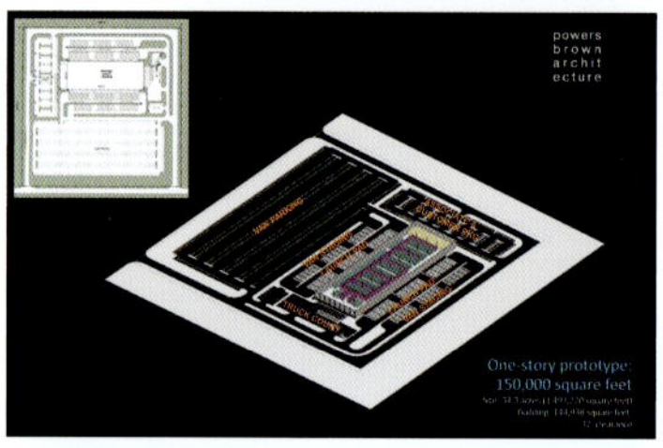

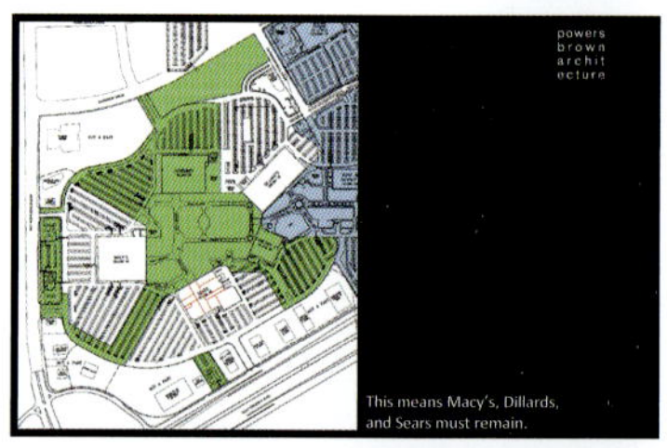

Explainer

Case study for Brookfield Properties.

Case study of a composite mall type

E X C U R S U S

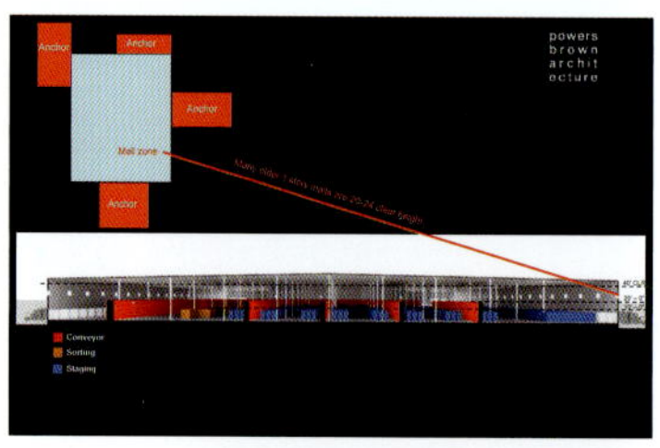

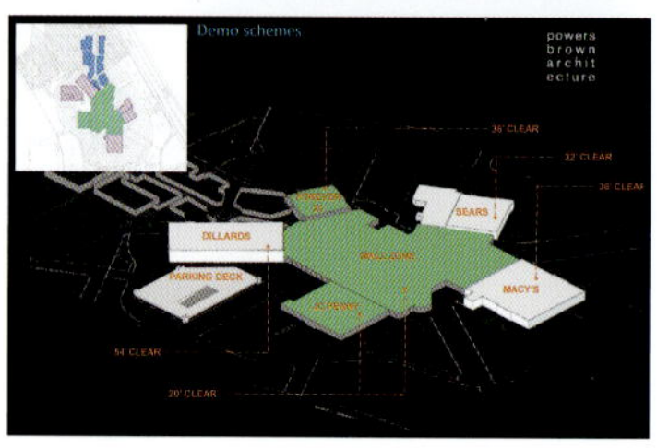

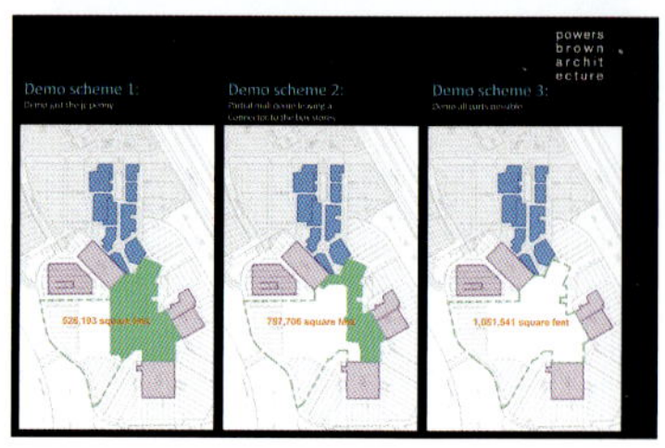

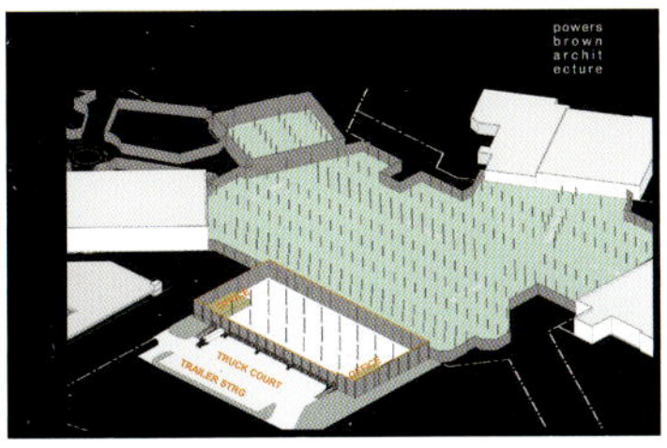

Explainer

Composite mall type with
e-commerce prototypes

Same exercise now with e-commerce building types inspired by Amazon criteria

E X C U R S U S

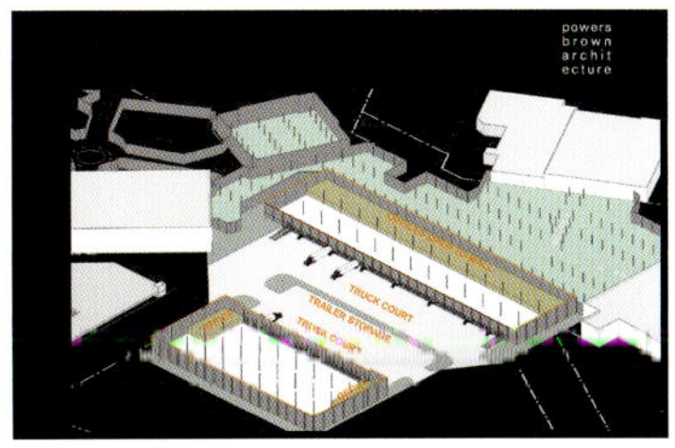

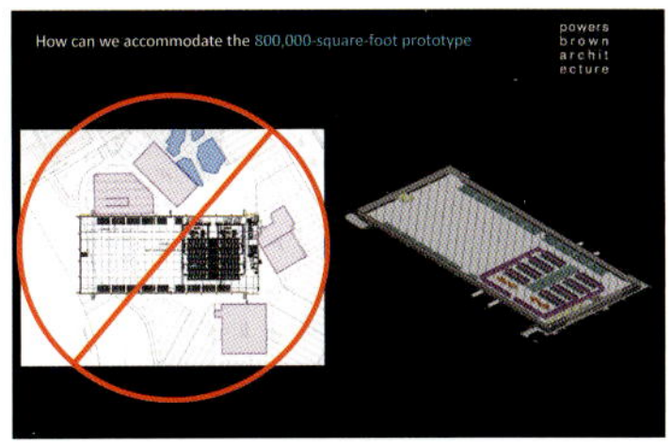

Explainer

Back to that interesting observation about provided clear height and actual used clear height.

E X C U R S U S

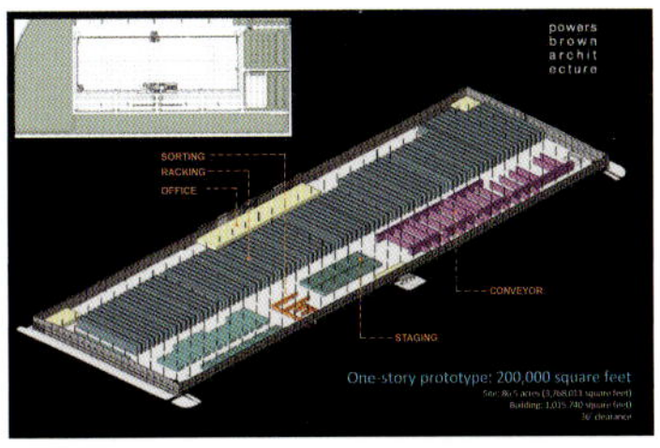

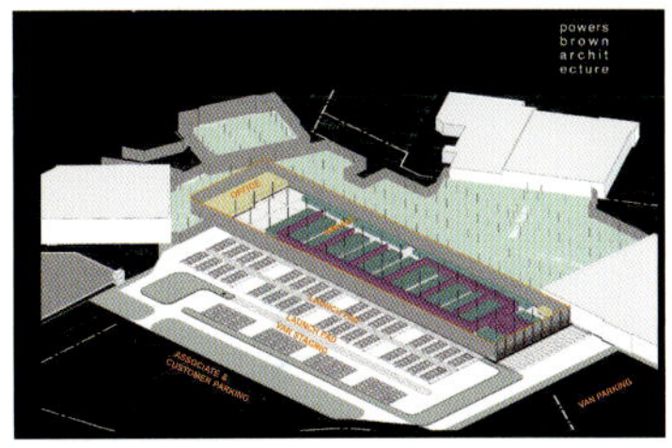

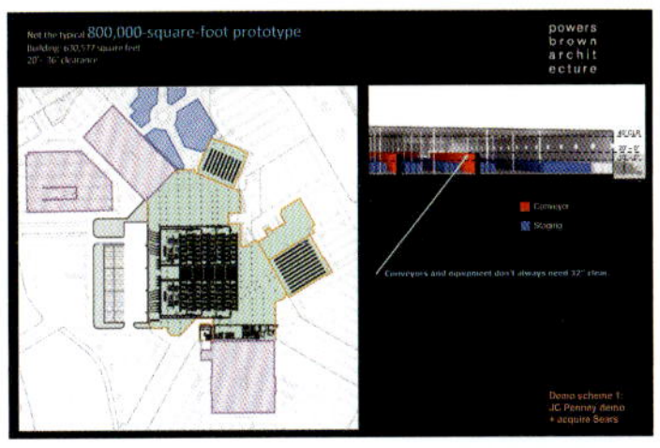

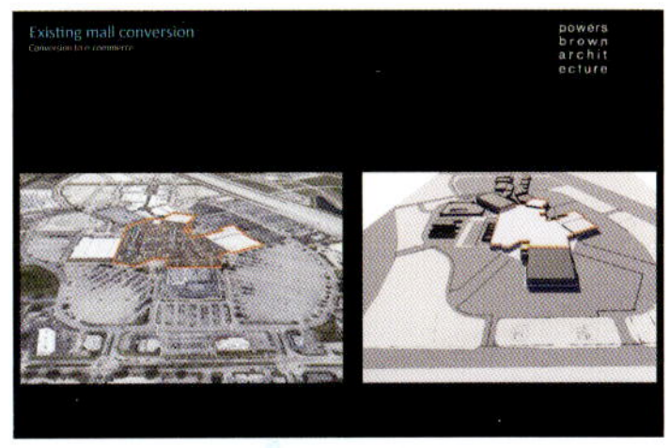

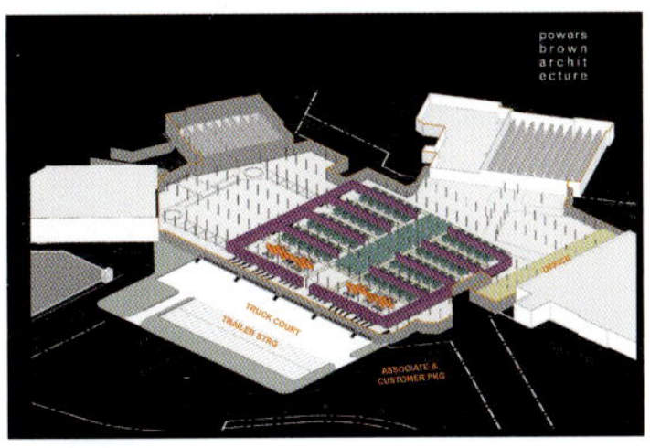

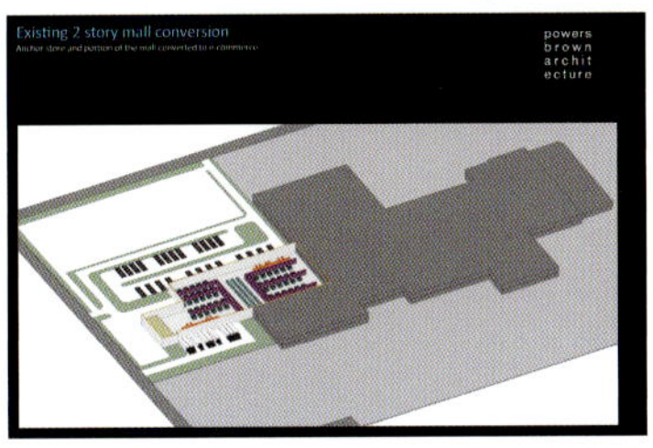

Explainer

Finally, we have been diving deeper on several opportunities around the country.

Mall Case Studies

Of over fifty malls studied for clients, here are some snapshots of actual real-world efforts that are moving forward to the next steps.

E X C U R S U S

Explainer

The following is 2020 market-based contractor-provided budgeting.

E X C U R S U S

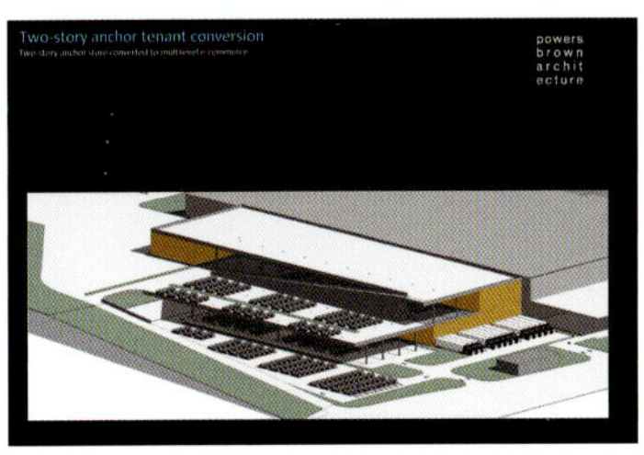

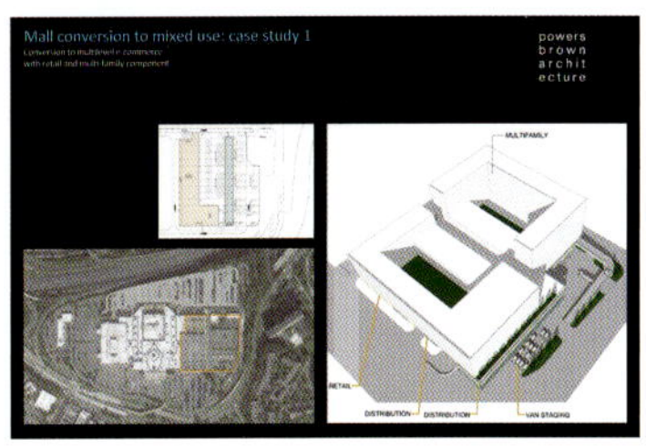

Compact describes the smallest building square footages we are capable of performing and making a profit on. They also circumscribe some of our best-known work. We have previously published our category of projects we call Small Smart Boxes™. SSBs are an approach to infusing an oblique ordinariness, via a specific low-cost construction technology, to elevate the formal possibilities on small business headquarters and facilities that normally would have been considered utilitarian structures. After twenty-five years of practice and growth we have to be mindful in identifying neglected problem types for potential, then "scale shift" our design process to optimize for very small projects. We are an international commercial practice and that comes with certain dangers to quality of design thinking. While the **Intermarine Operations Center** and the **Bank of Montreal (BMO)** utilize a clustering and bundling of interlocking volumes, the internal program of each bundling is very different. In the case of Intermarine it is the invocation of individual shipping containers without actually using them that defines the bundle, while it is an indexing to context and the materiality of nearby structures expressed in BMO. The **Gatehouse Medical Office Building** evokes audiology both in pattern and form, while the **Pinch Group** headquarters flips the work-at-home narrative to the reversed condition of home at work.

Compact

Houston, Texas | Operations center | 21,7654 square feet

Intermarine

Intermarine is a marine logistics and ocean transport provider focusing on the needs of break-bulk, heavy-lilft, dry-bulk, and project cargo with a fleet of more than fifty-five advanced multipurpose vessels. The operations center project is located at an industrial terminal—a 95-acre site directly adjacent to the Houston Ship Channel, functioning as Intermarine's primary load and staging center for cargo and projects.

We started the project with myriad site and building configurations to optimize the building's potential to serve as a business development strategy for the company. We sited the building at the terminus of Industrial Road and then dodged every existing subterranean obstacle imaginable with the building's relatively small foundation, approximately 5,000 square feet. It functions as both a terminal visitors center for Intermarine's clients and as a port operations facility.

We pondered the ability of a literal compilation of containers to equate to something architectural like Moshe Safdie's Habitat '67. But in the end, the literal use of containers provided something a little less than architectural form—untransformed.

We decided that artifice was the active catalyst to architecturalizing the containers, referring to the containers' opened iconographic and spatial opportunities that actually using them cannot provide; and the re-presentation and choreography of the visual vibe given off by the physical context. In this case, parsing the difference between what we want to see and what we want to see represented: the difference between a cartoonish reaction of stacking shipping containers versus creating an almost impressionistic iconography that by taking clues from a broader local physical/visual context offers a richer integration between form and program. In other words, architects have at times surfed the edge and come down on the wrong side of this difference.

We may like the idea of stacking shipping containers and indeed rediscover its "shock" value every half-generation or so, but the thinness of the gimmick always gives way quickly—it lacks transformation and, well, artifice. In the end, that is the *modus of architecture*—it is a purposeful intervention with authorship at stake. That is the subtle but important difference between a clever choreography of shipping containers and a careful evocation of aspects of them in service of a program that, in the former, can be contained by them and in the latter, transformed by the provocations they may provide.

(No shipping containers were harmed during the making of this building.)

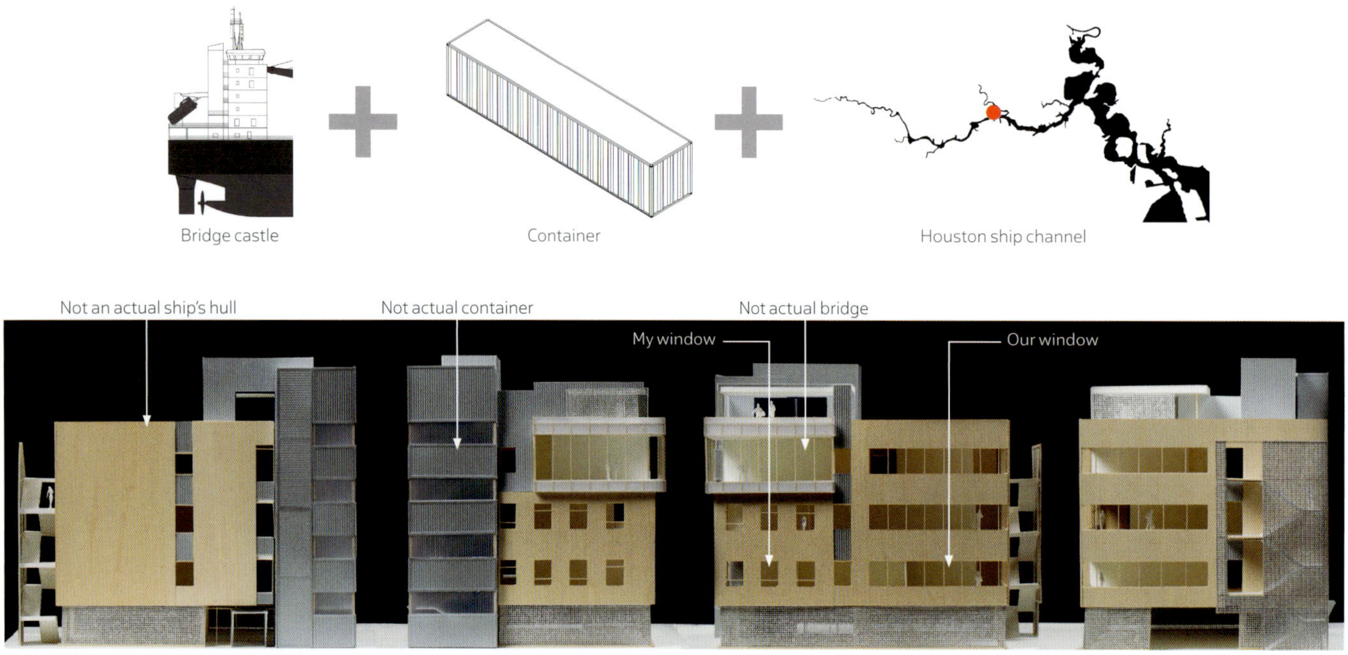

Concept and model

It should be tall enough for viewing ships like this unloading
A great spot for a cool building
Industrial rd

FDC

Fourth-floor plan

Terrace floor plan

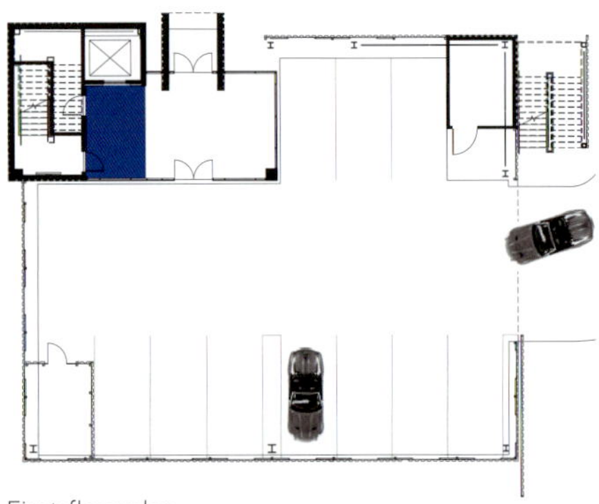

First-floor plan

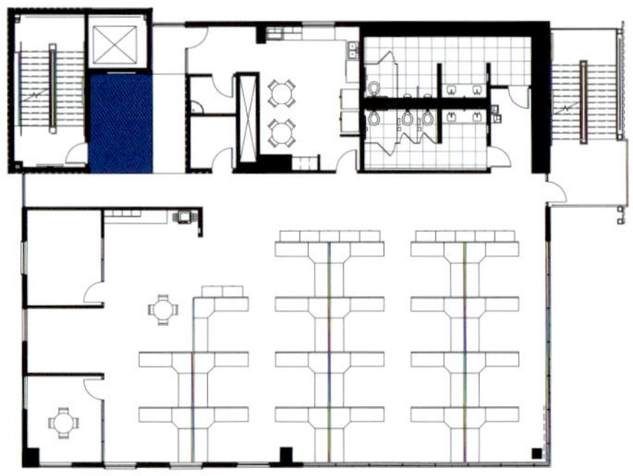

Second-floor plan

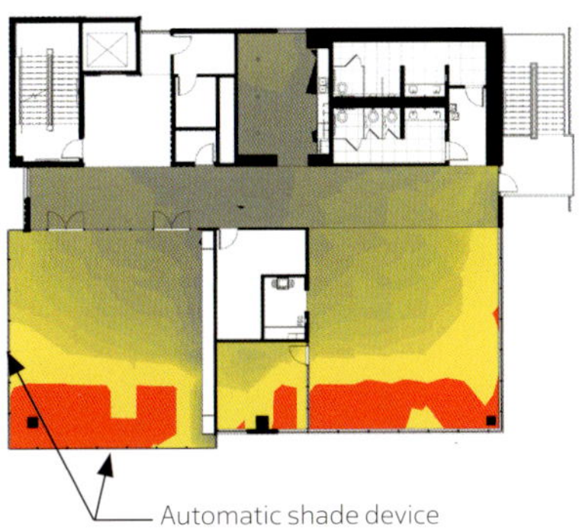

Fourth floor at 9 am

Third floor at 9 am

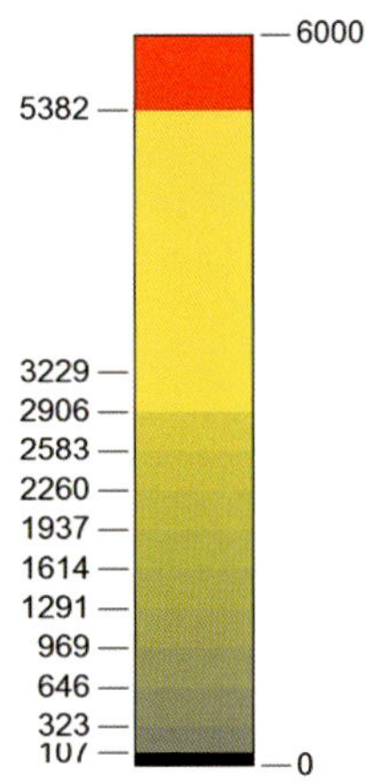

Results of lighting analysis

Fourth floor at 3 pm

Third floor at 3 pm

P1
P.2
Pkg#1436

BMO

The new Bank of Montreal (BMO) regional headquarters is located on a longtime vacant Water Street site in downtown St. John's that forms the boundary between the historic core and the more modern western end. Its form is a reflection of the unusually shaped site and the client's desire to provide a modern building with curtain-wall glazing, underground parking, and all the modern amenities while being sensitive to the adjacent historic building fabric. To address the surrounding heritage buildings, the shorter portion of the structure adjoining the neighboring buildings utilizes brick and traditionally scaled fenestration and details.

It was of the utmost importance that the building fully engage with its pivotal downtown location and to that end the pedestrian linkages that predate the development were incorporated into the design. Along the east façade an existing right of way and stairs were incorporated into the design, while along the west façade existing sidewalk stairs were refurbished, and a covered arcade was provided that connects to an accessible lift and a rear terrace overlooking Harbour Drive below. This openness at the rear façade combined with a variation in massing and scale and the provision of a required small retail space helped to create a streetscape along the waterfront. The building balances its pedestrian scale with the prominent presence the bank desired.

PREMISES

Jewel

Serving as the primary offices for a charitable foundation and their investment arm, the client brief was to create a "jewel-like" building that helped support their three key focus areas: childhood cancer research, creative arts programs at children's cancer centers, and public engagement around childhood cancer. These three functions were to be separate from but integrated with the office spaces required for the investment arm.

The current building the foundation is housed in is made up of primarily individual offices and cubicles that don't support their collaborative work environment needs. We proposed the new 15,250-square-foot building as a three-level space with an elevated interior courtyard that the offices for the foundation and investment group would be organized around. The program called for shared communal spaces between the two groups, with separate office and open work areas for each. To promote collaboration and serendipitous interactions, the communal spaces were placed in the corners on both levels of the office.

There was also a desire to have the ability to work outside and host post-work events, which led to the creation of two outdoor terraces on the third floor. The ground level of the project is a future leasable area that will also serve as an exhibition and fundraiser space to display children's art from the various children's cancer centers the foundation partners with.

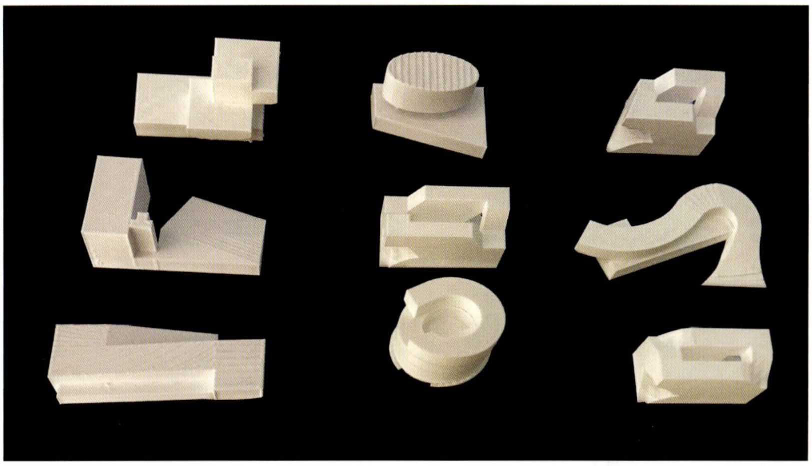

Gatehouse

This infill site building is anchored by an ear/nose/throat and audiology clinic. The building capitalizes on its allowable FAR and extensive setback requirements by using a strategy that separates the building into the retail base and the medical office building's "floating box." This creates covered parking as well as an attractive and prominent entry presence on busy Gallows Road in Fairfax. The Gatehouse Medical office building sits at the intersection of Gatehouse Road and Gallows Road, Merrifield, Fairfax, Virginia.

The client, an audiologist by practice, wanted a building that "spoke" of his work. The solution involved pursuit of a strategy that capitalizes on the nexus between a formal response to a very tight and geometrically challenged site and a narrative approach to the skin of the building.

The massing of the project is a relatively efficient office "box" slid over a socle. The base responds to the site geometry and resolves the poché into reasonable parking stalls. The box slides west over the base, creating a covered area, and aligns with the major feeder road geometry—an inviting approach that establishes a long-distance presence. A curtain-wall glass panel signals the office use and is expressed as the hollowed-out portion of a square tube; perhaps a metaphorical ear canal as observed by the client. The base function is a retail space in which hearing equipment is to be sold while the box above will accommodate the audiologist and several complementary tenants.

The shear between the base and top creates a green roof opportunity—neatly resolving an impervious coverage issue—and is answered by an occupiable garden roof atop the box, open to all tenants.

The skin of the building is inspired by a Doppler effect wave, a physical manifestation of sounds that grounds the building in its intended use; abstract enough not to require a literal reading.

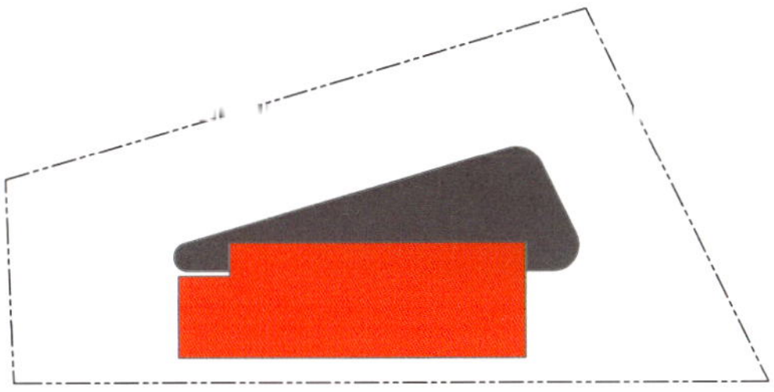

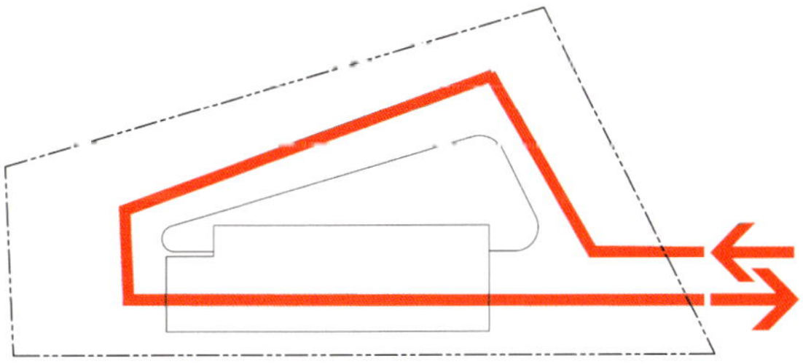

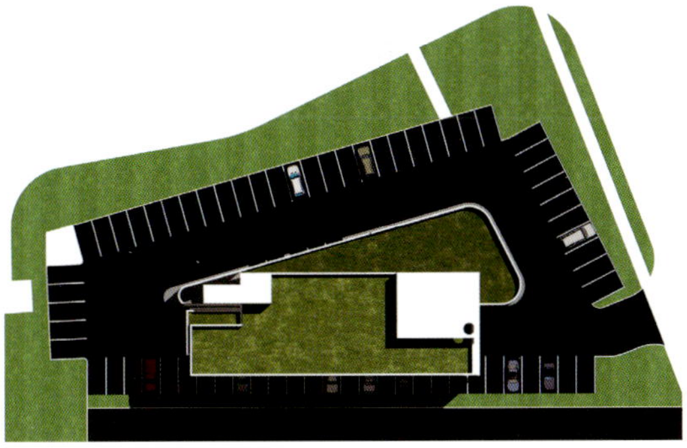

Pinch

The owners of the Pinch Group, a father and three sons, wanted in essence the reverse of the current trend of working from home: they wanted a space that didn't feel like an office to them or their longtime employee. The sons all have children, so they didn't actually want to *be* at home but rather they wanted to *feel* at home. And what held together their common vision for achieving this was an affinity for the environments of the television series *Mad Men*. We catalyzed this notion by introducing them to Case Study House (Googie Architecture) and roadside period architectures. We did so in the framework of accepting their desires somewhat literally and accepting our own interests in the role of creativity over the insane idea of the constant ongoing originality or invention that architecture perpetuates. We didn't feel like we needed to invent a new music but rather to work as mash-up artists, reinterpreting and recombining fragments into compositions. We thought of Picasso's famous reinterpretation of Velásquez's *Las Meninas* and Lady Gaga's "Alejandro" (how bizarrely like Madonna's "La Isla Bonita" it is and yet how very different).

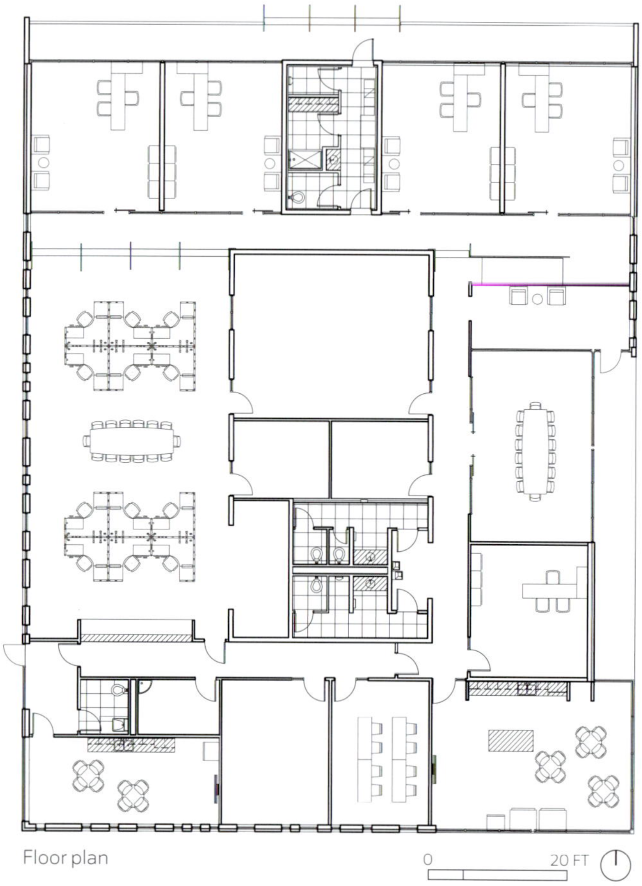

Floor plan

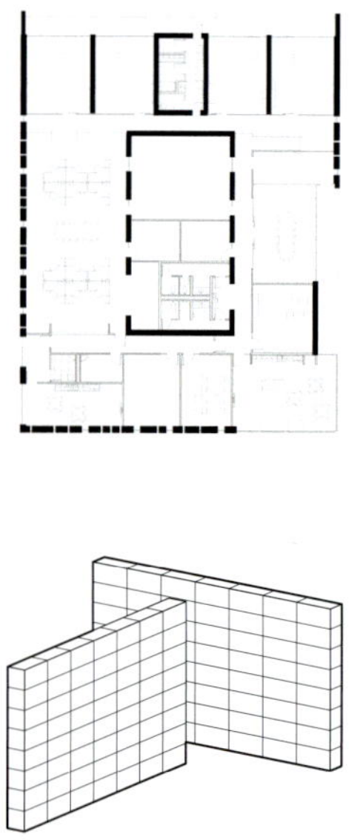
Burnished block

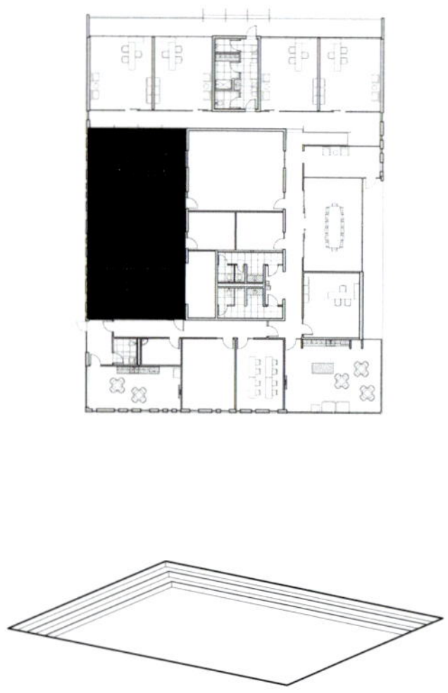
Recessed space

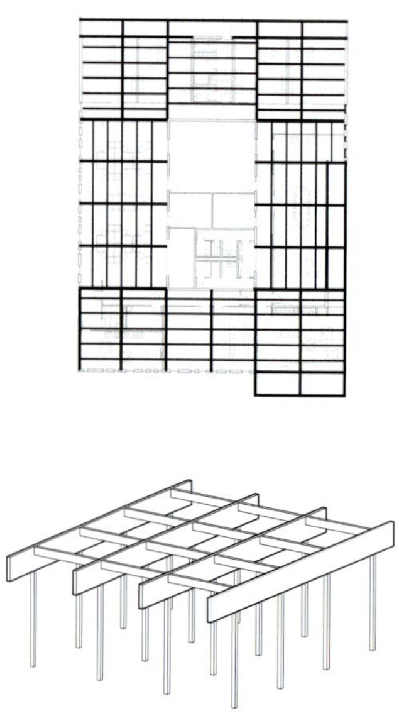
Expression of structure

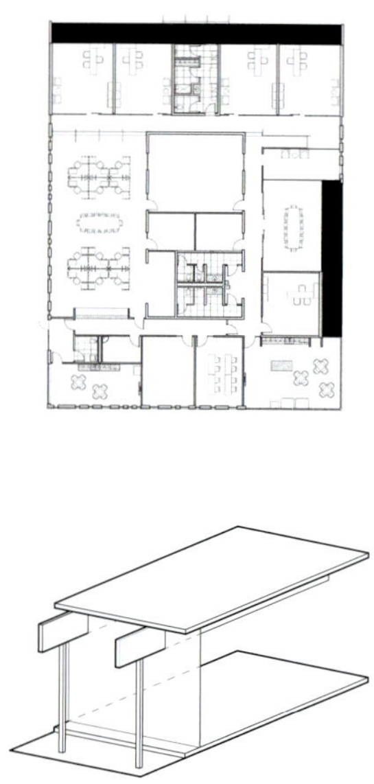
Expressed interior structure

We haven't abandoned our assiduity for research into tilt-wall construction. Our research on this subject is internally referred to as "bottom-up innovation." While our work in this subject is well known and published elsewhere, we continue to innovate in the possibilities of site-cast panel construction. Some of this work has been in the design of progressive collapse/blast resistant structures for the Department of Defense and General Forces Administration (GSA). The **Fort Bend Veterans monument** has received worldwide coverage for its evocative celebration of Korean War veterans, and it has now evolved to recognize all militairy service in its community. **Arch-Con** explores the urban infill potential of single-story stacking of tilt-wall panels without sacrificing the load-bearing capacity of the finished exterior structure. **GeoForm™** is our patented system for achieving dimensionally stable, reusable, curved site-cast forms. Working with a 3D-printing construction scaled start-up backed by a major chemical company providing a variable density foam, we systematized the formwork to produce millions of complex curved-edge variations over common tilt-panel heights, utilizing only three radii. Our patent supersedes the current method employed in tilt-wall for site-prepared curved panel edges, which is wire-cut foam done on-site by hand. **Woodlands** represents the vertical design potential of tilt-wall construction in achieving a first in the world 4+2 vertical stack exterior load-bearing, six-story structure. We are proud others have begun to emulate this low-cost, high-design approach to mid-rise structures. Finally, **Credit Union of Colorado** (CUC) exhibits the complex formal geometry and expression possible in a bespoke building type for a corporate headquarters in a harsh climate zone.

Tilt

Monument

We include this monument as an illustration of the reward that comes through the process of committing to and executing a pro-bono effort. As a trade organization, the Tilt-up Concrete Association (TCA) holds an annual convention. Each year the group looks for an opportunity to do a community project that will also demonstrate the possibilities of tilt-up construction as a method.

When approached, our firm embraced this as a unique chance to get involved in a new way for us. We teamed up with the Parks department of the city of Sugar Land, Texas, to augment a fledgling and underfunded Veterans Memorial park that it had begun. Much of the form and layout was in place but not much had progressed by way of a memorial.

They had teamed up with a philanthropic group, The Legacy Foundation, to seek urgent funding for a memorial for the Veterans of Fort Bend County, as many veterans of the Korean War, in particular, were reaching an age where it was time to honor their service (even though the monument was to be ecumenical in nature). The head of the foundation happened to be a tilt-up contractor and a team was formed.

As architects, we began the process with an internal design competition to let the intern staff participate and see the value of in-putting forth pro-bono work. An intern in our Washington, DC, office won the competition with the basic concept that we then executed and refined as an office. (The contractor, the Parks department, a historian, and the TCA acted as jurors for this effort.)

The contractor worked with us on the details and the drawings were completed in three weeks. Along the way nearly thirty sub-consultants, vendors, subcontractors, and suppliers donated their services, goods, and input.

The Parks department in conjunction with the Planning department received permission, after our presentation to the City Council, to expedite permitting and inspections. The entire project was built in twenty-nine days with almost nonstop construction and an on-site staff led by two former veterans who worked for the contractor.

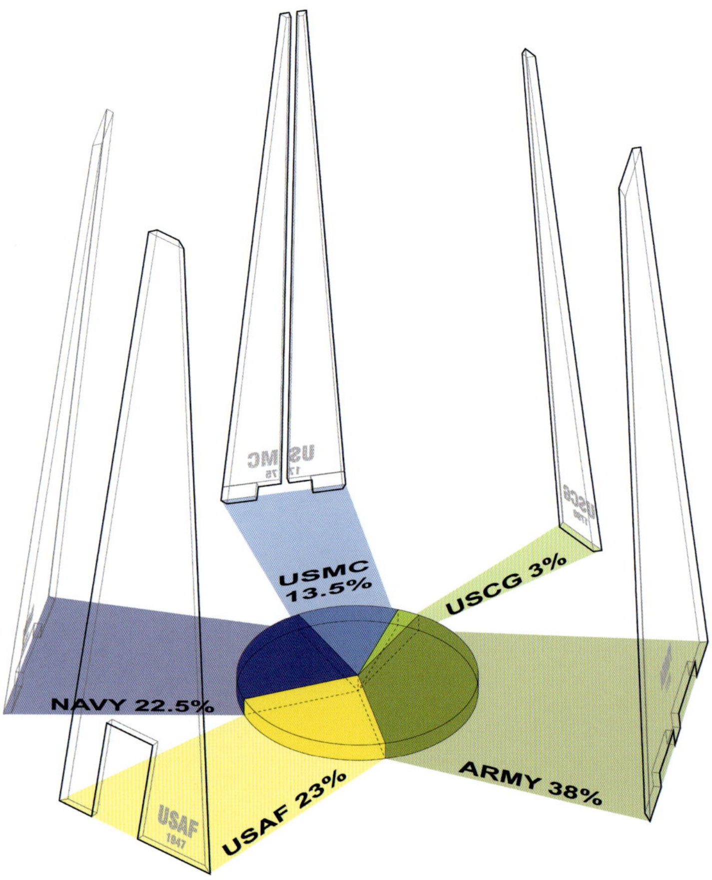

USMC
1775

USMC

USAF
1947

NAVY
1775

USMC
1775

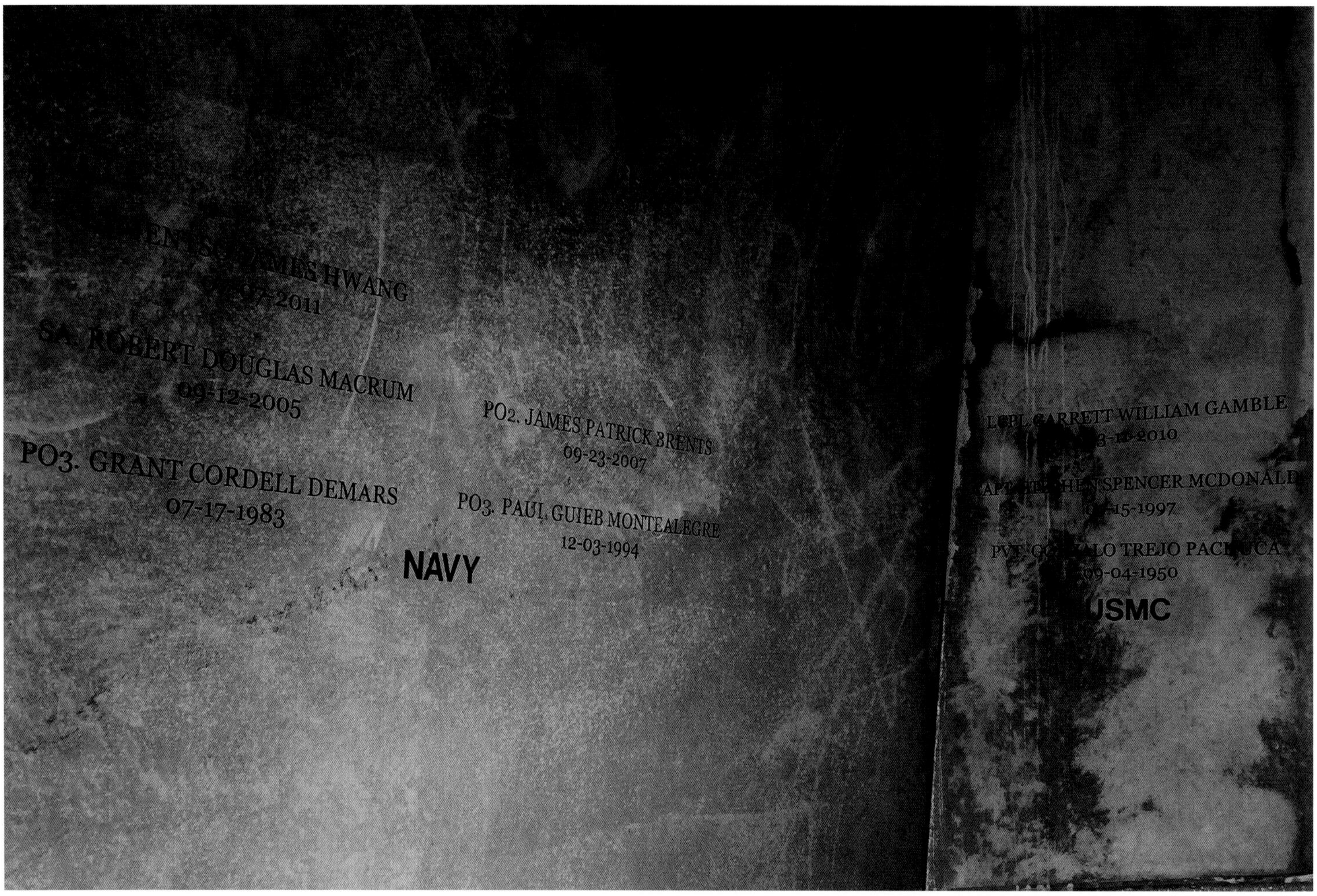
SA. ROBERT DOUGLAS MACRUM
09-12-2005
PO3. GRANT CORDELL DEMARS
07-17-1983
PO2. JAMES PATRICK BRENTS
09-23-2007
PO3. PAUL GUIEB MONTEALEGRE
12-03-1994
NAVY
09-04-1950
USMC

DEPARTMENT OF THE ARMY
UNITED STATES OF AMERICA
1775

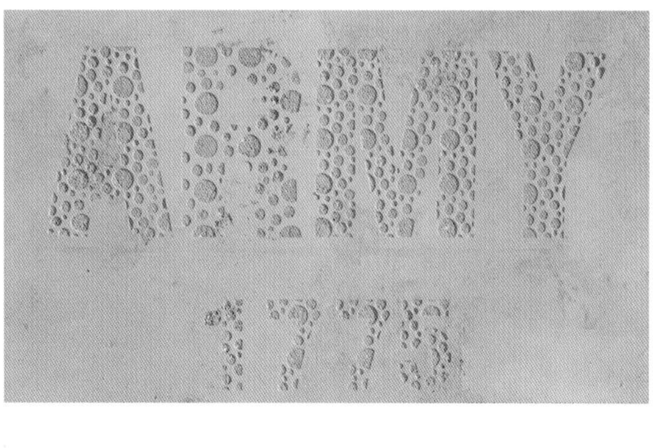
ARMY
1775

USCG
1790

Houston, Texas | Corporate headquarters | 35,400 square feet

Arch-Con

The innovation in this project isn't really the single-story stacking of the site-cast panels, which has rudimentary roots in the 1980s in Ottawa, Canada. Rather, this building exhibits the ability for hyper-urban applications with small sites, zero lot lines, and the need for maximum transparency in a load-bearing exterior skin system. In this project the panels were conceived to have gravity loads pass through the grout between panels. Out-of-plane shear, in-plane shear, and uplift were through the connections.

GeoForm™

As a low-cost, low-technology construction method, tilt-up concrete has become one of the fastest growing solutions for addressing lowered budget constraints. Recently, it has gained a foothold with architects as an innovative way of form-making for other projects.

It may appear strange to extoll the virtues of load-bearing wall construction in the twenty-first century after post-industrial revolution inventions such as the skeleton-frame structural systems of steel and cast-in-place concrete. However, load-bearing wall construction, particularly tilt-wall, has never had more potential to respond to market challenges and capitalize on technological advancements. Recent innovations in the science of concrete composition and engineering advancements like helical fiber reinforcement have enormous implications for all aspects of the material.

Yet almost all innovations are technological. Our effort here is to advance the aesthetic potential of this ubiquitous construction system to allow it entry into new building types and make it an option for designers rather than a last resort. It is currently not possible to make reliable, dimensionally stable curved edges, or meaningfully deep compound surface curves. The current method requires hand cutting of foam ballast. This in turn makes repetition difficult, and shop fabrication of windows impractical, and creates numerous other barriers. This invention solves those issues.

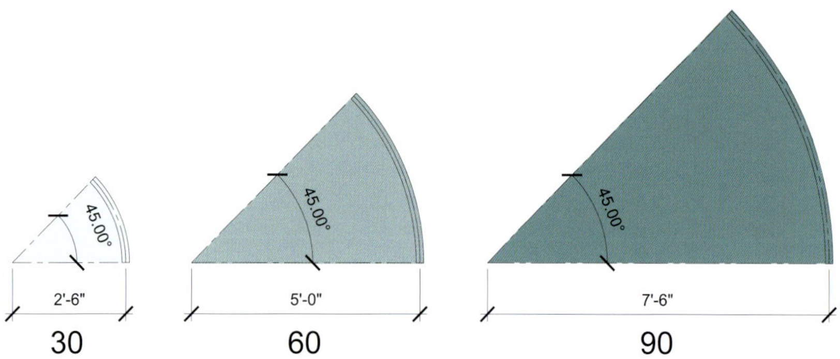

The system requires the fabrication of a limited number of forms that can be combined and either sold to subcontractors or rented out, very much the same way braces are, as equipment. It is simple, easily maintainable and if ever needed, easily extendable as a product line.

Three shapes systematically determine the level of optionality achievable with tilt-wall design ...

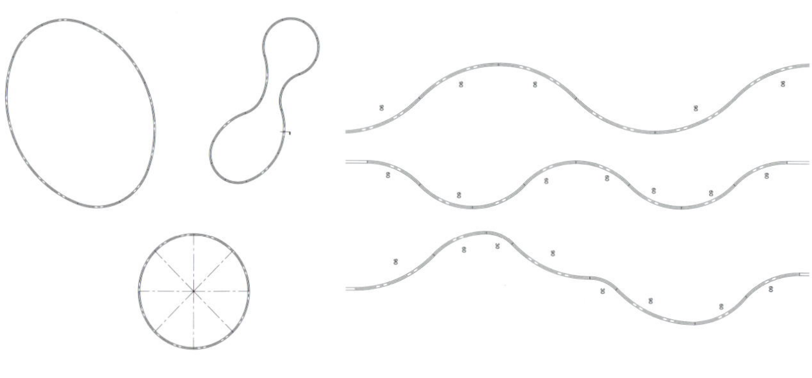

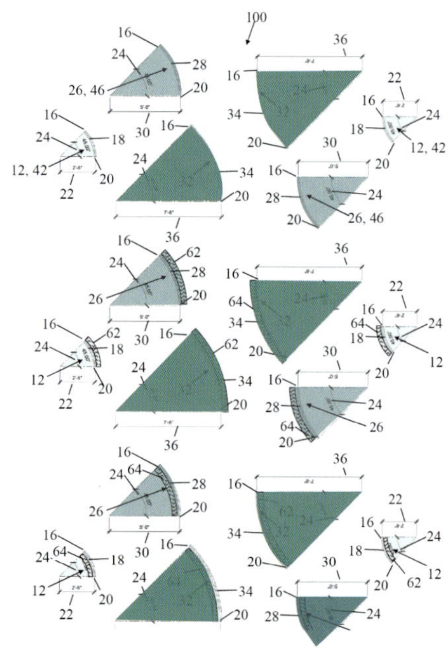

... these shapes can be assembled as closed shapes and panel joints.

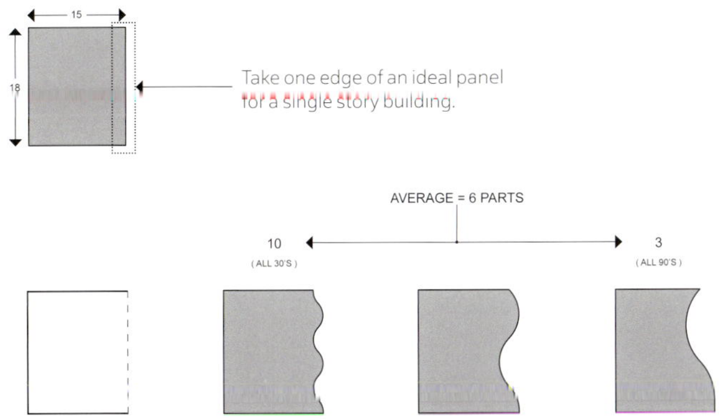

A limit of six pieces used on a single-story panel yields 729 possible edge conditions.

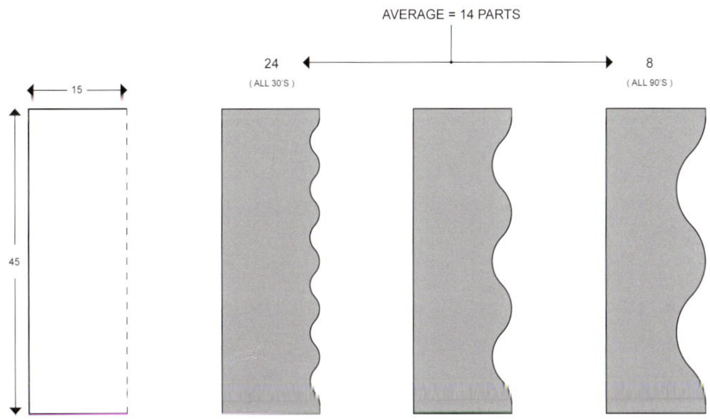

A limit of fourteen pieces used on a three-story panel yields 4,782,969 possible edge conditions.

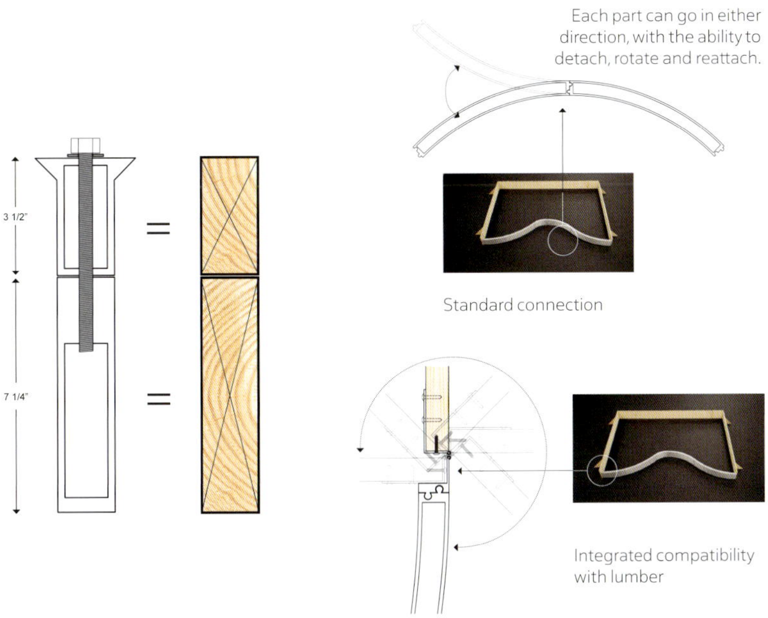

Details / connections

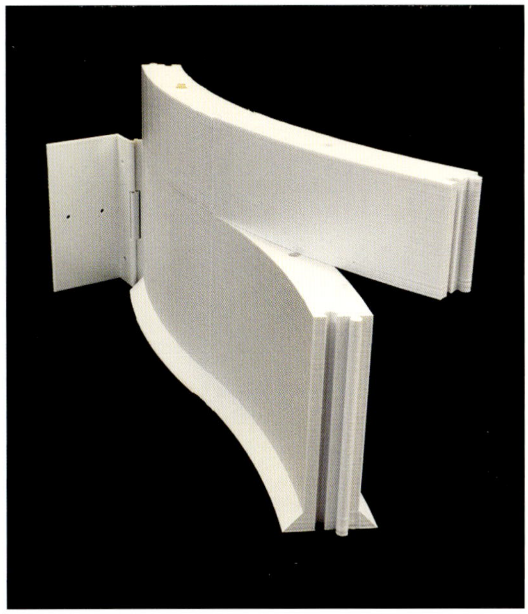

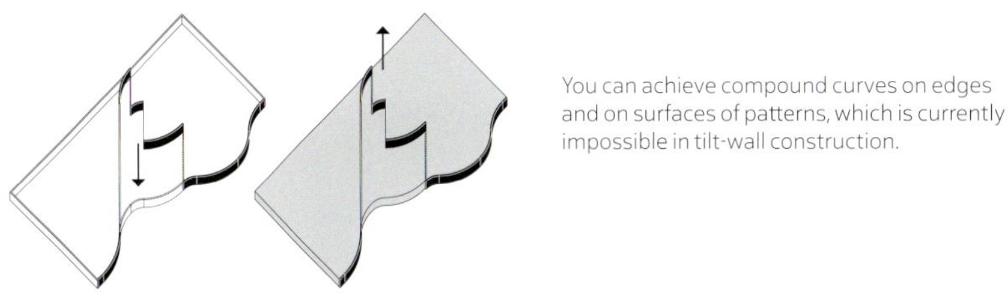

Connection allows for vertical setting and removal of parts.

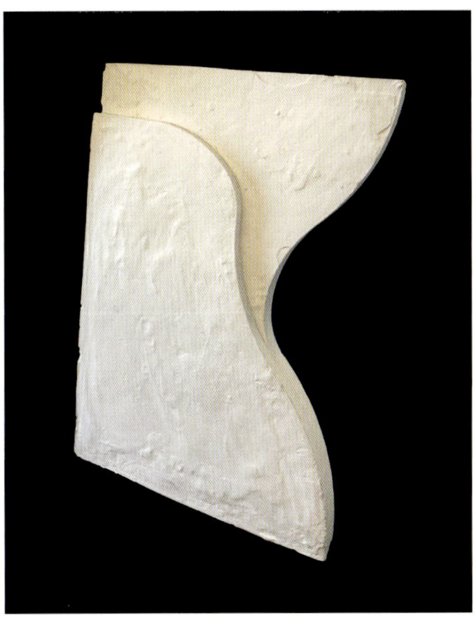

Top-cast panel intallation mock-up

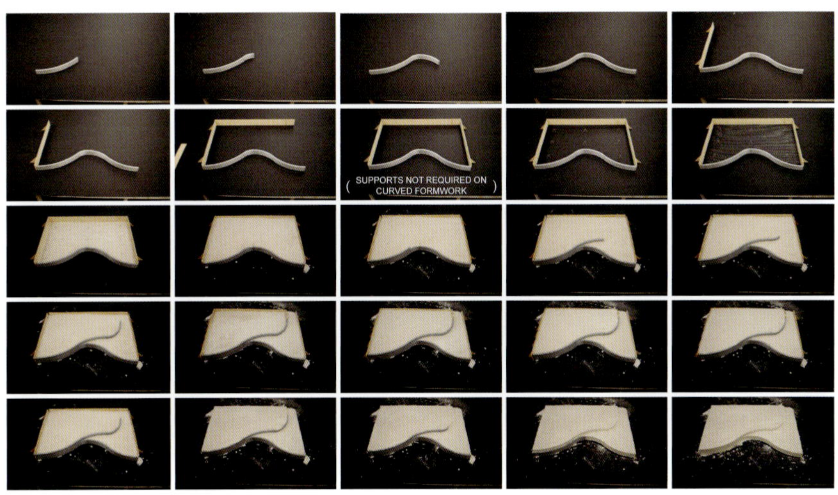

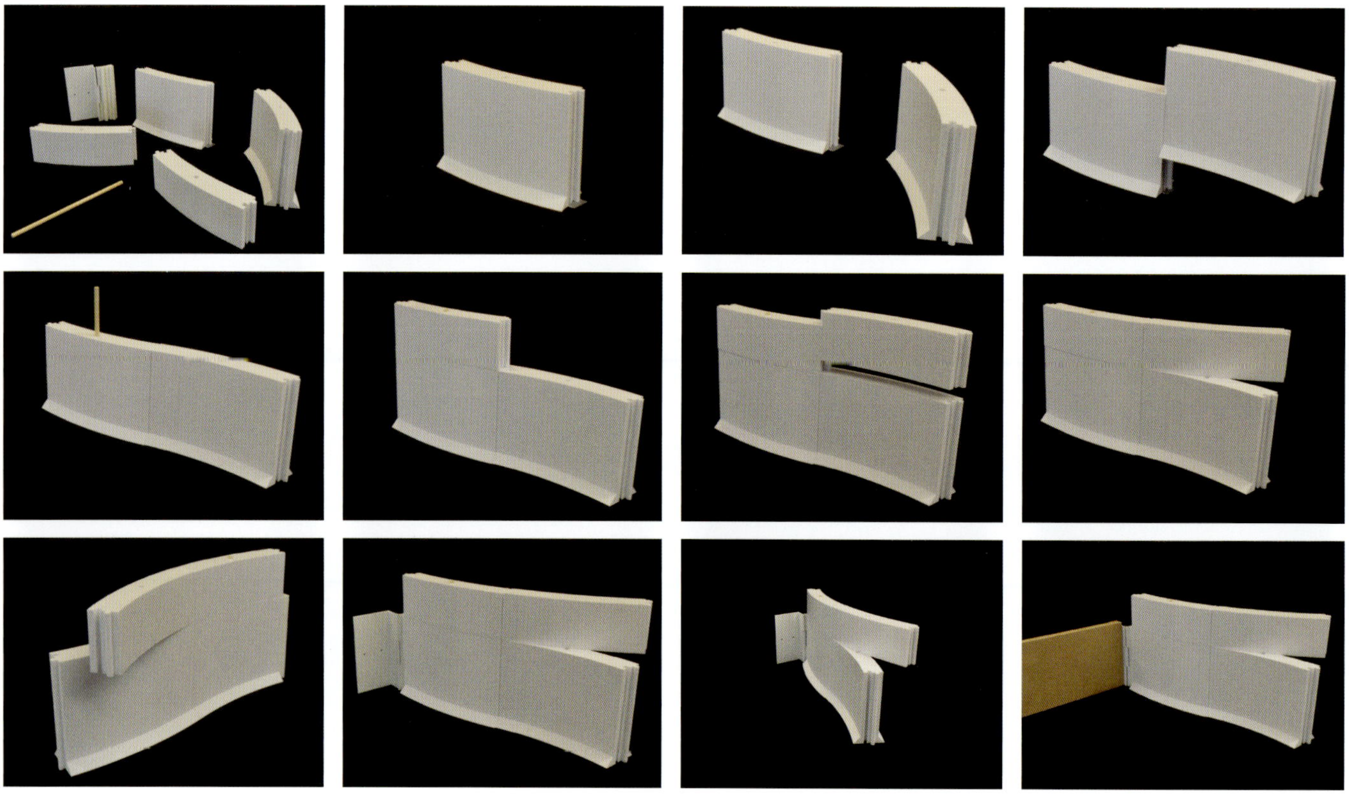

GeoForm™ system components

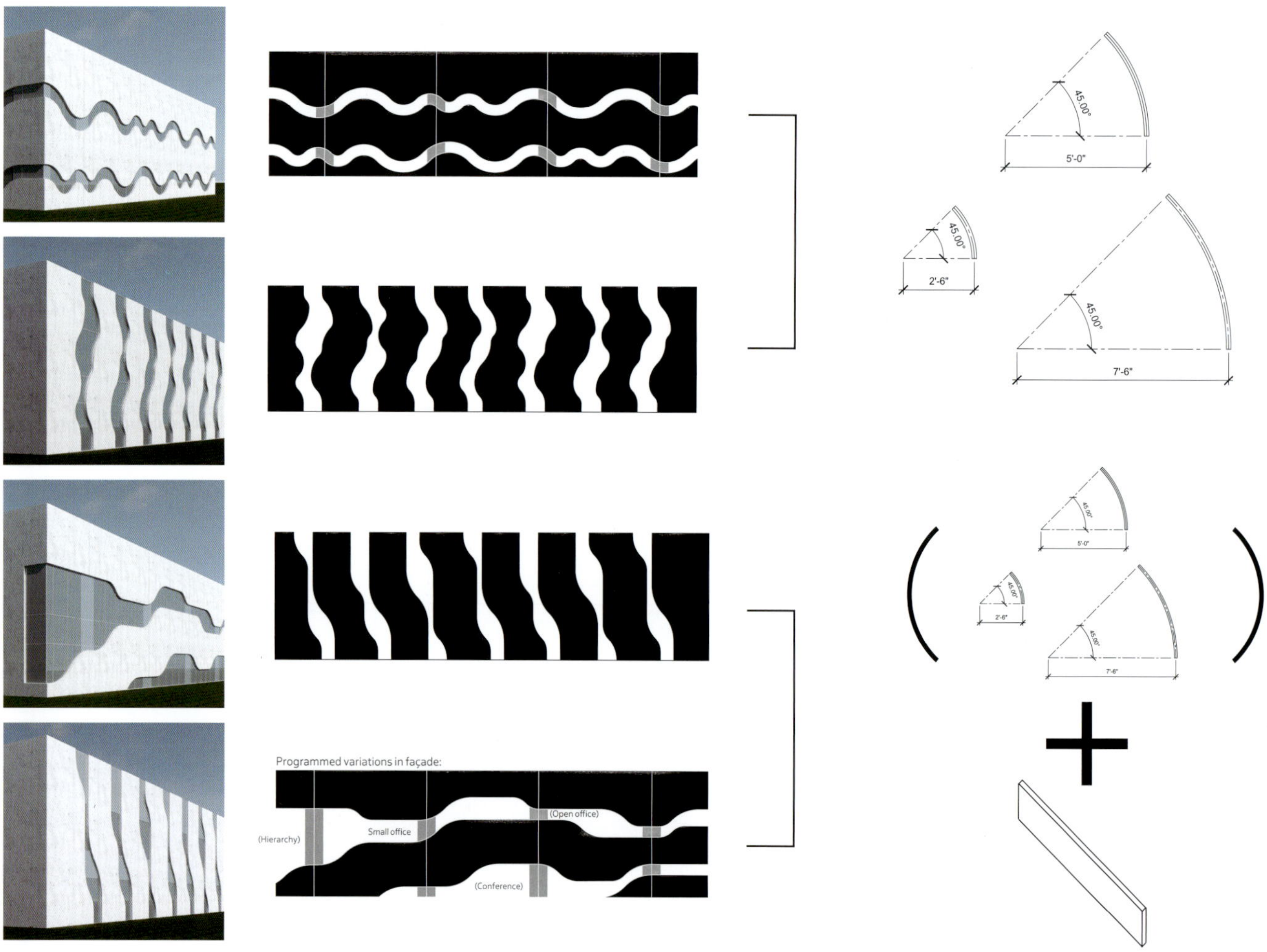

Variety of wall compositions

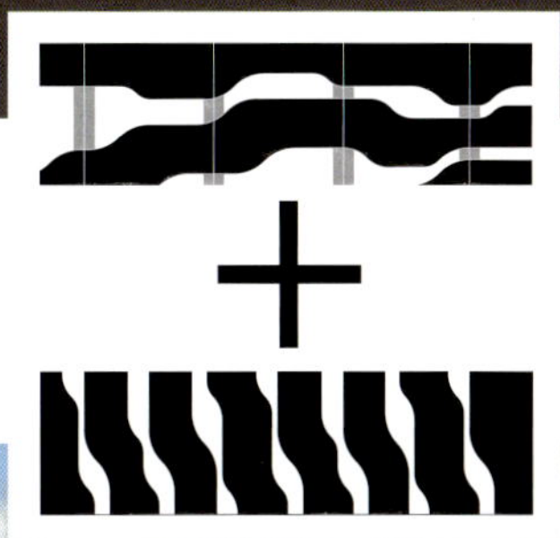

The Woodlands, Texas | Speculative office | 180,000 square feet

Woodlands

We were the first architects to stack a six-story building in a 4+2 stacked panel configuration. The first five floors were placed in the bottom stack with 30-foot-wide by 60-foot-tall panels. Once the fifth floor was placed, which secured the structural diaphragm, the two-story panels were "edge picked" and stacked on the perimeter edges of the base panels. Steel framing ties the structural diaphragm at the roof level and is braced mid-span by the sixth floor as well.

CUC

Having outgrown its existing facilities, the Credit Union of Colorado (CUC) sought the establishment of a new headquarters that would not only foster future growth, but also become a beacon for new talent while accommodating the new hybrid work styles of the current staff. To achieve 110,000 square feet of space, the decision was made to create a three-story building consisting of 36,600-square-foot floor plates. The program contains office space as well as a gym, multiple breakrooms, and a retail bank component.

Moving from the original location in downtown Denver, the new site was purchased in Denver's Central Park neighborhood, six miles east of the city center. The parcel sits at a convergence of architectural and commercial building types, industrial to the east, residential to the south, and commercial/retail to the north and west. But more importantly the site sits emphatically elevated above the I-70 transit corridor, which it fronts. With its proximity to one of the largest arteries into Denver, the site provides the opportunity to create a structure with formal prominence and exposure.

To capitalize on the design potential of the tilt-wall, which was dictated by the budget, we employed a folding-like articulation of planar elements. This broke down the rigidity of the basic linearity. A fractured, shifting, kinetic form was inserted behind the more cartesian enclosing walls. Deviating from orthogonality in a minor key, the geometry helps to define the westerly mountain views, establishes the hierarchy forming the entry, and screens the mechanical equipment. It is a multifunctional ribbon within the more staid exterior walls, creating a tension that quickly announces the character of the building for passing drivers.

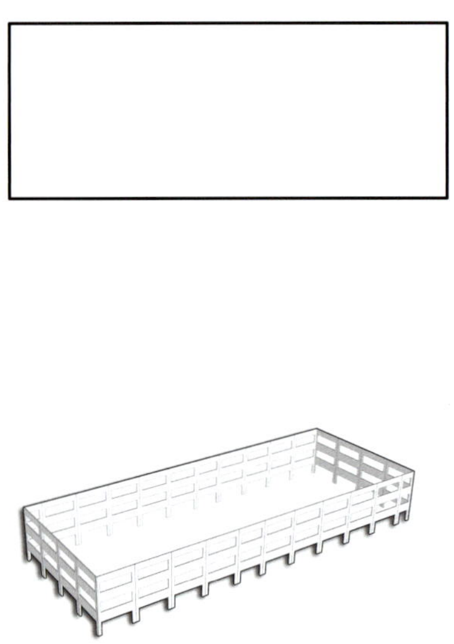

Base floor plate

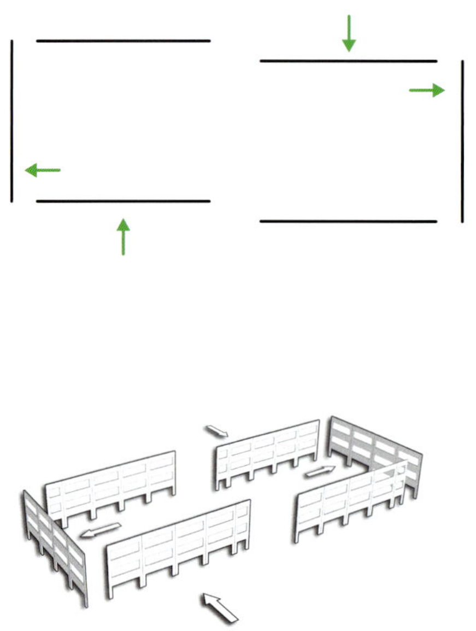

Fractured and shifted

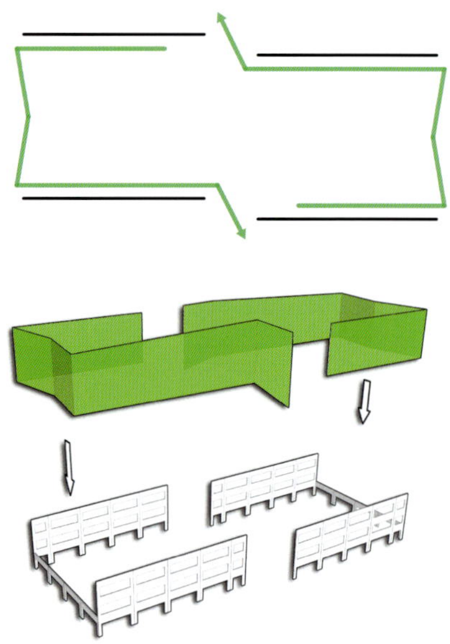

Ribbon creation and insertion

8959

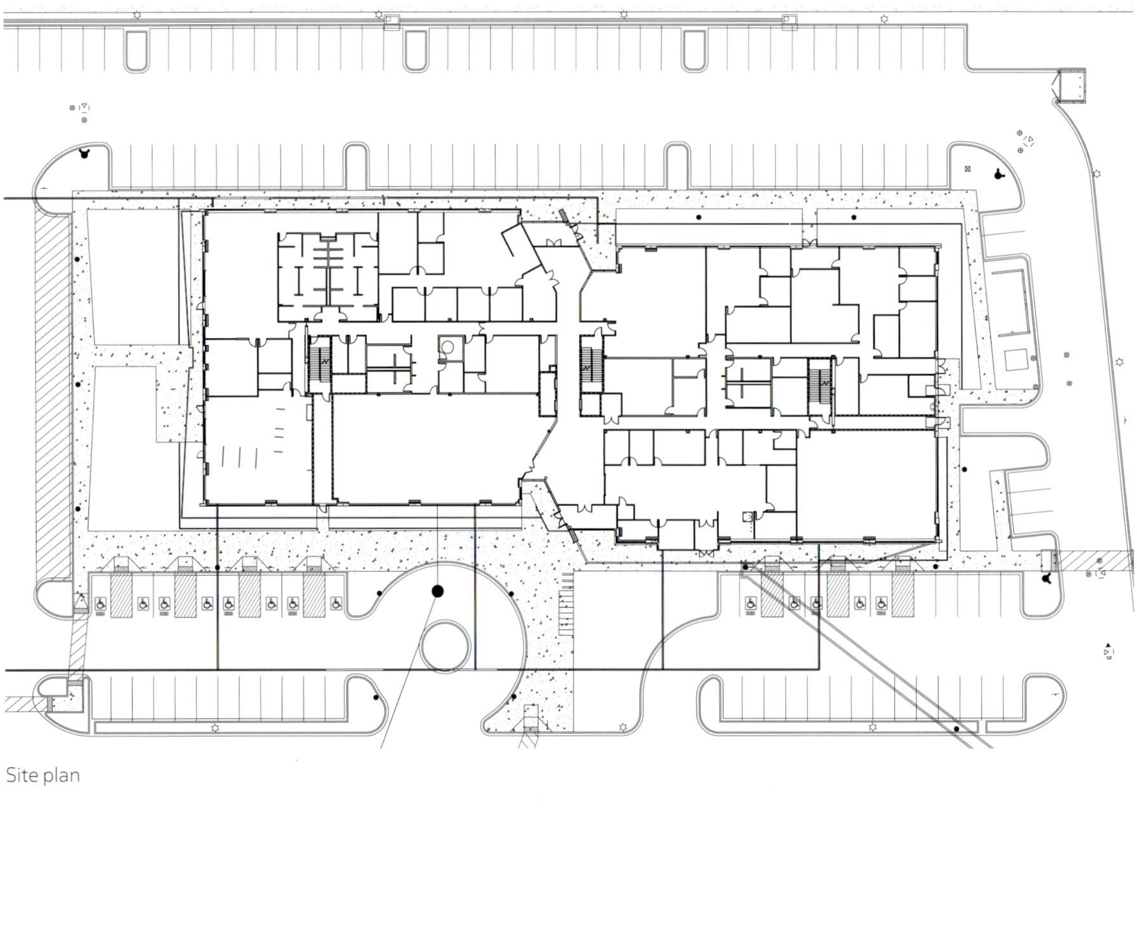

Site plan

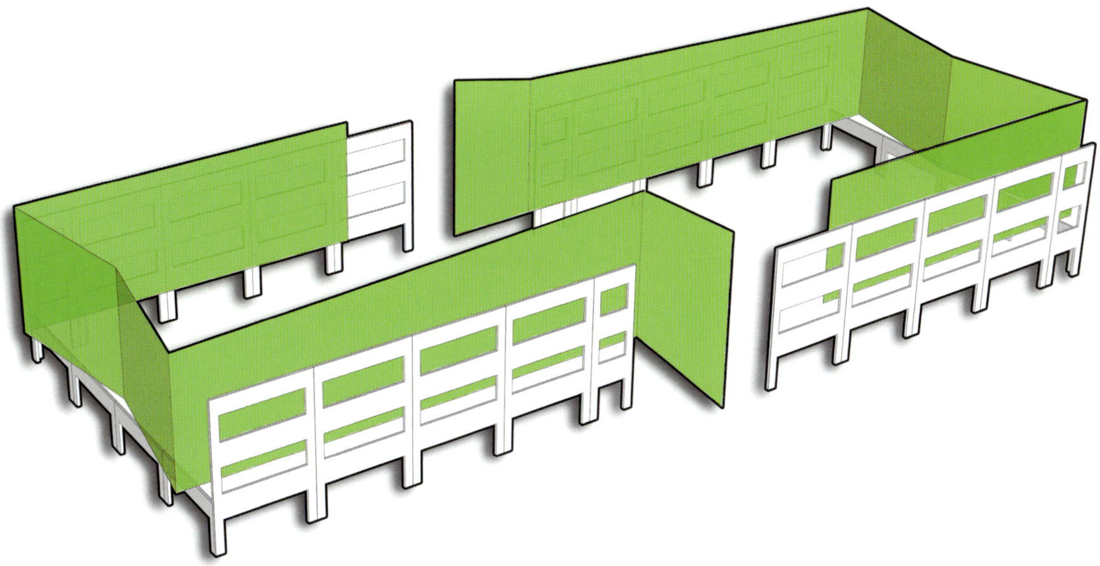

Final concept

Roger Sherwood's 1978 publication *Modern Housing Prototypes* established in catalog survey form the alignment of modernism to an obligation to provide high-quality affordable housing. Late and postmodernism—let alone "neo" forms of modernism—appear to have abandoned that alliance. We remain committed to pushing low-cost housing up the high-architecture ladder even when budgets are restricted. Our "for rent" Canada housing has inspired our efforts to imbricate big-move architecture into the least of projects. The work has also been fueled by a series of government subsidy programs stimulating developers to undertake more attainable living units. Much of this need comes from Canada's program to enhance immigration, growing the country from 33 million to over 40 million souls in a short timeframe, causing near-term housing shortages. Design strategies aimed at suppressing low-cost mechanical elements in the façades, democratic deployment of amenities, and consideration of vernacular influences are among the tools we deploy in approaching this type of work. In the **Hamilton** apartments we capitalize on the prominent site with two towers set on a base that scales down to the local neighborhood. **Churchill Square** is a mixed-use addition to an aggregated urban artifact. In **Shortall** we scale up the jelly-bean-and-white-frame vernacular architecture to an affordable complex overlooking a park. We also include examples of ongoing projects for affordable housing in the United States, like the **Sandrock** low-income housing project in suburban Houston. Other building types include student housing; the **University of Houston** housing project is an example of the specific amenities and room types off-campus housing takes on. **Adara** is yet another variation for rent housing, in this case a cultural version. The project serves a Vedic community in suburban Houston with large multi-generational unit types including Punja rooms and expansive amenities. Finally, at **Ivy** we explored high-density microhousing in the near town EaDo (East Downtown) neighborhood. The units range from 300 square feet to 750 square feet, all with kinetic furniture and customizable kitchen, study, and storage components for each tenant.

Rent

Hamilton

The Hamilton Avenue Apartments are much-needed residential towers that provide 192 apartment units to a small town with a large housing shortage. The project is located on a sloping site in a primarily single-family residential neighborhood just south of downtown St. John's. To the immediate northeast of the site is a view to St. Johns Bay, which contains a working commercial harbor with a narrow straight that leads out to the Atlantic. These site conditions became the main drivers in our design approach for the project.

With only a small portion of the site economically suitable to build on, the two towers needed to be aligned next to each other along Hamilton Avenue. The towers were then shifted slightly to maximize views of downtown and the bay from both buildings. Given this site's orientation the project became an exercise of aspect and prospect: the view from downtown of the East tower down the main avenue and the views from the West tower towards the bay. To address this idea, a single corner from each tower begins to open as the tower rises, creating larger apartments on the higher floors with open corners of floor-to-ceiling glass. The balconies on the bayside elevations of the towers are angled for optimal views to further accentuate this directional idea.

The adjacent context of multicolored wood-sided, two- to three-story, single-family homes led us to conduct a series of façade studies with the goal of breaking down the scale at the base and relating to the material and color variation of the houses while not having a disconnected architecture on the towers. The solution was a grid that could adjust in scale to the height of the tower as well as the smaller architecture desired on the podium. The façade of the base the towers sit on is organized by a "grid and infill" strategy, that relates to the existing residential dwelling scale surrounding the site. We chose a modern emulation of horizontal wood siding due to the harsh environmental conditions. This backdrop is punctuated by small punched openings also making reference to the windows in the nearby houses which is then extended to the logic of the tower cladding as well.

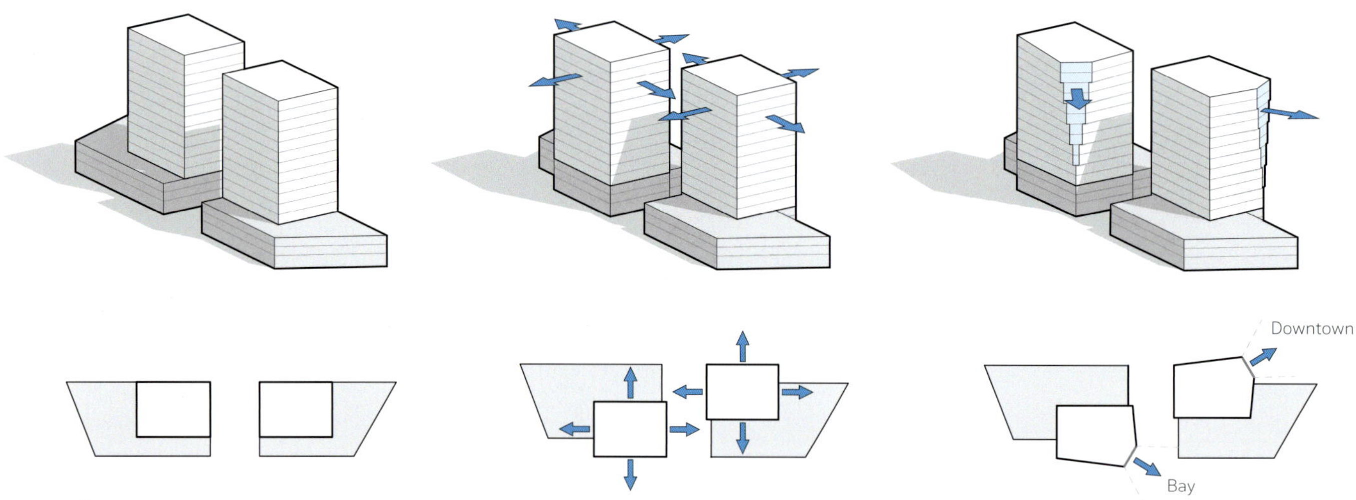

Concept to maximize veiws

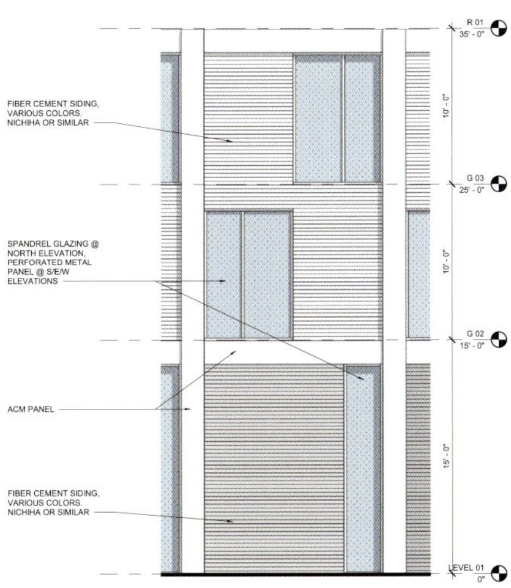

Typical podium grid

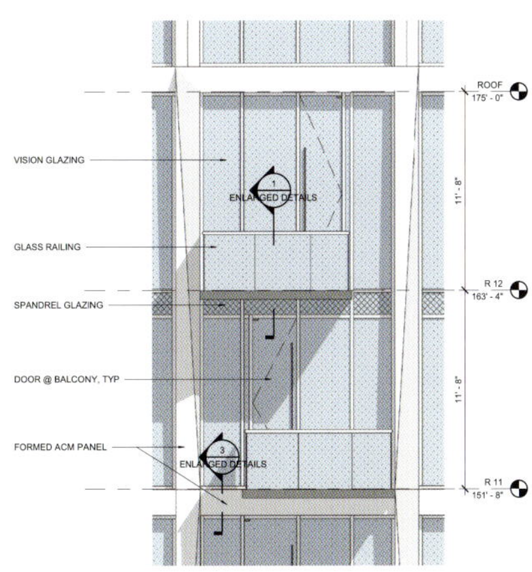

Typical tower grid (north/west)

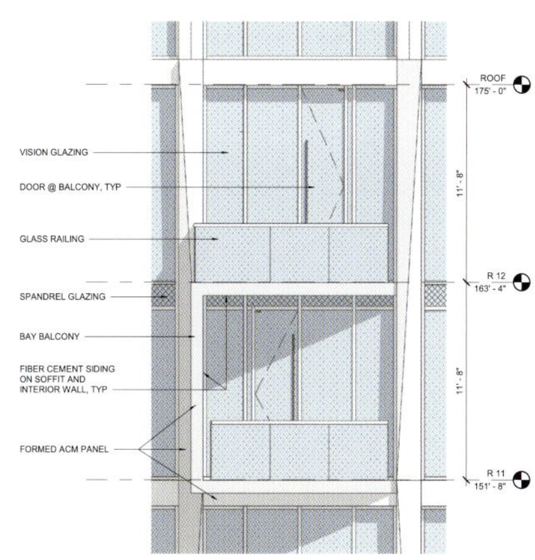

Typical tower grid (south/east)

Sandrock

The Sandrock Apartments is an affordable housing complex located in South Houston and consists of 144 units across three buildings. With large detention and parking requirements on the site, coupled with very odd easements, the buildings thread through the unbuildable gaps as a series of linear "tubes" connected by bridges on a narrow L-shaped strip of land. Multicolored fiber cement board siding on the exterior indexes the neighboring apartment complexes and helps keep costs down. White siding on the outside of the "tubes" is punctuated by the interior accent siding to indicate entry locations, vertical circulation, and social gathering spaces.

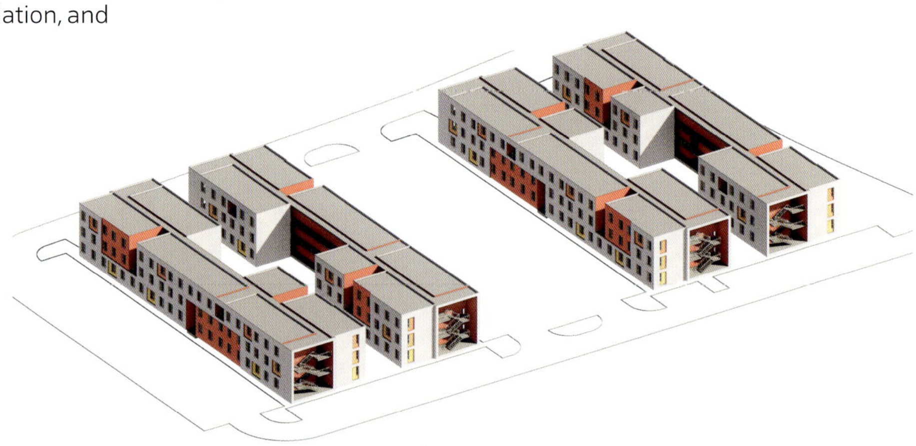

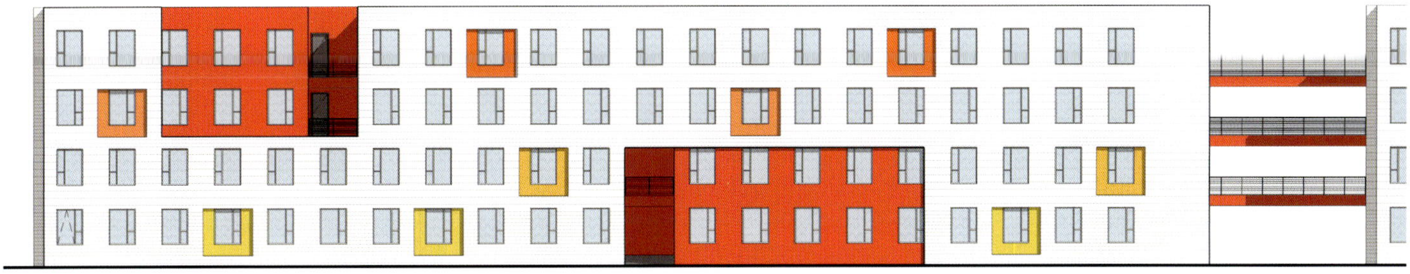

Overall south elevation

Overall north elevation

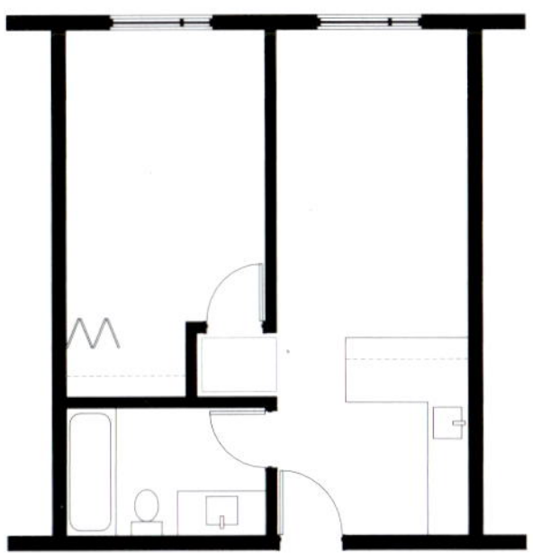

Unit: 1 bed / 1 bath (500 square feet)

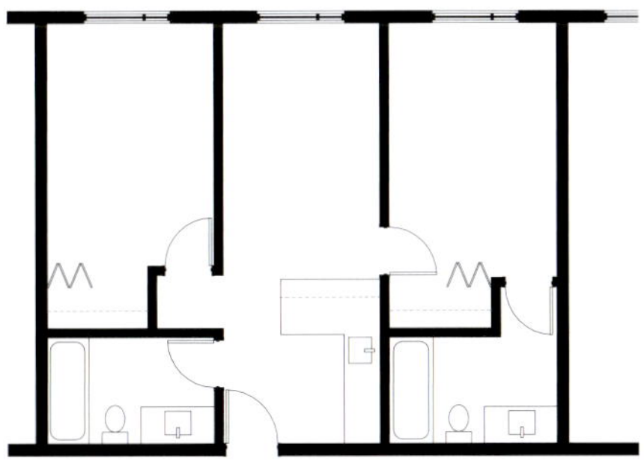

Unit: 2 bed / 2 bath (750 square feet)

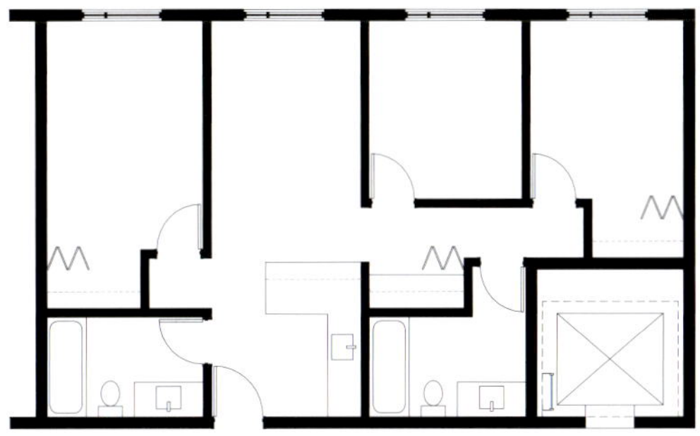

Unit: 3 bed / 2 bath (910 square feet)

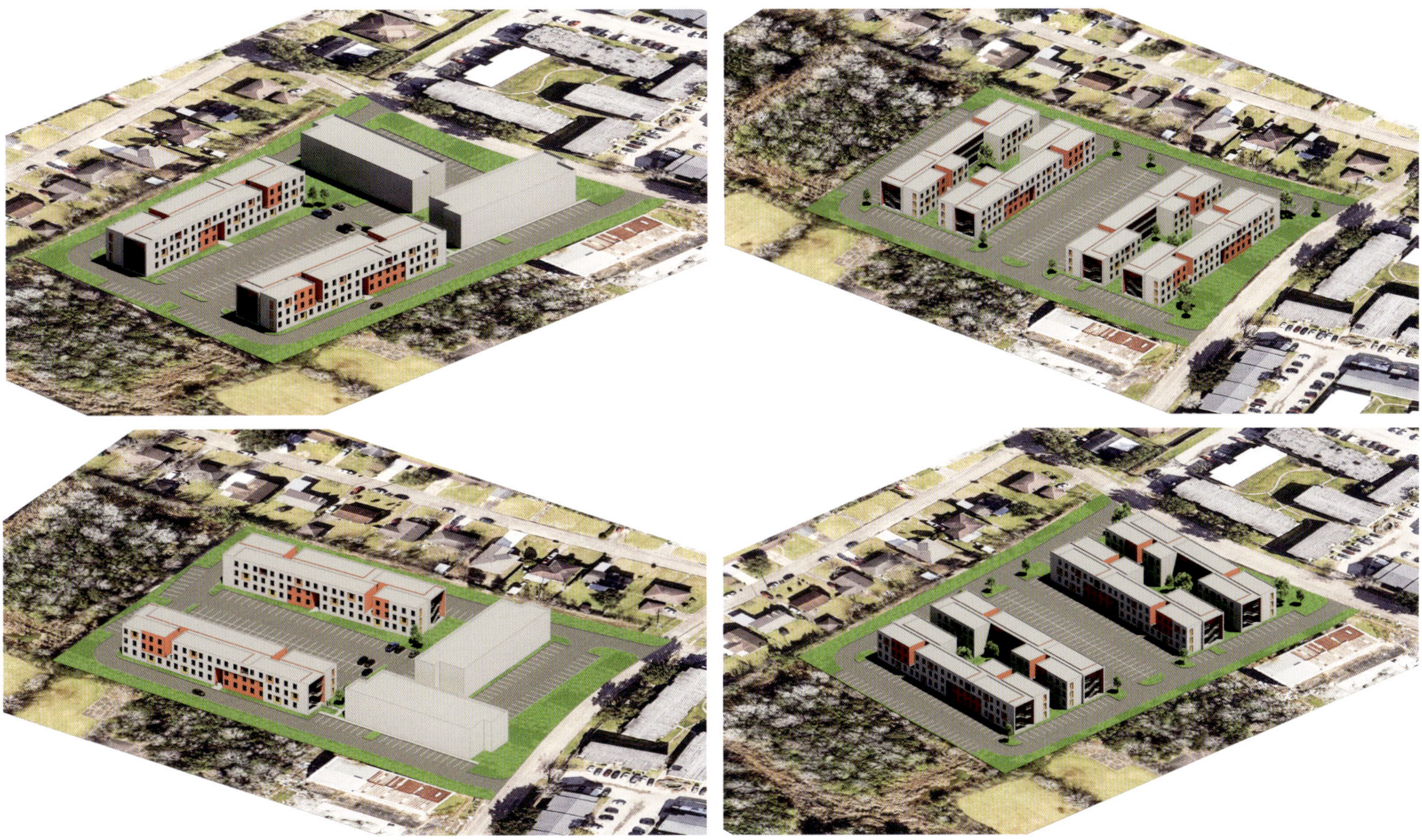

Campus

The University of Houston Student Housing project is a fifteen-story building consisting of 197 units and 502 beds. The building is organized around an internal courtyard comprising full amenities. The courtyard opens on the prominent corner to obtain views to the adjacent main campus from units that would normally face inward. This opening in the building façade creates a layering effect and is the defining formal characteristic of the building.

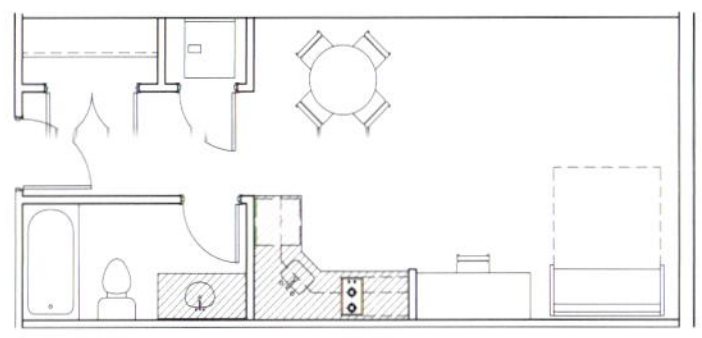

Efficient unit plan

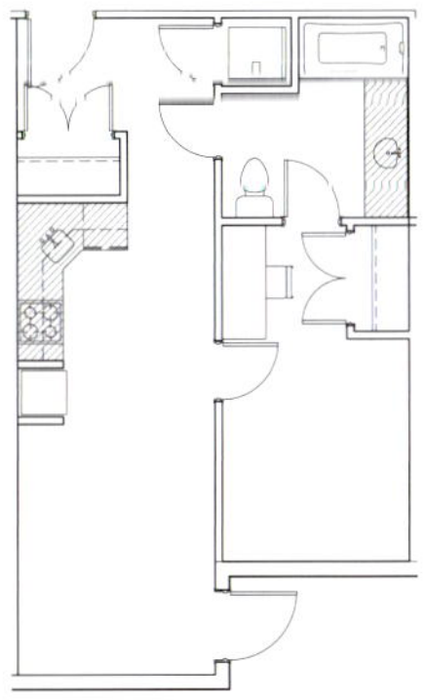

One-bedroom-unit plan

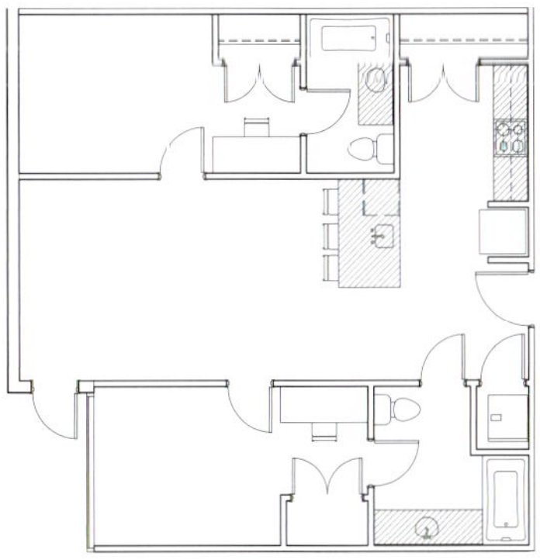

Two-bedroom-unit plan

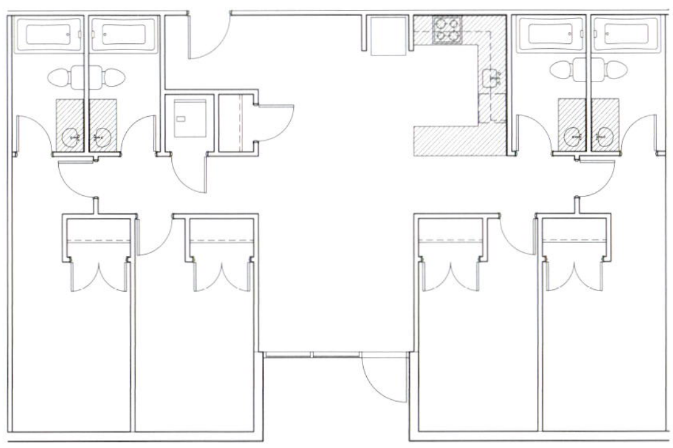

Four-bedroom-unit plan

Sixth-floor plan

Typical (7–12th) floor plan

Fifth-floor plan

Ivy

The microdwelling concept has taken hold in major cities across the United States, redefining and revolutionizing city living. This project was slated to be built in Houston's exciting EaDo (East Downtown) neighborhood for its inherent charm, as well as its unbeatable proximity to the city's cultural and business centers. Home to a thriving arts and entertainment scene, popular shopping districts, and the city's most celebrated restaurants, EaDo is one of the most sought-after areas in Houston.

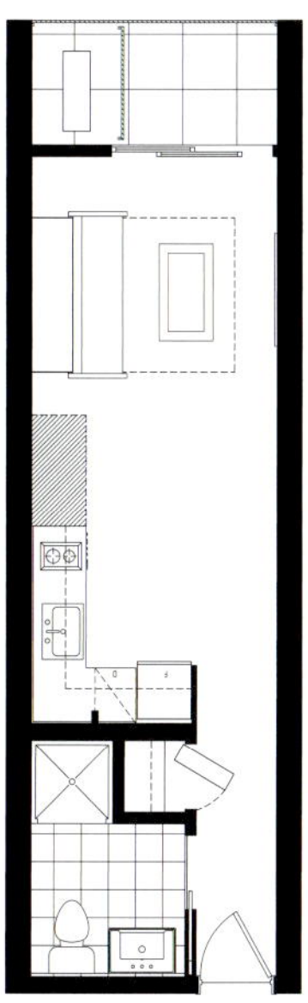

Studio floor plan

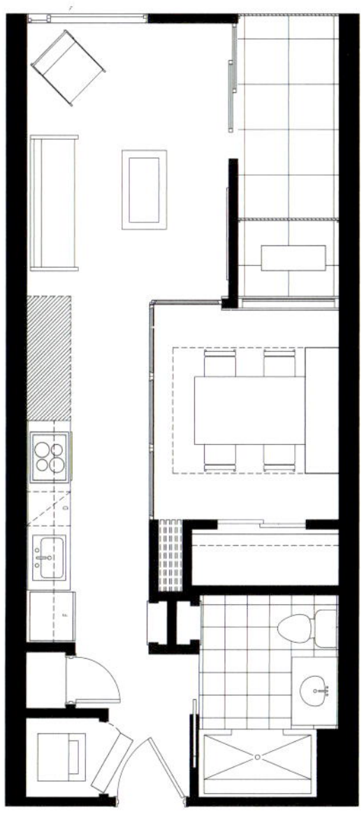

One-bedroom floor plan

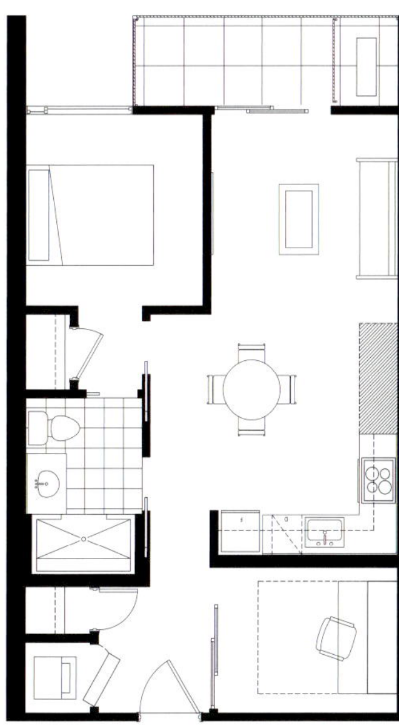

One-bedroom-plus-den floor plan

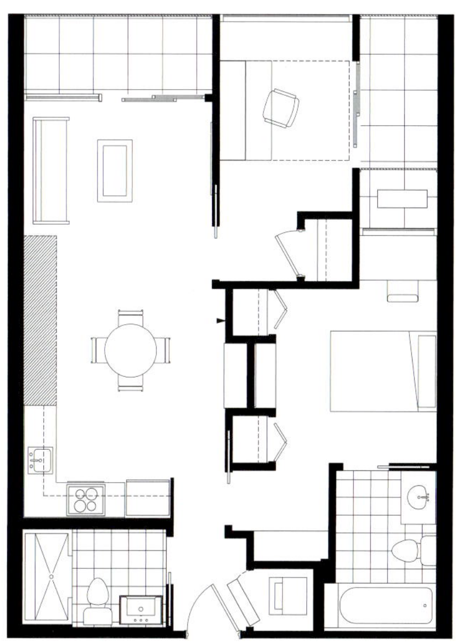

Two-bedroom floor plan

Churchill

This six-story multifamily facility with ground-level retail shops and two levels of underground parking is located Churchill Square in St. John's, Newfoundland. Churchill Square contains two parallel rows of shops on each side of a parking area and for years has remained much more uniform on the east row, which contains apartments on the upper levels. The entire complex forms a square "U" shape very much like an urban inset plaza, yet the complex is an object in space, reading as a single building rather than a façade containing a public space. Given this unique condition, replacing the small over-parked retail facilities with the proposed building balances out the object quality of the composite megabuilding with the increased density of mixed-use development. The façade uses a "switch" strategy to take advantage of preferred views from the upper levels while maintaining privacy for each residence.

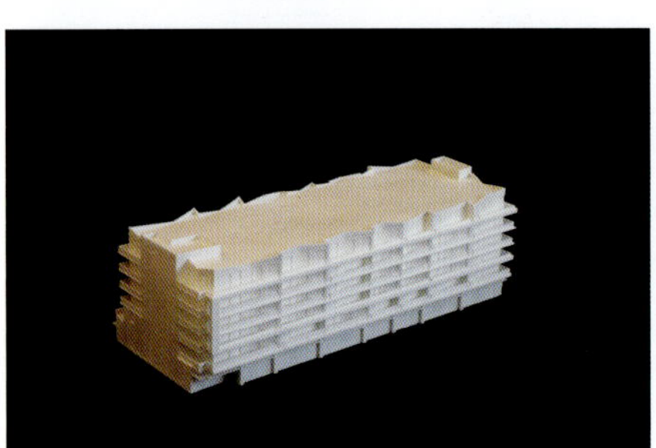

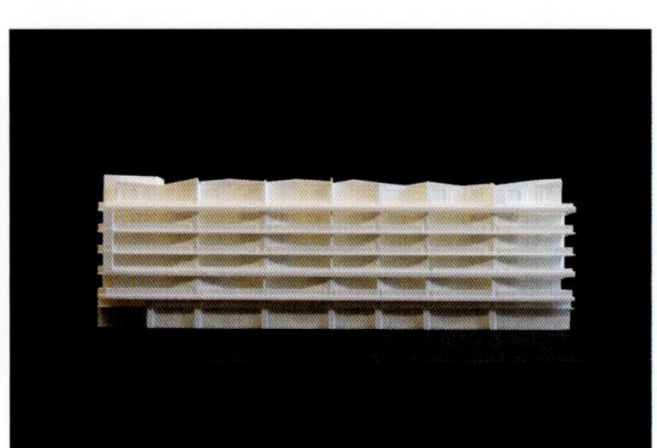

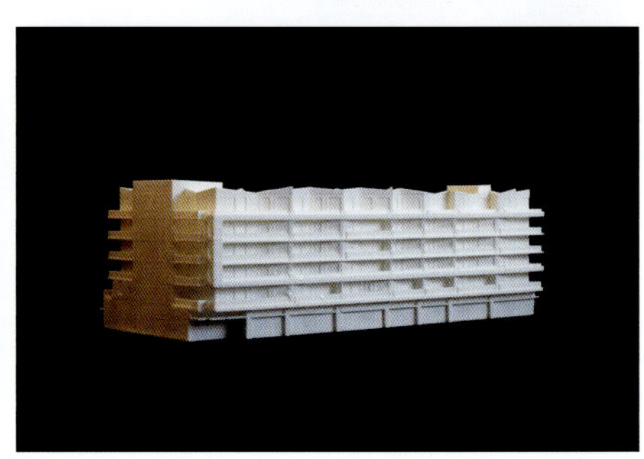

Second-floor plan

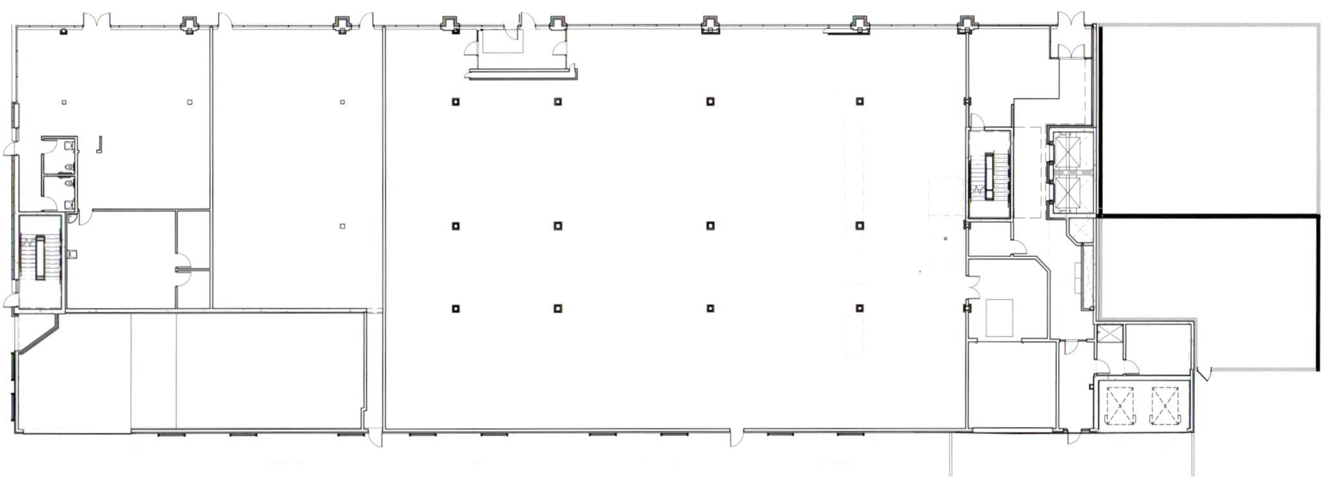

First-floor plan

Inside-out reciprocity used to be a reliable heuristic for the generating of elevations in academics post-establishment of the teaching movement known as the Texas Rangers. The survey of the beginnings of the ability to actually teach modernism by Alex Caragonne, titled *The Texas Rangers: Notes form an Architectural Underground*, codified certain formulae like big room/big window or big window/public internal space alongside small window/private internal space, and so on. Of course, this works when one controls the inside and the outside simultaneously. This is often the case on our *interiors* projects—at least it is how we categorize certain projects as "interior." When we control both we call it "architecture in congress" with the profession. We otherwise simply communicate that we did not control the outside in this category, or that if we did do the outside, as in an office building, and a tenant broke continuity in controlling both. Interior projects have their own logic of "interiority." The conditions of public/private are nuanced in new ways, the progression of collective to individual cannot be expressed on a surface like a façade, but rather becomes an experience written in materials, acoustics, spatial hierarchy, and often theme. The client has purchase in these types of projects in different ways from exterior projects. Often the client wants an expression or manifestation of some kind of culture—work culture, escape culture, etc. This culture framework can be seen in **Verafin**, a large financial tech company's gathering and training facility located on the first two floors of a speculative office building we did in St. John's in Canada. In the case of **Summit Utilities**, it is "brand" that is the organizing framework for the environment. **Logica** is a formal reaction to rectilinear neutrality of the existing building it occupied, inviting a game between the Cartesian grid and non-rectilinearity.

Inside

Summit

The concept behind the interior design of the Summit Utilities headquarters is inspired by its core business of creating pipework for the oil and gas industry. The design encapsulates the interconnectedness of its work product, weaving sinuous lines of pipework that choreograph staff and visitors through the space while simultaneously organizing and defining distinct areas within it. Visitors are immediately greeted by a life-sized geode, evoking the wonder and awe of what lies beneath in the realm occupied by the company's products. Pipes have been incorporated not only as a representation of its services, but also as functional elements, providing low-voltage power to workstations while acting as a spatial organizing element. The company's brand is subtly present in the design, with the geode wall acting as a beacon at the entrance and an LED map in the breakroom, showcasing the locations of their main pipelines. The predominant blue and green logo colors further reinforce the headquarter's identity.

Responding to the desire of the executive board for a more collaborative work environment, the breakroom was strategically positioned to capture the best mountain views, creating an inviting space for employees to gather and interact. It features custom wall-covering displays of the company's values, illuminated by LED neon lights in the shape of its main pipelines from different markets. To foster connectivity, huddle booths establish pathways and inviting spaces for focused discussions. Inside the booths, recessed lighting casts a textured pattern that allows the staff to occupy "work caverns" that inspire and provide privacy.

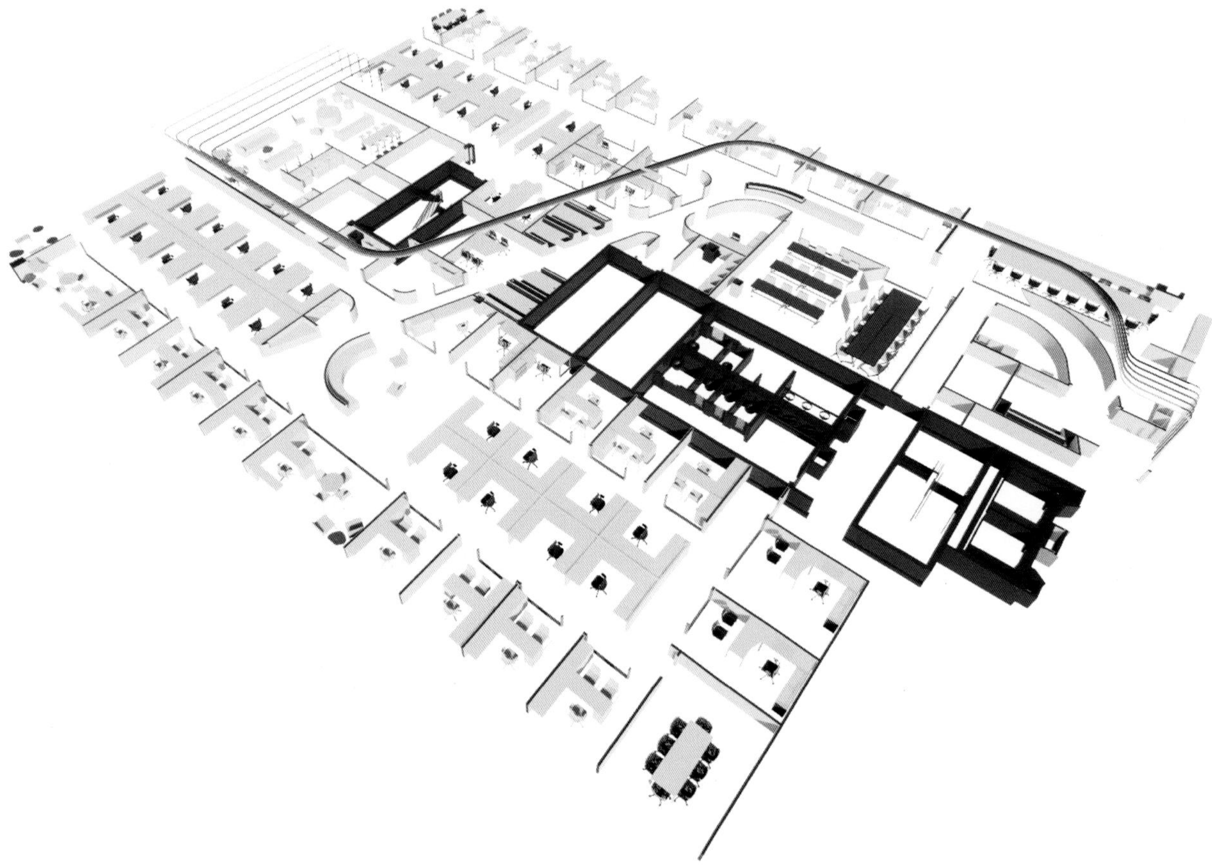

Pipe diagram

Summit
Utilities

COPPER

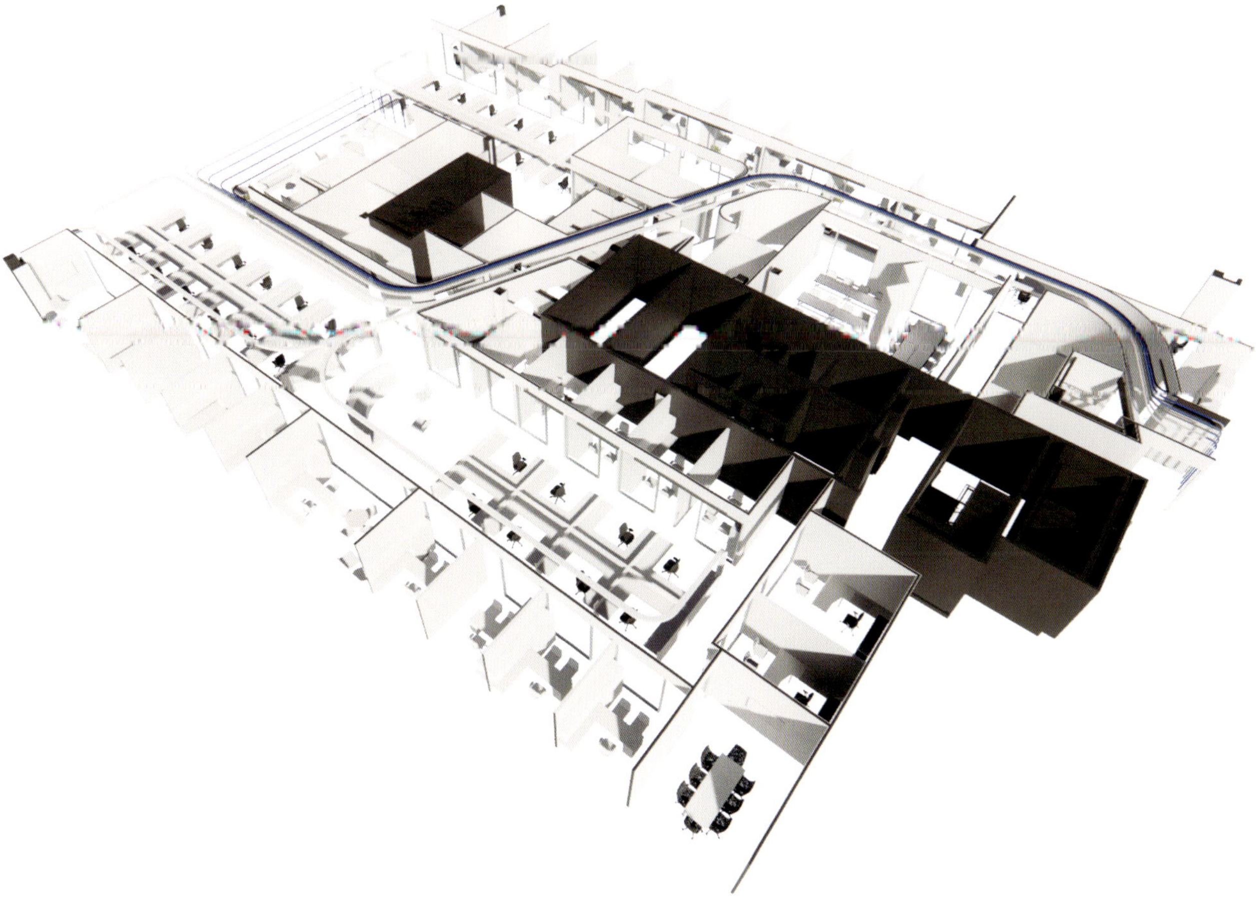

Floor plan

Logica

This collaborative company, whose mission statement is "Brilliant Together," often hosts clients in-house to assess needs and/or train on its customized software products. As such, this statement pertains to both staff and clients.

The scheme for this security-oriented digital design/ software company relies on a uni-surface wall that unites the space while simultaneously creating specific zones and articulation between functional work families. The organic form of the wall is carefully choreographed to react to the verities of the existing building skin. The compression and relief created between the exterior envelope and wall is the key in creating static workspaces and kinetic circulation connections. Each work function is established by circular overhead lighting clouds and is metaphorically interconnected by direct pathways expressed as wood-planked circuits. This floor pattern ignores the core zone established by the uni-surface wall in service of emphasizing the often-hidden interconnectivity of differing groups in the company.

The black ceiling emphasizes the form of the wall. The wall, a shine-finish white Venetian plaster, acts as a scaffold as well as a spatial organizer. It is conceived as datum on which a clip system of custom-designed bamboo millwork accommodates flex-use hotel desks, bench seating, task lighting, and accent brand lighting. Coves are created in the bends of the wall to allow for intimate conversation lounges and copy work areas.

The support functions are located within the wrapped core area, including employee welfare areas such as a café and coffee bars, and functional spaces h as IT/server rooms, and mail and other processing spaces.

In most ways ,the programming process was conventional in so far as we toured the existing space for size and function, and conducted interviews with department to determine needs, using the tour as a baseline for functional improvements and size adjustments. We overlaid cultural elements such as social space, public–private definitions, and use itineraries onto the base program prior to beginning to speculate about formal organization. Here there is a dialogue between the appearance of openness with underlying hidden connections.

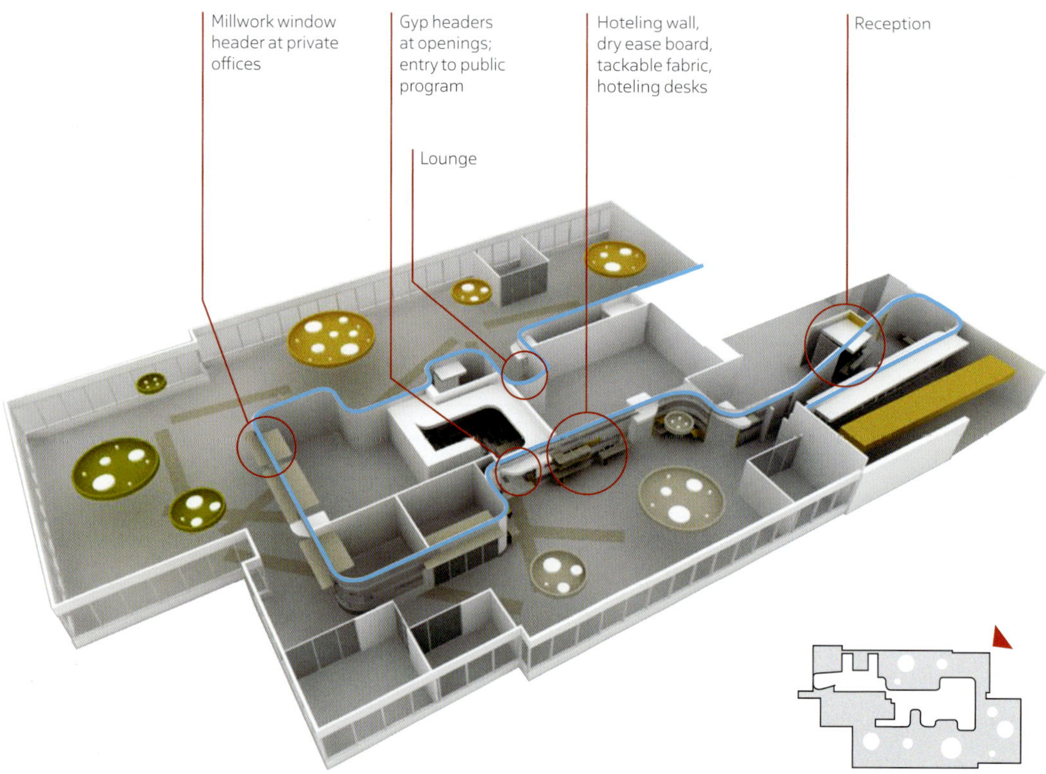

Committed
Innovative
Open

Desks

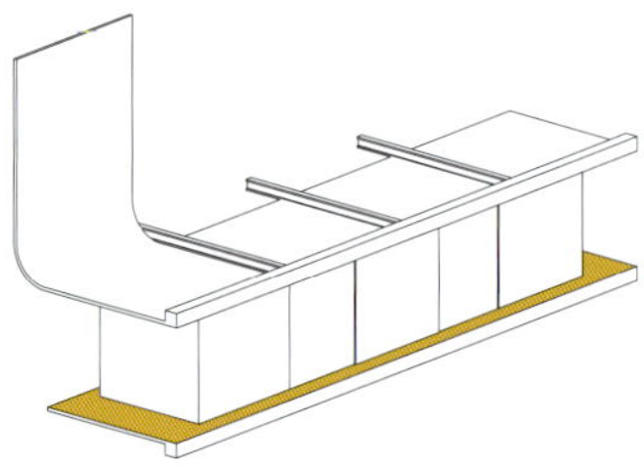

Shelf

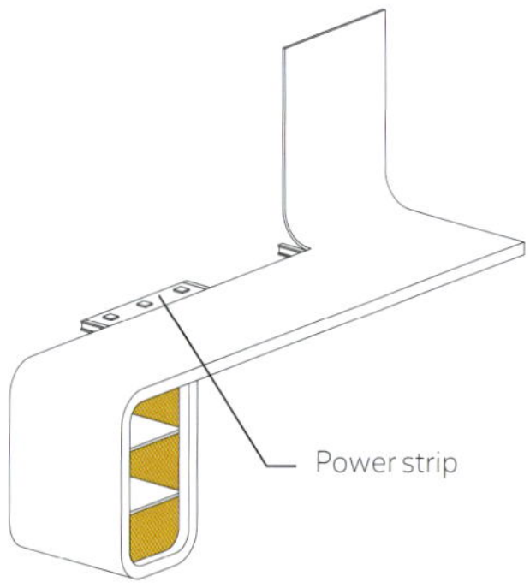

Desk

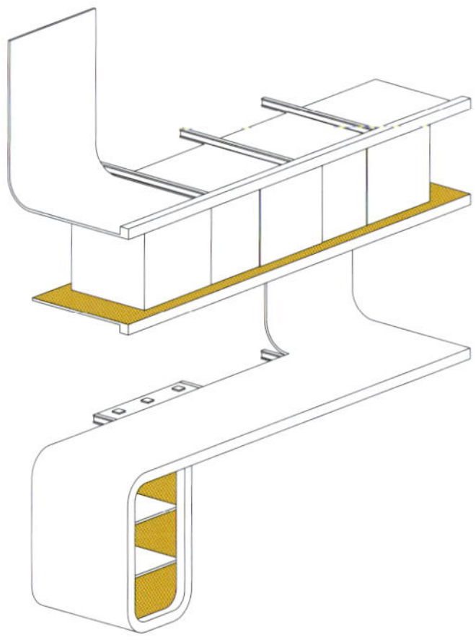

Desk with shelf

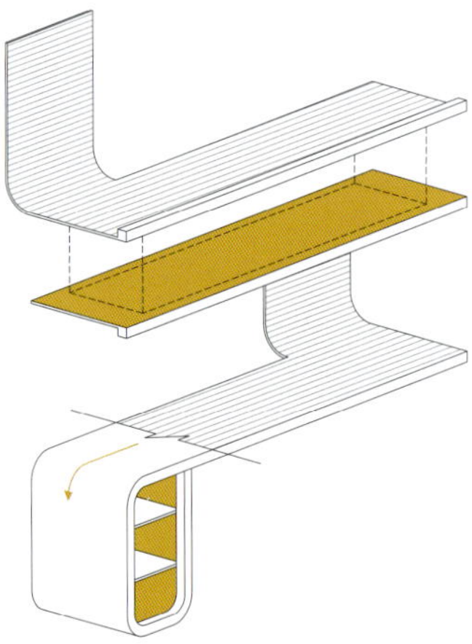

Millwork grain

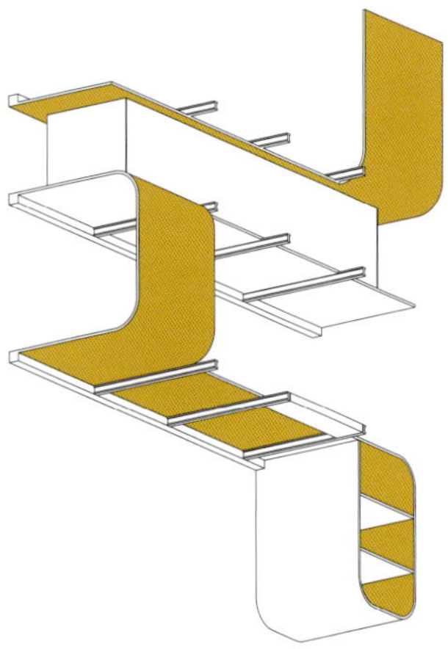

Millwork grain

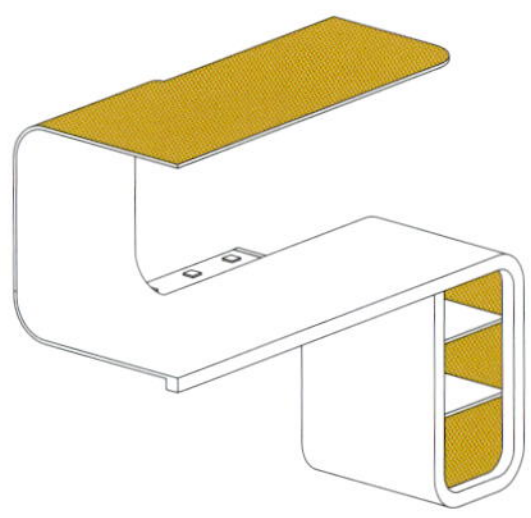

Desk with overhead shelf (lights mounted on underside of plane)

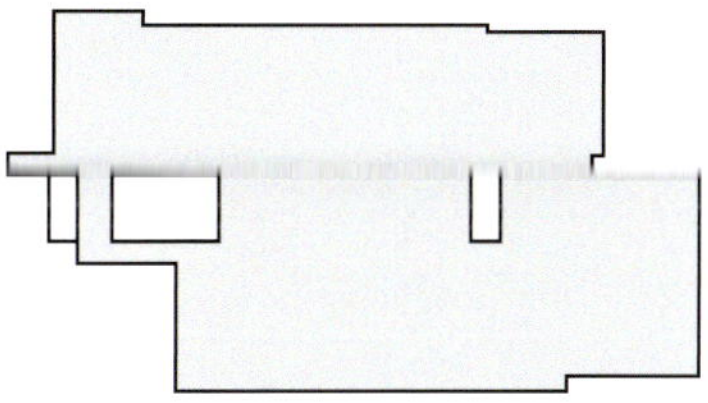

Work

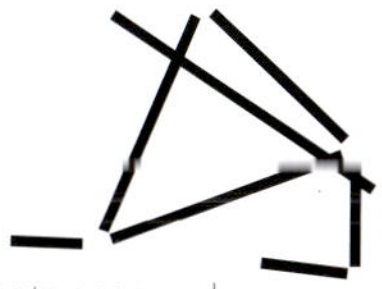

Connection to open work area neighborhoods

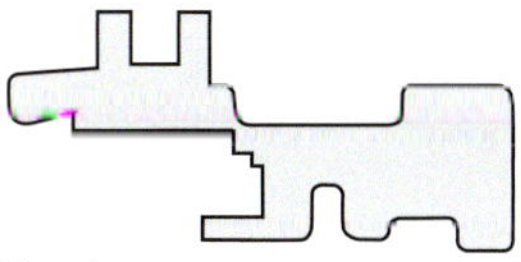

Closed program

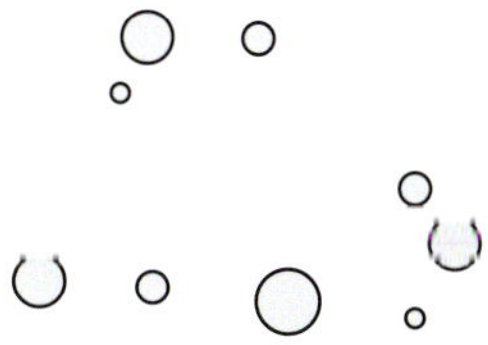

Destination: lighting clouds neighborhoods

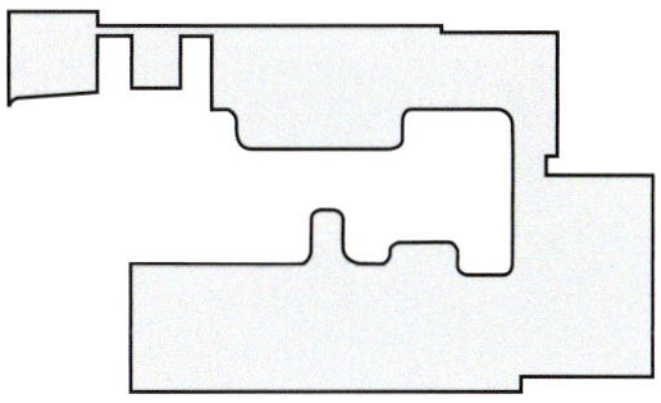

Open work area

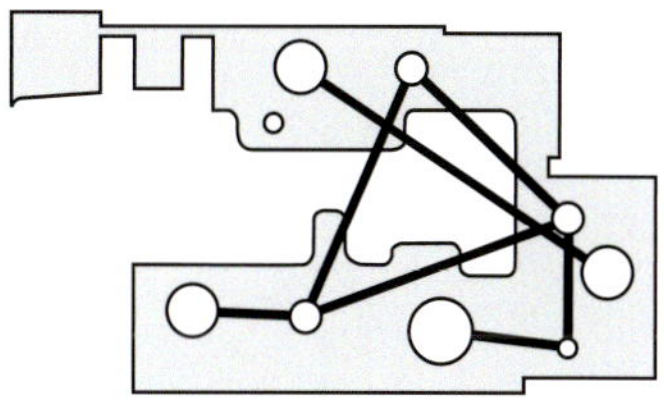

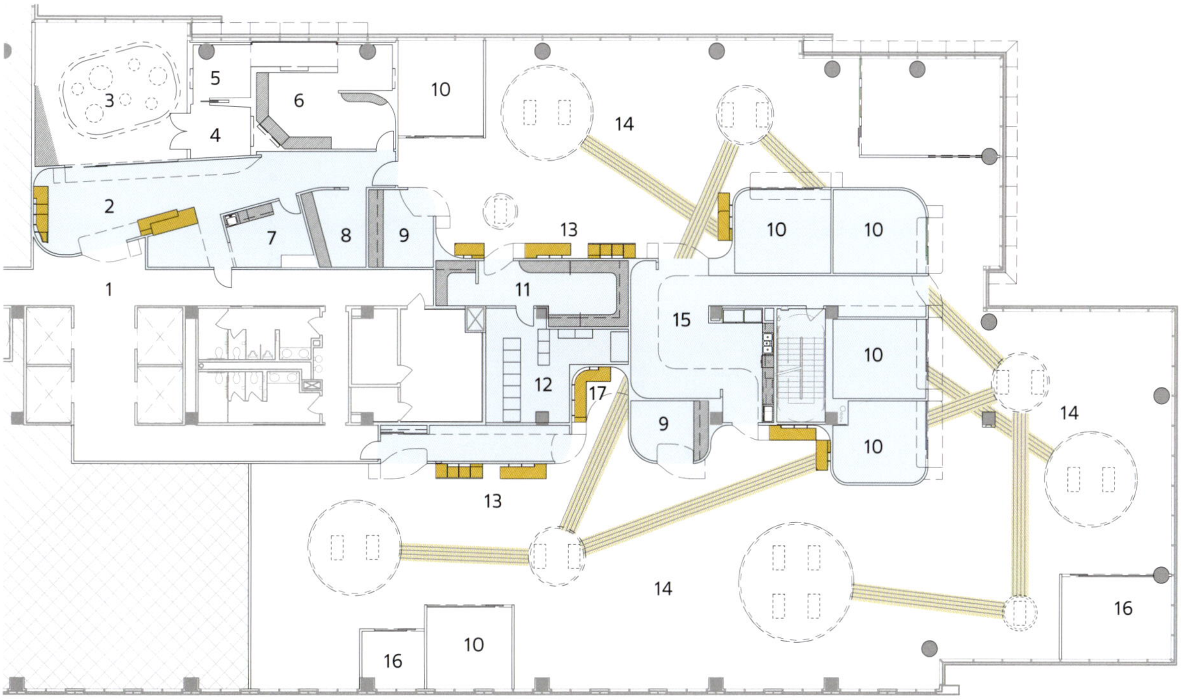

Floor plan

1 Entry
2 Reception
3 Conference
4 Reset room
5 Demo room
6 Collaboration room
7 Mail room
8 Visitor offices
9 Work room
10 Private offices
11 IT room
12 IT storage
13 Hoteling wall
14 Open offices
15 Breakroom
16 Small conference rooms
17 Lounge

Bamboo flooring

Lighting fixtures

Verafin

Verafin Inc. is a fraud detection technology and anti-money laundering software subsidiary of Nasdaq, Inc. based in St. John's. The company originally took space in one of our speculative value office projects in the Newfoundland building; it was the first of its kind in that market. The company leased the first two floors, totaling 50,000 square feet. The company wanted an inspiring and collaborative environment for collective training in a social environment expected by their employee demographic, much like any tech company. Timing took the design process through a side tour of alternative configurations forced on the client by COVID-19. This evolved into a silver lining of sorts as the prolonged uncertainty of what a post-COVID workplace might look like allowed us to fully engage with Verafin's culture over a period of time.

We were enmeshed deeply in the deliberation the leadership had about how training and work should be configured ideally and how to adapt that to the circumstantial. In the final configuration we trimmed the square footage down to 23,000 square feet by carving a two-story space out of the floor plates. Employees stay connected while positioned at open bench-style workstations down the center axis of the building. The narrow width of the building floor plate allows for a juxtaposition of view planes with city views out through the clusters of treetops facing the opposite direction. Frameless glass corners and transom windows allow natural light into the meeting rooms toward the center of the workspace. Break-out spaces are integrated with AV/IT systems and offer employees a nomadic style of working. An employee lunchroom, telephone rooms, and washrooms are centrally located on each floor with environmental graphic icons as a wayfinding method throughout the office. The space also included a 200-seat assembly and training room.

Harsh Parmar
How Can I Help You?
Harsh Parmar
How Can I Help You?

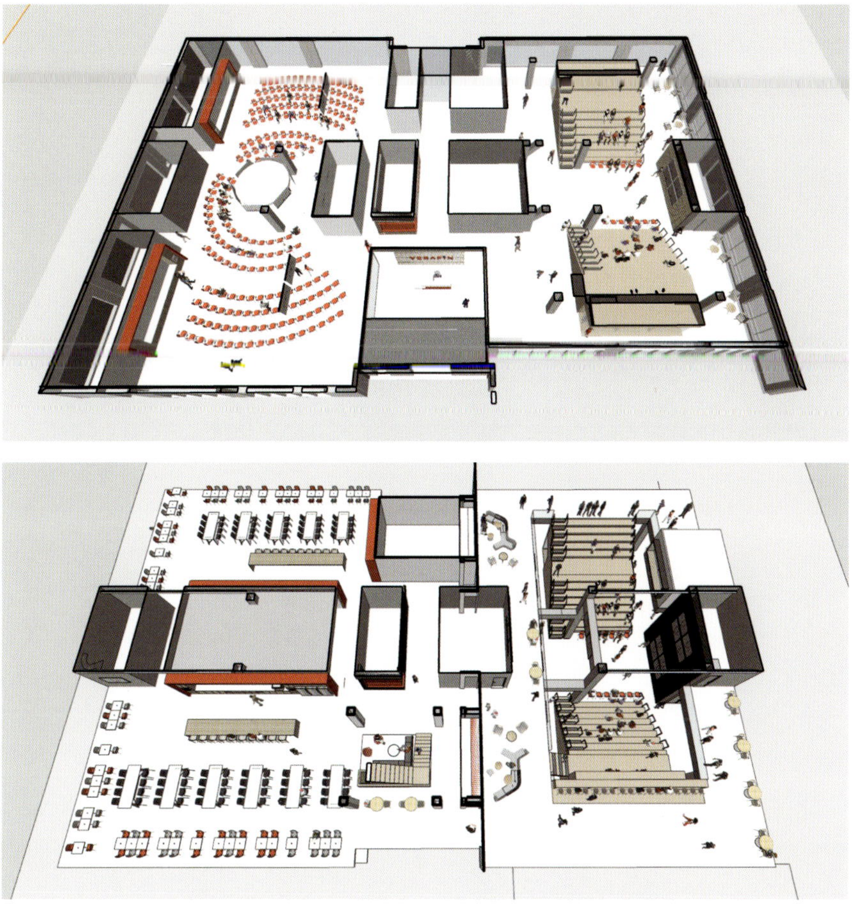

Alternative layout concepts

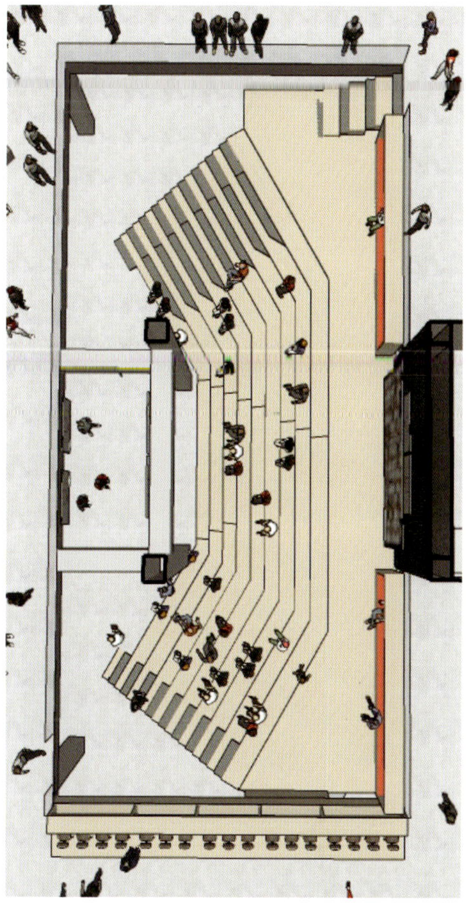

Seating and stage plan

Interview

University of Houston professor and author Donna Kacmar, FAIA spoke with CEO / Creative Director Jeffrey Brown, FAIA in early 2024 about the origins of the firm through the lens of twenty-five years of history and his thoughts on the practice of architecture in general.

This conversation is edited for clarity, brevity and format.

Donna: Thank you for spending time with me today.

Jeffrey: If we don't keep it loose, I will start laughing. But, I always enjoy our "from time to time" conversations. My first memory of our meeting was in the dean's office in 2000. You were reading your student evaluation at the mailbox and you were frustrated if not agitated; and I had thrown mine in the trash. You pointed out to me that those were the student evaluations and I said, "I never read them." Asking students for an evaluation during final reviews invites retribution as far as I could tell. I read one of them that said, "Professor is not very familiar with theory" or something like that and so I just stopped reading them. Then we started to have conversations. We have pretty close birthdays, and are about the same age. You had started your practice as had I mine. I knew your work from design awards, including your original home, and had read your Victor Lundy book, and *Big Little Houses*. That's why I was so grateful for you to agree to do this, because that conversation started between two people starting out about the same time and continues on to where we are now in our careers.

Donna: How did the firm evolve after the other founding partner retired? If he had the business focus and you were focused on design, did you learn more about running the business after he left?

Jeffrey: We had a great succession plan when we designed the company and it worked all the way up until Joe retired. We were born in 1999, and blessed with 2001 right after that so nothing to do for a while and the minute we recovered from that then about 2008 we had the Great Recession and then many people miss this around the country but in 2014–2015 there was the "Shale Gale" recession in Houston where we started. So, he was retiring kind of at a point of beginning. Once I bought Joe out, I became the sole owner of a company with a structure that was siloed in that the partners in Washington, D.C. and Denver were partners with me in kind of a franchise structure of Powers Brown Architecture. I ran the company as originally organized for about two years after Joe retired, then during 2019 reorganized it. We had a great toolbox but we really moved to having a Home Depot-level of tool chest post-reorganization; we had a lot more resources. We brought all the partners together in a single partnership. It made the company easier to grow and I have since tripled the size of the company.

Donna: Do you have any strategies for checking in with your firm or practice and adjusting the organization that allows some flexibility?

Jeffrey: We are able to shape career scenarios or office culture scenarios around an individual or a class of people. For example, we were very hesitant to say that we're "onshoring" in St. John's so we developed programs that allow growth beyond the internal training program called PBA University where they can advance. Toronto is a lot more like the US, it's mostly architects there. I think another part of your question is how my role changed. I had to move from being Creative Director to being CEO. We're working our way through that right now. It's been four or five years and we have an annual summit meeting and a large part of the discussions we have are that as I move down towards 50 percent ownership and below that, are there things that I'm doing as CEO that I can offload now to the folks who are buying the company and get back in a role where my heart is and my skill set is. I'm trying to evolve a little to accept I'm always going to have to be a bit of a CEO.

Donna: How do you make personal adjustments and find ways to both support the firm and support a person who's done so much for your firm? How are you allowing the company to adjust? I imagine it might be difficult, after growing the practice and shifting it multiple times, to know allow others to be in charge?

Jeffrey: You accept it's going to change naturally. Joe didn't have to accept the changes I made after he retired; the current partners have to. A good example is that our commitment to the AIA 2030 Initiative, which we signed onto with a great plan for implementation. I heard a great talk at the AIA, where a panelist on 2030 noted, "Your spec book is your checkbook." We came back and are making the specification optional carbon-zero. It's been a project we started last year and are just finishing it up right now. Our plan for 2030, which not all the partners agree with but accept, is now woven into our culture. So, you make changes not everybody agrees with but they are going to follow that leadership and it gets woven into the culture. It makes it easier to let go.

Donna: How will you feel when you only have 5 percent ownership? How do you transition yourself for that?

Jeffrey: When I took it over as CEO I didn't have a choice. That was the next logical step or the thing to do. I learned when I was deeply immersed in the business is you have to, if you're selling the stock to somebody and you have any moral/ethical boundary that's larger than just yourself, that you must make sure you leave it valuable to them as well. I'm now going back down to becoming an employee; it's my partners, job to take that over. That makes it a lot easier to become an employee again; to feel like, instead of doing what I really wanted to indulge in, you did the hard work to implement progress. Then it's a lot easier to say, "Look, there you go. Here's the car, put it on the track and off you go." You don't feel too bad about it because you did your duty.

Donna: Can you define practice versus the work so as you transition from ownership of the company and the practice of the company, perhaps you are moving more towards the work again? How do you distinguish between the practice and the work?

Jeffrey: We had one of the most productive discussions we've had in years about that at our summit meeting. The creative discussion we had this time is better than we've had in years from this point of reference: we've had so many new partners and partner-track people and business challenges and the pandemic that we focused on the "practice" of architecture, trying to stay alive and keep jobs. But because of that imbalance, I've been grumbling for eighteen months that if we're not careful, we're going to lose our way here, we're going to be a mere "business". We're going to be a thing that is about efficiency and profit extraction and all the terms of art like "value add" that you hear in the marketplace, not the studio.

I wanted to get us back to "What are we if we're an architecture firm, but we're not an architecture business?" I had a series of prompts like "Are we part of something bigger?", "Is there a through-line from project to project in terms of ideas?" And when ideas sit at the table that defines purpose, what is the message? Adam Gazzaley in *The Distracted Mind* tells us that you never multi-task; your mind doesn't multi-task, it task-switches. We had a big task-switch moment this February in those discussions about what we do and how we used to do it. Part of it is just heuristics in terms of how we identify the things we are willing to take a loss or a risk on.

We agreed in that conversation on where we had missed some opportunities where we used to make our design reputation. I think it touched everybody a little bit. We've already noticed an uptick in the number of projects that get to the core design team to balance the commodity aspects of a practice like ours.

Donna: In your essay, you talk about the mundane or the background buildings. I might call these ordinary buildings, but can you talk a little bit about the importance of those types of buildings and how they can be pushed forward?

Jeffrey: I can tell you exactly where I was when I began to think about the mundane building types. I was standing on the stage of the Igloo Factory on I-10 [on the outskirts of Houston] with my wife and we were up on stage with a lot of other people at the factory opening. A woman approached, as the owners were welcoming everyone to the plant, and said, "I just wanted to thank you." There were tears in her eyes and she said, "You saved our jobs. They were going to move all our jobs to China". I thought to myself, I didn't have anything to do with saving your job, but it hit me how impactful these mundane projects are beyond "design." That was the beginning of thinking nonstop about all these mundane buildings, which I wrote about later in Neglected Territory.

Everyday and everydayness and anything that has really been written about it isn't about everyday architecture. Its talking about the everyday as a source for the avant-garde to mine rather than interpreting the mundane it its own terms like commodification or the market. Frampton, in his *Theory of Critical Regionalism* says, "How does modern architecture become infected by local climates and local building technologies?". Venturi et. al in *Learning from Las Vegas*, observed something in mundane building types and how they are organized and aggregated, but then complexity and contradiction spin off into a kind of avant-garde theory: a duck's a duck, and a shed's a shed. It's understudied and I'm not sure I'm capable enough or smart enough to study this kind of thing with a foothold in only practice. I will tell you it is way too hard to pitch a book when you are not an academic.

Donna: Can we talk a little bit about that difference between creativity, originality, and innovation?

Jeffrey: Colin Rowe wrote an essay called "Ideas, Talent, Poetics". There are architects with great ideas, like John Hejduk; there are architects who have talent, like Richard Meier; and then from time to time you get somebody that brings that all together as poetics like Ando. There is an odd parallel in creativity and originality. There's way too much of a premium in architectural design studios in school on originality. Very little is original; it's hard to do; impossible to teach I think; but you can definitely teach creativity. Otherwise, the notion of doing what you can, with what you have, where you are in that moment. Creativity is often the reorganization of things that are already there.

Innovation to me is a little bit different. Innovation has a technical dimension to it you could map on to either of those concepts. You could map it onto originality but you could also map it onto creativity, which is what we do. My patent is about that. There is often potential that has not been juiced out of the "same old thing" which is why it continuously appeals to the same old group, but if you innovate within it, creativity occurs. There's nothing original about my patent beyond what it takes to get a patent, but it is an innovation inside of a system about which people have said, "That works great, we don't need to change anything about it."

Innovation can invade either one of those concepts but I think it's much harder for it to invade originality; it's easier for it to invade creativity.

Donna: How do you balance your leadership and collaboration within the firm to allow this kind of bottom-up innovation?

Jeffrey: We try to build a culture around it. For one thing, you have to make it visible around the company, so if you look on our website there is a section called Excursus where we are continuing to design but we're not drawing anything. It's divided into three areas and I'm the major protagonist for Design. It includes our resiliency side, that's Jesse (Hunt) who runs our sustainability group. Jeanette (Shaw) runs our practice group regarding QA/QC. She is currently the first female president of the CQEC (Construction Quality Executives Council) which is really a contractor-driven organization. She's got this whole program on how you educate architects inside of a firm and how you deal with quality.

Donna: I really enjoyed what you had to say about the differences between a starchitect versus an influencer versus a master architect. I'm wondering, as a personal note, are there other master architects you look to, including Ando and Piano, whom you already mentioned? Are there other architects at the top of your list?

Jeffrey: Zumthor. I believe I own all of his collected works and I'm not sure if I love any of his buildings but it's just amazing dedication to process. He is in direct lineage with Carlo Scarpa. Scarpa made just a few buildings but everything is crafted in them, it's that sort of medieval overlap of "the guild craft of architecture" which we don't have any more, or you get firms like Kieran and Timberlake who will talk about mass customization. Not realty close.

Donna: Great! Here's another kind of singular question: what are you reading or listening to right now?

Jeffrey: *Ninth Street Women* by Mary Gabriel. What I like about *that book* is that it describes that moment when the center of gravity shifted in painting and in art and in avant-garde thinking from Europe to the United States. Abstract expressionism, Pollock on down. It is actually about the women behind that movement. Otherwise you would have never heard of Jackson Pollock without Lee Krasner. Paradoxically this movement is a rare case of originality. Parallel to that is Louis Menand's book *On Freedom* that's looking at all of the other avant-garde disciplinary movements; abstract expressionism, but also deep language theory and all of the ideas that were born during the Cold War and in a very tight period of time. It takes what's happened in *Ninth Street Women* and puts it into the context of language theory and cultural theories and how they manifest and populate. There was a very famous photograph exhibition called *The Family of Man*. It was taken to all the World Fairs. When you look at what's behind it and what's left out of it, given the politics of the time, it shows how imperfectly they were able to use the structures that they invented, especially around language or culture, anthropology and so forth. But radiated by what was acceptable, the market adjusted cultural findings. Those are two of the big things I've been reading that's influential in a sense.

As far as listening to, I got caught up on a podcast, "I would prefer not to", mentioned in my essay, around how to choose not to do projects. It's counterintuitive and I became obsessed with listening to it. You're listening to this interlocutor interviewing people talking about why they won't do certain projects, why they turned this down or why they started a project and didn't finish it. I became fascinated by it.

Donna: Is there anything that you'd like to talk about that speaks to architectural education and anything you personally, or as a firm leader, need changed, or a possibility that you see that isn't being addressed?

Jeffrey: I substituted for Dean Joe Mashburn on a panel at Texas Tech some time back. It was one of those deals where you are sitting on the stage and the lights are so bright that you can't even see anybody. A question came around, "What do students need to be doing to be better prepared for practice?" I did what Dave Hickey would do and turned the question upside down. I said the real issue is practice isn't ready for the students! Practice is clinging to this old-fashioned guild notion that "these people don't know anything" so let's suppress their wages. The AIA has reported this in detail. Then you look out at the vast level of mediocrity in what I describe as the marketecture business and you say to yourself, "Well maybe the problem in this equation of students to practice is practice not education, maybe your mediocre work is due to the fact that you're not taking advantage of a person who's at their creative peak the minute they graduate."

Donna: It's much easier to look at what they can't do, perhaps we should look at what they are bringing. I think younger architects and designers can bring something completely different to the work of more experienced architects.

Jeffrey: I can just tell you, empirically, that always the best young employees we have are the people that are hired specifically to work on the design team. They're always successful because they're doing what they're best at in this peak part of their career. But it also goes back to my exploration of the schism in practice itself and how, or if, it silently is entering new territory without even knowing it.

Rear View

This afterword is meant to honor work that many, if not all, firms do not show you. This book has been a tour by sample of our signature works, not previously published. But an everyday practice like ours openly engages the commodity side of architecture, such as it applies to *building types*. There has been much ink spilled on how and why architects must avoid commodification, some of that writing by Kenneth Frampton, perhaps nowhere better consolidated than in his anthology, *Commodification and Spectacle in Architecture*. He reminds us of the post-Marxist critique of capitalism in architecture and the dangers of architecture succumbing to the economic determinism aiding the popular taste of the free market. It's a concern right out of Greenburg's notion of kitsch from the postwar definition of the avant-garde in abstract expressionist painting. Both of them set up a position opposing commodification in general, Frampton specifically in architecture.

But the building types of architecture ***are*** commodified, simplified for easy consumption and common use, and traded as assets, meeting the most basic definitions of "commodities." Particularly, warehouses, office buildings, and certain aspects of for-rent housing. While starchitects are constantly riding the drift of the latest style as it applies to various special building types, often generating what we will be told is *an all-new style*, the everyday architect has both the responsibility and opportunity of finding design methods and processes on neglected building types. The kind of projects and buildings types that offer very little surface and floor area for invention with budget constraints set by banks and investors. Work done for the aesthetically distracted client, who avoids any controversial design statement that may hinder the building as an investment, as an asset to sell. Isn't this as much a condition of "cultural expression" as much as "museum architecture." Isn't ***any*** "cultural content," even one derived from the forces of commodification, a project for design operations? The following collage illustrates our commitment to the problems of all architecture. The acceptance of design opportunity, even in small parts of large anonymous projects, buildings actually occupied by humans doing their jobs, and perhaps taking pride in where they do them. It represents 100 unique designs for the corners of warehouses ranging from 150,000 to over 1,000,000 square feet. The designs were done over a thirty-month period. They represent the same problem over and over and yet have been subject to internal design strategies and processes that allow them to be unique to site and purpose. Each project is "real" to the extent that by the publication of this book, they will all be constructed.

Acknowledgments

Making the architecture we have included in this book, particularly in trying to show works not previously published and covering a span of twenty-five years, involves the efforts of many individuals. Former and current employees, partners, and collaborators alongside our consultants and specialty advisors are all important to us, with a special acknowledgment to photographers Dror Baldinger, FAIA, and Mark Johnson. We, collectively, would of course not have the opportunities to work together in various ways without a gracious and engaged client group. We will inevitably miss some names and collaborators, but every effort has gone into getting as accurate as our records affirm, thus apologies to those accidentally overlooked.

Much of the credit in keeping this effort on our side goes to Vianney Gonzalez and Desta Kimmel. This effort went on consistently for nearly a year on our side with a few caesuras followed by frantic recalibration and research, adding to the effort of editing, higher resolution image hunting, and so on. Logan Springer, John Taylor, Mark Delpilar, Mike Fecco as well.

The opportunity provided by the IMAGES team to publish yet a third book focused on our work and research is not something we take for granted. Thanks to Honorine for the offer, Ryan for the design, and both Gina and Jeanette for their patience in editing what is definitely not a coffee-table book, which was our greatest fear.

The essay in this book and theme of our practice is nothing new to the many lateral helpers in this effort. Long conversations with Randal Hall PhD, over many years, on the iterative and evolving themes around which we have organized the practice and our own understanding of it, exposed to the gamma rays of an outsider's critique and queries, to say nothing of his and patient editing, are catalytic. Having colleagues from the academy provides a different but no less important baseline. In this matter Donna Kacmar, FAIA has been there all along. Sometimes dormant, always active when it really matters. We have much in common including our career timeline and I often wondered if I had followed her path academically just what that would have looked like. Thanks to them both. Of Stephen Sharpe all I can say is we are lucky. Stephen was kind enough to follow us in his twelve years as publisher of *Texas Architect* magazine. He knows our work, but more importantly he is a journalist rather than an architecture critic and always asked just slightly different questions. We thank him for taking on one more assignment and are lucky to have him.

If an academic critic/friend is important, so is an industry outsider. That role is played for us by Mitch Bloomquist, Executive Director of the TCA. Mitch is an architect and a designer and a critic, yet lives in the world of trade associations and navigates the neglected territory of the market place, not of ideas as much as commodities. I deeply value his ability to bridge worlds. While much between us has focused on tilt-wall, as a reader and critic of all I wrote for him and for others, he has been a clear honest voice, sometimes less than flattering and thus crucial.

My partners need singling out in so far as my transition back and forth from our Creative Director to our CEO often has us standing in the overlap of a great Venn diagram, trying to take a philosophical position on a business matter. I appreciate both the latitude and the grace they extend, almost always.

I was led to Houston twenty-six years ago by my wife to transition from practice into academia. Houston, it turns out, had different plans as it is one of the most welcoming and entrepreneurial cities in America. Soon I was doing both teaching and running my own small office in partnership with Joe Powers. While Joe is now retired, his ideas, plans, and standards are still operational in the firm. And to my other Joe, former dean Joe Mashburn, FAIA, solar architect. My time with him during hospice two Julys ago was peppered with him encouraging me to talk publicly about our private conversations, which I have done now. His thesis was that I was saying and describing what most architects think. We will see if he was right.

Finally, I am grateful for my wife, Hether, and my daughter, Aelish, and all those afternoons watching the play of the setting sun on the marsh in total silence together and separately, focused in congress.

Project Credits

Private

Frank's (pages 28–35)

Team Joe Powers, Scott Thompson, Jeanette Shaw, John Cadenhead, Jaon Gilbert, Ashley Elks, Garrett Taylor, Trupti Mehta, Vanessa Sotil, Steve Oliver, Phin Stubbs

Engineering *[Structural]* Pinnacle Structural Engineers; *[MEP]* DBR Engineering; *[Civil]* Ward, Getz & Associates

Landscaping Wong & Associates

General contractor Gamma Construction

Photography Mark Johnson

Pavilion (pages 36–37)

Team Jeffrey Brown, Mark Delpilar, John Taylor

Seismic (pages 38–41)

Team Jeffrey Brown, Bruce Walck, AJ Breneman, John Cadenhead, Jeanette Shaw, Barbara Novoa, Huy Bui, Alaina Dixon, Megan Ebert, Ron Fuertes, Steve Oliver, Jim Whitehead

Engineering *[Structural]* JQ Engineering; *[MEP]* Redding Lindon Burr (KCI Technologies); *[Civil]* TAC Engineering, LLC

Landscaping Clark Condon Associates

General contractor Rosenberger Construction

Photography Dror Baldinger (pages 38 right, 39–41), courtesy of Powers Brown Architecture (page 38 left)

Public

W & J (pages 44–51)

Team Jeffrey Brown, Reinaldo Venancio, Karla Contreras-Buquet, Samaneh Eslami, Randy Karn, Steve Oliver, Eduardo Sanchez, Chelsea Serrano-Piche, Sara Soleimanzadeh

Engineering *[Structural]* Dally + Associates; *[MEP]* DBR Engineering; *[Civil]* Widmer Engineering

General contractor Mosites Construction Company

Photography Dror Baldinger

Sunnyside (pages 52–53)

Team Jeffrey Brown, AJ Breneman, John Cadenhead

Hillel (pages 54–59)

Team Reinaldo Venancio, Stefan Dytrt, Randy Karn, Amanda Ragan, Stephanie Westrick, Karla Contreras-Buquet, Ryohei Saito, Eduardo Sanchez, Taylor Plumley, Isabelle Russell, Ngan Dinh, Steven Saltzman, Steve Oliver

Engineering *[Structural]* SK&A; *[Mechanical]* GPI Engineering; *[Civil]* Wiles Mensh Corporation

Landscaping Wiles Mensh Corporation

LEED Sustainable Design Consulting

General contractor Consigli

Photography Chris Spielmann

Highlands (pages 60-61)

Team Joe Powers, Jeffrey Brown, Jewels Carter, Ron Fuertes, Paul Butterfras, Alanna Strachan, Steve Oliver, Cary Els, Tammy Holmstrom

Engineering *[Civil]* Bury + Partners *[Structural]* Haynes Whaley *[MEP]* CHPA *[Landscape]* Asakura Robinson

Photography Dror Baldinger

Park

Roy Kelly (pages 64–75)

Team Jeffrey Brown, Bruce Walck, Nazir Khalfe, AJ Breneman, Jeanette Shaw, John Cadenhead, Amna Ansari, David Robinson, Stacy Driver, Ada Ho, Paul Butterfras, Raul Medrano, Roberth Mohler, Alaina Dixon, Angela Mayer, Ron Fuertes, Steve Oliver

Engineering *[Structural/Civil]* Walter P. Moore; *[MEP]* Infrastructure Associates

Landscape Clark Condon Associates

General contractor Harvey Builders

Photography Dror Baldinger

Galveston (pages 76–83)

Team Jeffrey Brown, Bruce Walck, Jeanette Shaw, John Cadenhead, David Robinson, Rudy Pagsanjan, Chelsea Serrano-Piche, Ashley Elks, Steve Oliver

Engineering *[Structural]* Rogers Moore; *[MEP]* Infrastructure Associates; *[Civil]* Walter P. Moore

General contractor Turner Construction Company

Photography Dror Baldinger (pages 78–83), Mark Johnson (page 76)

UHG (pages 84–93)

Team Jeffrey Brown, Bruce Walck, Jeanette Shaw, Amna Ansari, Stacy Driver, Steve Oliver, Ada Ho, Angela Mayer, Huy Bui

Engineering *[Structural]* Haynes Whaley Associates; *[Electrical]* E3 Electric; *[Plumbing]* Elite Plumbing Corp.; *[Civil]* Walter P. Moore

General contractor EE Reed Construction

Photography Mark Johnson

Home

Arabella (pages 96–103)

Team Jeffrey Brown, Bruce Walck, Jeanette Shaw, John Cadenhead, Carl Magill, Rudy Pagsanjan, Branden Leger, Garrett Taylor, Ramon Ramos, Shawn Adams, Elizabeth Longstaff, Steve Oliver

Engineering *[Structural]* SCA Consulting Engineers; *[Electrical]* Hargrave Electric; *[Mechanical/Plumbing]* Kilgore Industries; *[Civil]* Brooks & Sparks, Inc.

General contractor GT Leach Constructors, LLC

Photography Dror Baldinger (pages 97, 98, 101, 103 top), Mark Johnson (pages 100, 102, 103 bottom)

Innovation (pages 104–105)

Team Jeffrey Brown, Bruce Walck, John Cadenhead

Marlowe (pages 106–13)

Team Jeffrey Brown, Bruce Walck, AJ Breneman, Jeanette Shaw, Kristen Stapper, Carl Magill, John Cadenhead, Cesar Diaz, Branden Leger, Ramon Ramos, Derrick Kately, Steve Oliver

Engineering *[Structural]* SCA Consulting Engineers; *[MEP]* The PDC Group; *[Civil]* Brooks & Sparks, Inc.

General contractor GT Leach Constructors, LLC

Photography Mark Johnson

Stay

Hemisfair (pages 116–17)

Team Jeffrey Brown, Bruce Walck, Scott Thompson, Jeanette Shaw, Logan Springer, Mike Fecco

Engineering *[Structural]* Lundry & Franke Engineers; *[MEP]* DBR Engineering; *[Civil]* Pape-Dawson Engineers

Landscaping TBG Partners

General contractor Jordan Foster Construction

Thompson (pages 118–29)

Team Jeffrey Brown, Scott Thompson, Jeanette Shaw, Kristen Stapper, John Cadenhead, Rudy Pagsanjan, Garrett Taylor, Branden Leger, Katy Broussard, Stacy Driver, Jamal Banan, Soheb Javaid, Chelsea Caldwell, Diana Rivas, Ashley Elks, Lindsay Bench, Alaina Dixon

Engineering *[Structural]* SCA Consulting Engineers; *[MEP]* DBR Engineering; *[Civil]* Pape Dawson Engineers

Interior design Mariana Valero, Amass & G

Landscaping SWA Group

General contractor Jordan Foster Construction

Photography Dror Baldinger

Breeze (pages 130–31)

Team Jeffrey Brown, Nazir Khalfe, Logan Springer, Jeanette Shaw

Recycle

Stratford (pages 134–35)

Team Jeffrey Brown, AJ Breneman, Jeanette Shaw, Ashley Elks, Ada Ho, Ron Fuertes, Steve Oliver

Engineering *[MEP]* Bansal & Associates

General Contractor EE Reed Construction

Photography Dror Baldinger

Red Gap (pages 136–37)

Team Joe Powers, Jeffrey Brown, Bruce Walck, Megan Ebert, Mei Zhang

Photography Geoffrey Lyons

POST (pages 138–43)

Team Jeffrey Brown, Scott Thompson, Jeanette Shaw, Rudy Pagsanjan, Austin Sandel, Jesse Hunt, Philip Elia, Jay Kim, Myra Peralta, Lamon Roberts Jr., Ashley Loftin, Carl Magill

Design OMA

Engineering *[Structural]* IMEG Corp; *[MEP]* DBR Engineering

Lighting Dot Dash

Landscaping Hoerr Schaudt

General contractor Harvey Builders

Photography Kat Ambrose (page 138), Lovett Commercial (page 139); Leonid Furmansky (pages 140 bottom, 142, 143); courtesy of Powers Brown Architecture (pages 140 top, 141)

Systems

MEDDNet™ (pages 146–49)

Team Jeffrey Brown, Logan Springer, John Taylor

Engineering *[Structural]* LJB Inc.; *[Medical]* Leo A Daly

Mall (pages 150–53)

Team Jeffrey Brown, Nazir Khalfe, Stacy Driver

Compact

Intermarine (pages 156–63)

Team Jeffrey Brown, Jeanette Shaw, John Cadenhead, Rudy Pagsanjan, Lisa Robins, Christina Zeibak, Elizabeth Longstaff, Steve Oliver

Engineering *[Structural]* Dally + Associates; *[MEP]* Brazos Valley Engineering, Inc.; *[Civil]* TAC Engineering, LLC

General contractor Rosenberger Construction

Photography Mark Johnson

BMO (pages 164–65)

Team Jeffrey Brown, Bruce Walck, John Holland, John Cadenhead, Madalena Cheung, Joanna Crabtree, Peter Jackson, Sara Sexton, Babak Gholizadeh, Shea MacDougall, Tristan Solis, Amanda King

Engineering *[Structural]* Morrison Hershfield; *[MEP]* RAN Engineering; *[Civil]* Pinnacle Engineering

Photography courtesy of Powers Brown Architecture

Jewel (pages 166–67)

Team Jeffrey Brown, Logan Springer, Nazir Khalfe

Gatehouse (pages 168–69)

Team Jeffrey Brown, Reinaldo Venancio, Joe Powers, Ricardo Hendi, Randy Karn, Matthew Stephens, Kimberly Belfour, Steve Oliver

Engineering *[Structural]* Structural Engineering Group; *[MEP]* DBR Engineering; *[Civil]* Rinker Design Associates, P.C.

General contractor Bognet Construction

Photography Mark Johnson

Pinch (pages 170–73)

Team Jeffrey Brown, Joe Powers, AJ Breneman, Jeanette Shaw, John Cadenhead, David Robinson, Ashley Elks, Steve Oliver

Engineering *[Structural]* Pinnacle Structural Engineers; *[Civil]* TAC Engineering, LLC

General contractor Burton Construction

Photography Dror Baldinger

Tilt

Monument (pages 176–83)

Team Jeffrey Brown, Jeanette Shaw, John Cadenhead, Matthew Stephens

Engineering *[Structural]* Pinnacle Structural Engineers; *[Civil]* Ward, Getz & Associates

General contractor EE Reed Construction

Photography Mark Johnson

Arch-Con (pages 184–85)

Team Jeffrey Brown, Scott Thompson, Christina Zeibak, Myra Peralta, Sara Sexton

Engineering *[Structural]* Pinnacle Structural Engineers; *[Electrical/Plumbing]* DBR Engineering; *[Mechanical]* Graves Mechanical

General contractor Arch-Con

Photography Michael Craft

GeoForm™ (pages 186–89)

Team Jeffrey Brown, John Cadenhead, John Taylor

Woodlands (pages 190–93)

Team Jeffrey Brown, Nazir Khalfe, AJ Breneman, Jeanette Shaw, Cesar Diaz, Rudy Pagsanjan, Rahl Medrano, Nicole Cadenhead, Steve Oliver, Jonathon Matle, Phin Stubbs, Jesse Hunt, Jamal Banan

Engineering *[Structural]* LJB Inc.; *[MEP]* Wylie Consulting Engineers; *[Civil]* WGA

LEED Apollo BBC

Parking Walter P. Moore

Landscaping SWA Group

General contractor EE Reed Construction

Photography Mark Johnson

CUC (pages 194–99)

Team Bryant Mazzetti, Lauren Amber Prestenbach, Justin McCarthy, Mike Fecco, Garrett Taylor, Brandon Byrd, Milan Manurung, Natalie Mediate

Engineering *[Structural]* LJB Inc.; *[MEP]* Jordan & Skala Engineers; *[Civil]* Kimley-Horn & Associates, Inc.

General contractor Adolfson & Peterson, Inc.

Photography Brad Nicol

Rent

Hamilton (pages 202–205)

Team Jeffrey Brown, Bruce Walck, Logan Springer, John Taylor

Sandrock (pages 206–207)

Team Logan Springer, John Taylor

Campus (pages 208–209)

Team Jeffrey Brown, John Cadenhead

Ivy (pages 210–11)

Team Jeffrey Brown, John Cadenhead, Mike Fecco, Stacy Driver

Churchill (pages 212–13)

Team Jeffrey Brown, Bruce Walck, John Holland, Jeanette Shaw, Peter Jackson, Madalena Cheung, Stacy Driver, Paul Valesky, Jay-Lord Agliam, Alex Barnes, Ashley Jordan, Zachary Layman, Sara Sexton, Destiny Pardy, Amanda King

Engineering *[Structural]* Design Works Engineering; *[MEP]* Design Works Engineering; *[Civil]* Pinnacle Engineering

General contractor Allied Construction Management

Photography courtesy of Powers Brown Architecture

Inside

Summit (pages 216–21)

Team Lauren Amber Prestenbach, Garrett Taylor, Tessa Fay, Addie Bush, Jill Dau Klug, Nicole Potter, Natalie Mediate, Jennifer Schmidt

Engineering *[Structural]* Peak Engineering; *[MEP]* IMEG

General contractor RAND Construction

Photography Brad Nicol

Logica (pages 222–25)

Team Jeffrey Brown, AJ Breneman, Jeanette Shaw, Barbara Novoa, Alaina Dixon, David Robinson, Amna Ansari, Megan Ebert, Ashley Elks, Jim Halloran, Steve Oliver

Engineering *[Mechanical]* Graves Mechanical; *[Electrical]* Melton Electric; *[Plumbing]* CE *Anderson Inc.*

General contractor Harvey Builders

Photography Dror Baldinger

Verafin (pages 226–29)

Team Bruce Walck, Stefan Dytrt, Sara Sexton, Stephanie Westrick, Colby Farrell, Marisa Vinson, Tessa Fay, Amanda King

Engineering *[Structural]* Jewer Bailey Consultants; *[Mechanical/Electrical]* Jewer Bailey Consultants

General contractor Allied Construction Management

Photography Andrew Garland

Recognition

Selected Design Awards

2023 American Institute of Architects Houston, Design Awards: Architecture Greater than 50,000 Square Feet: POST Houston, Houston, Texas (with OMA)

2023 Texas Society of Architects, Design Award: POST Houston, Houston, Texas (with OMA)

2023 Houston Business Journal Landmark Awards Industrial: Empire West Phase II, Brookshire, Texas

2023 Preservation Houston Good Brick Award: Printhouse, Houston, Texas

2022 Third Place Overall: IIDA Product Runway

2022 Award of Merit NAIOP DC|Maryland: George Washington University, Hillel, Washington, D.C.

2022 Award of Excellence, NAIOP DC|Maryland: University of Maryland at College Park 4600 River Road, Riverside, Maryland

2022 PSMJ 2022 Circle of Excellence Award

2022 Tilt-Up Achievement Award: 8000 Redstone Gateway, Huntsville, Alabama

2022 Houston Business Journal Landmark Awards Rehabilitation and Renovation, POST Houston, Houston, Texas

2022 American Concrete Institute (Maryland Chapter) Excellence in Concrete: Matan Westview South Business Park, Frederick, Maryland

2021 Tilt-Up Achievement Excellence Award: 8600 Redstone Gateway, Huntsville, Alabama

2021 Tilt-Up Achievement Award: Hines Empower Phase II, Houston, Texas

2021 ENR Baltimore Regional Best Projects Awards, Small Project Under $10 Million: Hillel at the George Washington University, Gewirz Center, Washington, D.C.

2021 Houston Business Journal Landmark Awards Industrial: Parc 59, Houston, Texas

2020 American Institute of Architects Houston, Design Award: Divine Detail, GeoForm™

2020 North Alabama ABC Award of Excellence—Commercial $10M–$25M: 8000 Redstone Gateway, Huntsville, Alabama

2020 NAIOP Colorado, Industrial Development of the Year: Parc Santa Fe, Littleton, Colorado

2020 Tilt-Up Achievement Award:
- Camwest Office Building, Bryan, Texas
- I-97 Business Park Phase III–Millersville, Maryland
- Redi Carpet, Stafford, Texas

2019 Houston Business Journal Landmark Award Multifamily: Arabella, Houston, Texas

2019 Tilt-Up Achievement Award:
- 5801 University Research Court, Riverdale, Maryland
- EPL Airport Commerce, Park, Leesburg, Maryland
- American Omni, Katy, Texas
- Vital Heart & Vein, Humble, Texas

2018 Board of Trade Newfoundland, RBC Business Excellence Innovative Solutions Award

2018 American Institute of Architects Houston, Design Award: Architecture Less Than 50,000 Square Feet: Intermarine Shipyard Office, Houston, Texas

2018 Tilt-Up Achievement Award:
- Connection Park, Irving, Texas
- Enterprise Business Park, Building 6, Denver, Colorado
- INOVA II, Centennial, Colorado
- NALCO Champion, Sugar Land, Texas

2018 American Concrete Institute (Maryland Chapter), Excellence in Concrete: St. John's I-97 Business Park, Millersville, Maryland

2017 ENR Mountain States Best Project, Office/Retail/Mixed-Use Development: INOVA I, Denver, Colorado

2017 Houston Business Journal Landmark Award Industrial: Bay Area Business Park, Pasadena, Texas

2017 ENR Texas and Louisiana Best Project, Manufacturing: Daikin Texas Technology Park, Waller, Texas

2017 Tilt-Up Concrete Associate—Tilt-Up Achievement Award: Daikin Texas Technology Park, Waller, Texas

2016 ENR Mountain States Best Project, Manufacturing: Value Plastics, Loveland, Colorado

2016 Tilt-Up Achievement Award:
- INOVA at Dry Creek, Centennial, Colorado
- Havenwood Office Park, Spring, Texas
- Value Plastics, Loveland, Colorado
- Memorial Hermann MOB, Cypress, Texas
- Fallbrook Pines Business Park, Houston, Texas
- Powell Electrical Systems, Houston, Texas

2016 USGBC Maryland Award: 7880 Milestone, Hanover, Maryland

2015 Tilt-Up Achievement Award:
- Legacy at Fallbrook, Phase I, Houston, Texas
- Texas Instruments—Sugar Land, Texas
- Frank's International Alvin Office, Alvin, Texas
- Westway Park Office, Houston, Texas

2015 ENR Mid-Atlantic Best Project, Government/Public Buildings: Annapolis Junction Business Park, Building 8, Annapolis Junction, Maryland

2015 American Institute of Architects Houston, Design Award: Architecture Less than 50,000 Square Feet: Fort Bend Veterans' Memorial, Sugar Land, Texas

2015 Judge's Award, Metal Architecture: Intermarine Operations Center, Houston, Texas

2015 PaperCity Design Award, Outdoor Living Space, Garden, or Pool: Fort Bend Veterans' Memorial, Sugar Land, Texas

2014 Award of Merit, NAIOP Northern Virginia: Cuisine Solutions, Inc. HQ, Sterling, Virginia

2014 Tilt-Up Concrete Association's Irving Gill Distinguished Architect Award: Jeffrey Brown, FAIA

2014 Tilt-Up Achievement Award:
Annapolis Junction Business Park, Building 7, Annapolis Junction, Maryland
Fort Bend Veterans' Memorial, Sugar Land, Texas
Westgate Campus, Houston, Texas
Kelsey-Seybold Administrative—Office Building, Pearland, Texas
8 West Centre, Houston, Texas
Greenhouse Office, Houston, Texas
Wallis State Bank, Houston, Texas

2014 The Herlong Memorial Award—American Institute of Architects Northern Virginia: Fort Bend Veterans' Memorial, Sugar Land, Texas (awarded to Matthew Stephens)

2014 Golden Trowel Honor Award—Associated Masonry Contractors of Houston: Roy Kelly Multimodal Terminal and Parking Garage, Bryan, Texas

2014 Excellence in Concrete Construction—American Concrete Institute Awards (Maryland Chapter): Annapolis Junction Business Park, Building 7, Annapolis Junction, Maryland

2014 Most Creative Construction, NAIOP Maryland: Annapolis Junction Business Park, Building 6, Annapolis Junction, Maryland

2013 Tilt-Up Achievement Award:
EagleBurgmann, Houston, Texas
Annapolis Junction Business Park, Building 6, Annapolis Junction, Maryland
RDA, Manassas, Virginia

2013 Award of Merit, Best Suburban Office 1-4 Stories, NAIOP Maryland/Washington, D.C.: SAIC Lexington Park, Lexington Park, Maryland

2013 PSMJ Circle of Excellence

2013 American Institute of Architects Northern Virginia, Design Awards: Juror Citation, Conceptual/Unbuilt Architecture: Gatehouse MOB, Falls Church, Virginia

2013 Texas Society of Architects, Design Award: Roy Kelly Multimodal Terminal and Parking Garage, Bryan, Texas

2012 Tilt-Up Achievement Award:
North Gate Building E1, Aberdeen, Maryland
Sentry Gateway Building 100, San Antonio, Texas

2012 Citation, Architect Magazine Annual Design Review: Roy Kelly Multimodal Terminal and Parking Garage, Bryan, Texas

2012 Merit Award—ABC Metro Washington, D.C./Virginia: SAIC Lexington Park, Lexington Park, Maryland

2012 Excellence in Concrete Construction—Tilt-Up Buildings, American Concrete Institute Awards (Maryland Chapter): SAIC Lexington Park, Lexington Park, Maryland

2012 American Institute of Architects Houston, Design Awards: Architecture Greater than 50,000 Square Feet: Roy Kelly Multimodal Terminal and Parking Garage, Bryan, Texas

2012 Best Construction: IIDA Houston Product Runway

2012 Wintergreen Award (Maryland Chapter) USGBC: SAIC Lexington Park, Lexington Park, Maryland

2011 Tilt-Up Achievement Award:
Lufkin Automation Offices, Missouri City, Texas
The Reserve at Sierra Pines, The Woodlands, Texas

2011 American Institute of Architects Houston, Firm of the Year

2011 Most Outstanding Example of Design and Implementation for Renovation/Reuse: GRACRE Stratford University/Thalhimer Center, Richmond, Virginia

2010 Tilt-Up Achievement Award (20th Annual): Tramontina W. Airport, Sugar Land, Texas

2010 Washington UNBUILT Award Honor Award (American Institute of Architects|Washington, D.C.): Shell(ter) for Home

2010 Silver Medal Award for Distinction in Design (Upsilon Chapter): Tau Sigma Delta Honor Society

2010 Most Original Design—IIDA Houston Product Runway

2010 Tilt-Up Achievement Award:
Advance Polybag, Houston, Texas
Tilt-Up Achievement Award—Office/Pavilion, Houston, Texas

2009 PSMJ Circle of Excellence

2009 Real Estate and Construction Review (Texas Edition), Building of America Award:
Bayou Place, Houston, Texas
Klein ISD Network Operations Center, Klein, Texas

2009 Tilt-Up Achievement Award:
Southwest Bean Makers/Standard Meats, Saginaw, Texas
Laversab, Sugar Land, Texas
Corporate Centre Building 3, Houston, Texas

2008 *Texas Construction Magazine*, Construction Excellence Award: Private/Corporate—Laversab, Sugar Land, Texas

2008 American Institute of Architects Houston, Design Award: On the Boards:
Klein ISD High School, Klein, Texas
Arbor School, Houston, Texas

2008 Irving Gill Distinguished Architecture Award: Powers Brown Architecture

2008 Tilt-Up Achievement Award:
Tornier Medical Office/Warehouse, Stafford, Texas
PetrolValves, Houston, Texas
MNP, Houston, Texas
Pinch Office/Warehouse Facility, Houston, Texas

2007 Urban Land Institute—Award for Excellence

2007 American Institute of Architects Houston, Design Award: PetrolValves, Houston, Texas

2007 American Institute of Architects Houston, Design Award: On the Boards: Flower Market Square, Houston, Texas

2007 Tilt-Up Achievement Award:
RTRON Corporate Headquarters, Sugar Land, Texas
General Technologies Inc., Corporate Headquarters, Sugar Land, Texas

2007 *Texas Construction Magazine*, Construction Excellence Award: Private/Corporate, Bayou Place, Houston, Texas

2006 *Texas Construction Magazine*, Construction Excellence Award: Private/Corporate: Tornier Medical Office/Warehouse, Stafford, Texas

2006 American Institute of Architects Houston, Architecture Honor Award: Notation for Sustainable Design: Westchase Long Range Plan, Houston, Texas

2005 Urban Land Institute, Landmark Design Award: Best Industrial Development: Igloo Headquarters, Brookshire, Texas

2004 Urban Land Institute, Landmark Design Award: Best Industrial Development: Century Oaks Business Park, Stafford, Texas

2004 American Institute of Architects Houston, Architecture Merit Award: METRORail Maintenance and Administration, Facility, Houston, Texas

2003 American Institute of Architects Houston: Architecture Merit Award: RTRON Corporate Headquarters, Stafford, Texas

1999 Urban Land Institute, Award for Excellence

Exhibits

2017 "This City Celebrating Plan Houston," Blueprint Houston, HUB Studio, The Silos at Sawyer Yards, Houston, Texas
"Reimagining Architecture Center Houston," Architecture Center, Houston, Texas

2014 "Women in Architecture," Architecture Center, Houston, Texas (featured Jeannette Shaw and Chelsea Serrano-Piche)

2007 "Houston-Future Form," Architecture Center, Houston, Texas (featured Westchase District Long-Range Plan)

2006 "Garden City, Green City," The Museum of Fine Arts, Houston, Texas—David Crossley, curator, Gulf Coast Institute (featured Jeffrey Brown's research on Ebenezer Howard's Garden City)

2004 "5 @ 5" Powers Brown Architecture, Kava Kane Gallery, Houston, Texas

2003 "SNAPSHOT," sponsored by the Rice Design Alliance, Lawndale Art Center, Houston, Texas (featured current Houston design)

2001 "SNAPSHOT," sponsored by the Rice Design Alliance, Lawndale Art Center, Houston, Texas (featured current Houston design)

2001 "Art on the go," Museum of Fine Arts Houston, Houston, Texas (an exhibition of the collaboration between architects and artists on the METRORail, featured South Fannin Station)

Publications

2022 *Texas Tribune*, "Magic Island" by Ross Wienert

2021 *Demo Magazine*

2018 *Houston Chronicle*, "Trammell Crow/Clarion Partners to nearly double size of NW Houston industrial park"

2017 "Denver's Energy Benchmarking Ordinance: What it Means for the Denver Real Estate Market" by Jesse Hunt

2017 "Confirmation Bias: Architects and Their Relationship to Tilt-Wall Construction" by Jeffrey Blaine Brown, FAIA

2017 *CultureMap San Antonio*, "New Luxury Hotel and Residences coming to San Antonio's Museum Reach"

2017 *Houston Business Journal*, "Bay Area Business Park Named Industrial Winner in 2017 Landmark Awards"

2017 *Texas Architect*, "Stranded" (features Galveston Transit Terminal)

2017 *ReBusiness Online*, "Conor Commercial Real Estate Completes 213,864 SF Industrial Facility in San Antonio"

2017 *Houston Business Journal*, "First Look at Cemex's New U.S. HQ in Memorial City"

2017 *Houston Business Journal*, "New Southwest Houston Industrial Park Signs First Tenant"

2016 *The Post and Courier*, "Planned Road Changes Near Charleston Airport Spur $150M Real Estate Deal"

2016 *Houston Business Journal*, "New Co-Working Space to Open in The Woodlands"

2016 *Swamplot*, "The Many Faces of Sugar Land's Veteran Memorial, Stormwater Detention Basin, and Tilt-Up Concrete Demo Project"

2016 *Architizer*, "The Power of Simplicity: 8 Moving Minimalist Memorials"

2016 *Dallas Business Journal*, "Dallas Group Lands $43.5M in Funds to Build New Lancaster Logistics Hub"

2016 *BusinessDen*, "Concessionaire Firm Building New HQ in Northfield"

2016 *Baltimore Business Journal*, "St. John Properties Bets Big on Spec, Cites 'Continued Confidence' in Maryland Economy"

2016 *Houston Business Journal*, "Houston's First Major Micro-Unit Condo Project Shifts Direction"

2016 *Houston Business Journal*, "Memorial City Office Building Tops Out"

2016 *Washington Business Journal*, "COPT to Take a Gamble on the University of Maryland"

2016 *Realty News Report*, "Conor and USAA Develop Spec Industrial in Hot South Side Market"

2016 *San Antonio Express-News*, "Three Downtown Projects Get Support From HDRC"

2016 *San Antonio Express-News*, "Thompson Hotel Tower in the Works for River Walk"

2016 *Guidry News*, "Galveston Transit Terminal Grand Opening"

2016 *Houston Chronicle*, "East Downtown Micro-Units Marketed to Millennials"

2016 *BizWest*, "Denver Developer Plans Small-Bay Industrial Space in Louisville, Colorado"

2016 *Houston Business Journal*, "New Houston Campus Named Best Deal of 2015 by National Publication"

2016 *Reality News Report*, "Best Construction Project of the Year"

2015 *Houston Business Journal*, "New Details Revealed for First Micro-Condo Project in Houston"

2015 *Denver Urban Review*, "Construction Begins on INOVA Office Project"

2015 *Galveston County Daily News*, "Work Nearly Complete on Downtown Transit Terminal"

2015 *Colorado Real Estate Journal*, "INOVA Elevates Office into Agile Workspace"

2015 *Houston Business Journal*, "More Industrial Coming to the Port Area"

2015 *Houston Business Journal*, "Groundbreaking Set for New Condominium Tower in Houston"

2015 *Denver Urban Review*, "Beverage Distributors' New Home Breaks Ground in Stapleton"

2015 *ENR Mid-Atlantic*, "ENR Mid-Atlantic Announces 2015 Best Project Winners"

2015 *Baltimore Business Journal*, "St. John Properties to Build Spec Office Project at Annapolis Junction Town Center"

2015 *Denver Business Journal*, "United Properties Secures Big Lease, Plans More Development in Stapleton"

2015 *Denver Business Journal*, "More Spec Office Breaking Ground in Centennial Near Topgolf"

2015 *San Antonio Business Journal*, "UPS to Spend More Than $35M on Distribution Center Expansion in NE San Antonio"

2015 *Texas Architect*, "Of Note" (a review of *Tiltwallism: A Treatise on the Architectural Potential of Tiltwall Construction*)

2015 *Metal Architecture*, "2015 Metal Architecture Design Awards"

2015 *Houston Business Journal*, "Office Building to Rise in New Portion of Memorial City"

2015 *Houston Business Journal*, "Largest Houston-Area Architecture Firms"

2015 *Houston Business Journal*, "Check out the Major Projects Underway in Uptown Houston"

2015 *Houston Business Journal*, "Private Terrace-Top Pools Planned for New Galleria-Area Luxury Condo Tower"

2015 *Tilt-Up Today*, "World's Largest Tilt-Up Building Under Construction in Houston, Texas"

2015 *Houston Business Journal*, "New Business Leads"

2015 *Houston Business Journal*, "More Industrial Gears up to Break Ground"

2015 *Houston Business Journal*, "Exclusive: New Industrial Park Gearing up in North Houston"

2015 *Houston Business Journal*, "Beltway Crossing Northwest Named Industrial Winner in 2015 Landmark Awards"

2015 *Houston Business Journal*, "Southwestern Energy's Move to Springwoods Village Wins Landmark Awards' HQ Move"

2015 *Houston Business Journal*, "French Industrial Giant's Massive Move Earns HBJ 2015 Landmark Awards"

2015 *Houston Business Journal*, "Another Big Industrial Park Coming to Southwest Houston"

2015 *Houston Business Journal*, "Southwest Houston, the Next Industrial Frontier"

2015 *Houston Business Journal*, "REIT Snags Two Buildings in Energy Corridor"

2015 *Houston Chronicle*, "Hospitals Finding Healthy Market as Cy-Fair Medical Options Expand" by Lindsay Peyton

2015 *Houston Business Journal*, "Christian Brothers Automotive Moves HQ"

2015 *Houston Business Journal*, "Another Spec Office Park Underway"

2014 *Houston Business Journal*, "Meet the Fast 100: Growing Architecture Firm Quadruples Revenue, Tries New Venture"

2014 *Houston Business Journal*, "New Office Building to Rise Near Exxon Mobil Campus"

2014 *Houston Business Journal*, "Construction on Micro Center's New Site to Begin this Month"

2014 *Houston Business Journal*, "New Submarket Hot for Office Construction"

2014 *Houston Business Journal*, "New Mid-Rise Building Breaks Ground Near Grand Parkway"

2014 *Houston Business Journal*, "Sugar Land of Opportunity: Sweet for Some, Sour for Others"

2014 *Houston Business Journal*, "Illinois Developer Enters Houston Industrial Market"

2014 *Houston Business Journal*, "New Pearland Medical Facility Will Offer Physicians More Freedom"

2014 *Tilt-Up Today*, "Class A Six-Story Texas Tilt"

2014 *Tilt-Up Today*, "For the Dangerously Uninterested"

2014 *Tilt-Up Today*, "New Book Gives Insights into 'Everyday' Architecture..."

2014 *Tiltwallism: A Treatise on the Architectural Potential of Tiltwall Construction* by Jeffrey Brown (published by The Images Publishing Group)

2013 *Houston Business Journal*, "Texas Instruments' New Campus Heats up Fort Bend Market"

2013 *Houston Business Journal*, "On the Grow: Energy Firms Pump up Their Houston Space"

2013 *Houston Business Journal*, "Houston Architecture Firms Reach New Heights on HJB's List"

2013 *Houston Business Journal*, "Q&A with Jeffrey Brown of Powers Brown Architecture"

2013 *Houston Business Journal*, "2013 Landmark Awards: Cookiebar LLC"

2013 *Houston Business Journal*, "Intermarine Breaks Ground on Ship Channel Operations Center"

2013 *Houston Business Journal*, "Memorial Hermann Plans More Medical Office Buildings in Houston"

2013 *Tilt-Up Today*, "Small Smart Boxes"

2012 *Architect*, "2012 Annual Design Review" features Roy Kelly Multimodal Terminal and Parking Garage

2012 *Houston Chronicle*, "A Boom Looms on West Side of Town," by Nancy Sarnoff (features three buildings designed by Powers Brown Architecture)

2012 *Texas Architect*, "Delight in Restraint," by Jeffrey Brown, FAIA

2011 *Tilt-Up Today*, "Tilt-Up as a Re-Emerging Design Technology," by Jeffrey Brown, FAIA and Mitch Bloomquist

2011 *The Construction Specifier*, "Untapped Potential for Tilt-up Concrete," by Jeffrey Brown, FAIA and Mark Gardner, PE

2011 *Texas Architect*, "Extending the Brand", by Dan Searight (American Institute Architects article, features Logica's North)

2010 *Texas Architect*, "Stylized Urbanism", by Jeffrey Brown, FAIA

2009 *Texas Architect*, "Neglected Territory: Notes on the Architectural Potential of Tilt Wall Construction," by Jeffrey Brown, FAIA

2008 *Texas Architect*, "Reborn on the Bayou", by Stephen A. Jovicich, American Institute Architects article features the renovation of Bayou Place Phase II.

2007 *Powers Brown Architecture: Neoarchitecture*, edited by Melina Delyannis, The Images Publishing Group

2006 *2000 Architects,* The Images Publishing Group features Powers Brown Architecture

2005 *Upstairs Downstairs*, edited by Aisha Hasanovic, The Images Publishing Group features Tramontina USA

Biographies

Jeffrey Brown, FAIA, is the Founding Principal/CEO for Powers Brown Architecture. Practicing architecture for more than thirty years, Jeffrey has an array of experience working on multiple building types for both public and private entities. He is an accomplished designer with unique graphic communication and strategic planning skills, and his ability to design utilizing an interactive process of project definition and interpretation has resulted in distinguished design awards and published works.

Jeffrey was elevated to the AIA's College of Fellows in 2016 and the TCA College of Fellows in 2019. He has been instrumental in leading the firm to numerous awards including a citation in the Annual Design Review from *Architect* magazine as well as accolades from the Texas Society of Architects, American Institute of Architects Houston, AIA DC|Washington, Design Excellence Awards and the Urban Land Institute. The firm's work has been widely covered in magazines and books including his latest tome, *Tiltwallism: A Treatise on the Architectural Potential of Tiltwall Construction*, which is available through booksellers nationwide. Brown received a patent from the United States Patent and Trademark Office for his GeoForm™ invention in 2022.

He has authored numerous articles on architecture/criticism for *Texas Architect Magazine* and other publications. He has led numerous research projects including work published on high-rise tilt-wall, and progressive collapse and blast resistance in tilt-wall. He also led the COVID-era collaborative and multi-disciplinary research project MEDDNeT™ which proposed a systems approach to disaster medical deployment.

Jeffrey has a passion for shaping architecture and the architects of tomorrow. He has taught as an assistant to Fred Koetter at his alma mater, Harvard University's Graduate School of Design, and as an adjunct professor at both The University of Houston Gerald D. Hines College of Architecture and Prairie View A&M University. He has been a guest critic at the above-mentioned institutions, Rice University, Roger Williams University, and the University of Texas at Arlington. He is also active in numerous organizations including The Harvard Alumni Association, a board member of The Houston Philosophical Society, NAIOP, and the Tilt-Up Concrete Association, where he serves as the president of their nonprofit foundation TILTLAB.

Joe Powers, AIA was active in the Houston, Austin, Washington, D.C., and Denver markets during his career. While working at another firm, Joe approached Jeffrey Brown and pitched the idea that with his business acumen and Jeffrey's design talent, they should start their own firm. Twenty-five years later, it turns out he was on to something. In his more than forty years of architecture, Joe demonstrated the ability to design and document buildings that were attractive, economical, and durable. His familiarity with his project markets were key in making strategic decisions for the projects, ranging from construction type to building layout issues, as they pertained to future flexibility and code compliance. Joe's focus on balancing project budget issues with durability and quality made him the go-to architect for clients throughout many markets. In 2017, Joe retired from the firm and architecture to spend time on his Texas farm.

Stephen Sharpe writes about architecture from his home in Austin. Under his leadership as its longest serving executive editor, *Texas Architect* magazine won several regional and national awards for excellence in its coverage of the architecture profession. In 2012 he was awarded for his efforts with an honorary membership in the American Institute of Architects. Sharpe began his career as a newspaper reporter and later as a graphic designer. Most recently, he earned a master's degree in urban planning from the University of Texas School of Architecture.

Donna Kacmar, FAIA was educated at Texas A+M University and graduated with a Bachelor of Environmental Design in 1988 and a Master of Architecture in 1992. Donna is a National American Institute of Architects 2004 Young Architects Award recipient and was elected to the College of Fellows of the American Institute of Architects in 2009. Donna has served on multiple boards including the Houston AIA, Avenue CDC, Rice Design Alliance, Architecture Center Houston Foundation, Texas Society of Architects, and AIA Strategic Council. Donna has taught at Rice University, and Texas A&M University, and is currently a Professor at the University of Houston where she teaches architecture design studio. She also founded the Materials Research Collaborative (MRC) in 2009 and directed materials research for 10 years. Her Fisher Street House, a small 544-square-foot dwelling, received a 2013 AIA Houston Design Award and led to her first book, *Big Little House*, published by Routledge in 2015. Her edited book on the work of Victor Lundy was published in 2018 by Princeton Architectural Press and her most recent book, *Big Little Hotel*, was published in March 2023. Donna is the principal of Architect Works, PLLC, and her architectural practice focuses on residential and small-scale commercial projects in the Houston, Texas area.

Firm Profile

AEC CARES
projectHouston 10.5.18
hanley wood
AIA

CREConverge
powers
brown
archit
ecture

Collaborators List

Names in **bold** indicate Principals and Associates.

Parandis Abdi, Brian Adams, Dominic Adams, Shawn Adams, Jay-Lord Agliam, Daniela Aguilar, Eduardo Aguilar, Mine Aksoydan, Jason Aleman, Sheena Fe Alejandro, Courtney Alexander, Jade Allen, Katie Allen, Hanaa Ali, Keithen Andrews, Estafania Alzamora, Joan Anderson, Amna Ansari, Gregory Aranda, Carlos Arboleda, Abigail Archibal, Maria Armenta, Jose Arriaga, Fernando Autrique, Daniel Ayad, Sareh Bakhtiari, Kimberley Belfour, Heidi Barriga, Jamal Banan, Denise Barberis, Chris Barboza, Alex Barnes, Lindsay Bench, Audrey Benglis, Kendall Benjamin, Stacey Bension, Erin Begneaud, Courtney Bishop, Cristhian Bisso, Logan Blandino, Matthew Boeske, Deleon Boyd, **Grant Brandenburg**, **AJ Breneman**, Doug Brooks, Katy Broussard, **Jeffrey Brown**, Paul Buchanan, Huy Bui, Mariah Buras, Brynn Burda, Brian Burnett, Taylor Burrow, Addie Bush, Paul Butterfras, April Buvinghausen, Brandon Byrd, John Cadenhead, Nicole Cadenhead, Matthew Caines, Chelsea Caldwell, Skylar Caldwell, Gly Callahan, Samantha Callender, Deborah Campos, Breaujah Carter, Jewels Carter, Cristina Castanon, Cristle Castillo, Eleonora Cenacchi, Dave Chan, Meyer Chaskin, Madalena Cheung, Summer Churchill, Kayla Clancey, Caroline Cobb, Esperanza Cobo, Lacy Collier, Barry Conner, Keith Conrad, Karla Contreras-Buquet, Jerad Cowan, Joanna Crabtree, Sohel Cruz, Ladan Dana, Amy Darrow, Towana Davilmar, Rudy Del Bosque II, Garrett DeLano, Maria Delgado, Mark Delpilar, Caelan Denley, Cesar Diaz, Sally Diaz, Seidy Diaz de Leon, Huy Diep, Ngan Dinh, Alaina Dixon,Thuan Do, Stacy Dominguez, Daphne Dow, Stacy Driver, Gillian Dyson, Stefan Dytrt, Layla Eastin, Megan Ebert, Akemi Eden, Rebecca Eden, Philip Elia, David Elkin, Linda Elkin, Ashley Elks, David Ellis, Cary Els, Samaneh Eslami, Michael Fagan, Alam Farias, Colby Farrell, Tessa Fay, Mike Fecco, Kyle Fell, Emily Fitzgerald, Canston Fitzwater, Matthew Flis, Daphne Floran, Ernesto Flores, Lee Fly, Scott Forstell, Cynthia Foteh, Brandon Francis, Ericka Frias, Ron Fuertes, Rodolfo Garcia, James Gavin, Jason Geving, Babak Gholizadeh, Jody Gibson, Jason Gilbert, Mariana Gomez, Luis Gonzales, Baldemar Gonzalez, Vianney Gonzalez, Suzanne Goss, Corrina Green, Morgan Grindal, Gregory Grady, Nikiwe Grantham, Mason Gulliver, Jim Halloran, Robert Hardy, Jasper Harmon, Amy Harris, William Harris-Ryden, Luke Hart, Rebecca Hawkins, Robin Hayse, Mikki Heckman, Ricardo Hendi, Jocelyne Hernandez, Stacy Hernandez, Dominic Herrera, Mabel Herrera, Faith Hickey, Lauren Himsel, **Chad Hindi**, Homer Hinojosa, Ada Ho, Jaden Ho, Kirby Hobley, Bryan Hodge, John Holland, Megan Holland, Samantha Hollis, Barbara Holmes, Tammy Holmstrom, Chelsey Hume, Jesse Hunt, Dan Hutchinson, Alexis Jacobs, Peter Jackson, Ather Jaleel, Leslie Janes, April Janiszak, Soheb Javaid, Sogole Javanmardi, Natalie Jayawardene, Sarah Johnson, Katie Jones, Lindsey Jones, Ashley Jordan, Sheryl Joy, Meera Kachhla, Randy Karn, Derrick Kately, Gabriela Katusak, Erin Kelley, **Nazir Khalfe**, Jay Kim, Desta Kimmel, Amanda King, Richmond Kingsford, Maeve Kinsey, Jill Klug, Jay Knowles, Anne Kummer, Kimberly Lacson, Hernán Lazarde, Taylee Lawson, Zachary Layman, Hannah Leber, Branden Leger, Samantha LeDuc, Edward Lee, Lindsay Lehman, Lee Lemons, Dee Lewis, Keenan Linehan, Alexander Littlepage, Annette Littleton, Suou Liu, Ashley Loftin, Elizabeth Longstaff, Samantha Loyman, Ross Lukeman, Antonio Luna, Ashley Lynch, Mackenzie Lynch, Shea MacDougall, Brynn Macinnis, Laura Mackenzie, Deborah Madera, Carl Magill, **Ben Mahala**, Aiden Mai, Milan Manurung, Zirren Marin, Jake Marshall, Atzydy Martinez, Jimmy Martinez, Jose Martinez, Karen Martinez, Allan Masilang, Caveh Masum, Jonathon Matle, Anna Matsotska, Grace Matta, Christopher Matthews, Angela Mayer, **Bryant Mazzetti**, Justin McCarthy, Breandan McDermott, Richard McFarland, Kate McLean, Robert McMahon, John Meadows, Delia Meave, Natalie Mediate, Rita Medina, Alejandro Medrano, Raul Medrano, Trupti Mehta, Natalie Meinkoth, Roman Mendez, Lisa Metzger, Holly Metzger, Julie Mitros, Lars Moeller, Robert Mohler, Valeria Montenegro, Danielle Montross, Milton Moore, Erick Morales, Juan Morales, Jaime Moreno, Julia Morin, Nicholas Moser, Kseniya Nagornova, Zoha Naqvi, Neda Nikahd, Negar Nikouei, Frank Nolan, Barbara Novoa, Erik Okland, Steve Oliver, Dani Olivera-Gomez, Ashlee Owens, Rudy Pagsanjan, Scott Palermo, Armony Panighello, Destiny Pardy, Chhayal Parikh, MacKenzie Parr, Myra Peralta, Enrique Perez, Michael Peterson, Daisy Pichardo, Taylor Plumley,

Robert Plushnick, Stefano Poisl, Cassie Pond, Rahil Pote, Nicole Potter, Alex Poujol, **Joe Powers**, **Lauren Amber Prestenbach**, Steve Procter, Bailey Putnam, Melissa Quagliata, Catherine Quan, Amanda Ragan, Brandon Ramon, Ramon Ramos, Angelo Rapanos, Vineeth Ravinder, Destenie Reyes, Kim Rhoton-VanHoltz, Misty Richards, Megan Richardson, Chelsea Riggs, Diana Rivas, Charles Roa, Chris Roberson, Lamon Roberts Jr., Lisa Robins, David Robinson, Alaina Rodriguez, Iker Rodriguez, Miguel Rodriguez, Sunne Rodriguez, Alex Roestenburg, David Rowson, Chris Royster, Justin Ruiz, Isabelle Russell, Sarah Rust, Sadeq Sadeq, Elayna Sadorus, Talal Safat, David Sahagun, Ryohei Saito, Luis Salas, Gilbert Salazar, Jose Salinas, Mackenzie Salman, Steven Saltzman, Amanda Sanabria, Aimee Sanborn, Eduardo Sanchez, Austin Sandel, Dante Sandoval, Javier Sartorio, Kelly Scarberry, Jennifer Schmidt, Deena Schoenfeldt, Paul Schuette, Deon Scott, Roger Sekol, Chelsea Serrano-Piche, Kyle Seton, Sara Sexton, Ken Shanks, **Jeanette Shaw**, Hamna Siddiqi, Naomi Sims, Ayushi Singhal, Curtis Smallwood, Jordan Xavier Smith, Natalie Smith, Sara Soleimanzadeh, Tristan Solis, Vanessa Sotil, Logan Springer, **Kristen Stapper**, Matthew Stephens, William Stewart, Nicholas Stoutt, Alanna Strachan, Kevin Strohfus, Cameron Stubbs, Phin Stubbs, Jeanann Sundby, Emily Sutliffe, Michael Ta, Ashley Taetz, Silvia Tartaglione, Emmanuel Taylor, Garrett Taylor, John Taylor, Zachary Taylor, Amadeus Tec, Charles Tehauno, Sonia Tejada, Lindsey TeKrony, Brandon Terry, Anthony Thomas, Chris Thomas, **Scott Thompson**, Katie Thorell, Sofie Torabi, Hector Torres, Thomas Torres, Trent Torres, Cathleen Trechter, Hector Trevino-Palacios, Brian Tucker, Zubair Ulhaq, Ryan Upton, Gerardo Valdez, Paul Valesky, Marlene Vargas, David Velandia, **Reinaldo Venancio**, Francisco Vera, Dominik Vigil, Marisa Vinson, Cody ViPond, Hai Vu, **Bruce Walck**, Reed Walker, Erin Wallander, Nick Waterman, Tina Wesley, Brian West, Stephanie Westrick, James Whitehead, Jim Whitehead, Kimberly Wilkinson, Ryan Williker, Shane Wilson, Justin Winchester, James Wise, Miao Miao Xiao, Kylie Young, Yolanda Young, Haosheng Yu, Christina Zeibak, Mei Zhang, Yan Zhang

AJ Breneman

Grant Brandenburg

Chad Hindi

Nazir Khalfe

Ben Mahala

Bryant Mazzetti

Lauren Amber Prestenbach

Jeanette Shaw

Kristen Stapper

Scott Thompson

Reinaldo Venancio

Bruce Walck

Published in Australia in 2024 by
The Images Publishing Group Pty Ltd
ABN 89 059 734 431

Offices

Melbourne
Waterman Business Centre
Suite 64, Level 2 UL40
1341 Dandenong Road,
Chadstone, VIC 3148
Australia
Tel: +61 3 8564 8122

New York
6 West 18th Street 4B
New York City, NY 10011
United States
Tel: +1 212 645 1111

Shanghai
6F, Building C, 838 Guangji Road
Hongkou District, Shanghai 200434
China
Tel: +86 021 31260822

books@imagespublishing.com
www.imagespublishing.com

The Images Publishing Group Reference Number: 1712

All photography is attributed in the Project Credits on pages 240–43 unless otherwise noted.
Pages 2–3: Mark Johnson; page 4: Dror Baldinger; page 6: Dror Baldinger; pages 10–11: Michael Craft; pages 24–25: Mark Johnson; page 27: Dror Baldinger, Mark Johnson, courtesy of Powers Brown Architecture; page 43: Dror Baldinger, Chris Spielmann, courtesy of Powers Brown Architecture; page 63: Dror Baldinger, Mark Johnson, courtesy of Powers Brown Architecture; page 95: Dror Baldinger, Mark Johnson, courtesy of Powers Brown Architecture; page 115: Dror Baldinger, courtesy of Powers Brown Architecture; page 133: Kat Ambrose, Dror Baldinger, Geoffrey Lyons, courtesy of Powers Brown Architecture; page 145: courtesy of Powers Brown Architecture; page 155: Dror Baldinger, Mark Johnson, courtesy of Powers Brown Architecture; page 175: Michael Craft, Mark Johnson, Brad Nicol, courtesy of Powers Brown Architecture; page 201: courtesy of Powers Brown Architecture; page 215: Dror Baldinger, Andrew Garland, Brad Nicol; page 230: Mitch Bloomquist (Jeffrey Brown, FAIA and Donna Kacmar, FAIA); page 248: Calie Griebel (Jeffrey Brown, FAIA), Timothy Fulton (Joe Powers, AIA); page 249: Ava Sharpe (Stephen Sharpe), John Apogee (Donna Kacmar, FAIA); page 253: Mark Johnson (AJ Breneman), courtesy of Powers Brown Architecture (Grant Brandenburg), Matt Tibbo (Chad Hindi), courtesy of Powers Brown Architecture (Nazir Khalfe), courtesy of Powers Brown Architecture (Ben Mahala), Brad Nicol (Bryant Mazzetti), Brad Nicol (Lauren Amber Prestenbach), courtesy of Powers Brown Architecture (Jeanette Shaw), courtesy of Powers Brown Architecture (Kristen Stapper), courtesy of Powers Brown Architecture (Scott Thompson), Tina Leu (Reinaldo Venancio), courtesy of Powers Brown Architecture (Bruce Walck); pages 250–51: courtesy of Powers Brown Architecture; pages 254–55: Mark Johnson.

NATIONAL LIBRARY OF AUSTRALIA
A catalogue record for this book is available from the National Library of Australia

Title: Powers Brown Architecture: Commodity and Virtue in Architecture
ISBN: 9781864709827

This title was commissioned in IMAGES' Melbourne office and produced as follows:
Editorial Helen Koehne, Georgia (Gina) Tsarouhas, Jeanette Wall
Graphic design/project management Ryan Marshall,
Production Nicole Boehringer

Printed on 157gsm Chinese OJI matt art paper by Artron Art (Group) Co., Ltd, in China

IMAGES has included on its website a page for special notices in relation to this and its other publications. Please visit www.imagespublishing.com